COLLECTED POEMS
OF
IVOR GURNEY

WITHDRAWN

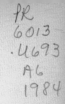

COLLECTED POEMS
OF
IVOR GURNEY

Chosen, edited and with an
Introduction by

P. J. KAVANAGH

Oxford   New York

OXFORD UNIVERSITY PRESS

1984

Oxford University Press, Walton Street, Oxford OX2 6DP

London New York Toronto
Delhi Bombay Calcutta Madras Karachi
Kuala Lumpur Singapore Hong Kong Tokyo
Nairobi Dar es Salaam Cape Town
Melbourne Auckland

and associated companies in
Beirut Berlin Ibadan Mexico City Nicosia

Oxford is a trade mark of Oxford University Press

British Library Cataloguing in Publication Data

Gurney, Ivor
Collected poems of Ivor Gurney.—(Oxford paperbacks)
I. Title II. Kavanagh, P. J.
821'.912 PR6013.U693
ISBN 0-19-211963-X

Library of Congress Cataloging in Publication Data

Gurney, Ivor, 1890–1937.
Collected poems of Ivor Gurney.
(Oxford paperbacks)
Includes bibliographical references and index.
1. Kavanagh, P. J. (Patrick Joseph), 1931–
II. Title.
[PR6013.U693A6 1984] 821'.912 84-738
ISBN 0-19-211963-X (pbk.)

Printed in Great Britain by
The Guernsey Press,
Guernsey, Channel Islands

ACKNOWLEDGEMENTS

I WOULD like to thank G. Matravers of Gloucester who first drew my attention to the existence of the Gurney manuscripts which have made such a difference to the preparation of this edition, and Mrs Ronald Gurney who passed the manuscripts through me to the Gurney Archive now held in Gloucester Public Library. The letters of Ivor Gurney to Edmund Blunden, from which I quote in my Introduction, are in the possession of the Humanities Research Centre, The University of Texas, who, as owners, kindly consent to their use. I would also like to thank the following for their help and encouragement: Geoffrey Grigson, the late Leonard Clark, Mrs Joy Finzi, Michael Hurd, Robin Haines, the Librarian and staff of Gloucester Public Library, and above all Kate Kavanagh for her help with the Notes, with indexing and typing and suggestions. I would also like to acknowledge the financial assistance of the Phoenix Trust.

P. J. K.

CONTENTS

An asterisk (*) indicates a previously uncollected poem

POEMS

I. From *Severn and Somme* (1917)

From *War's Embers* (1919)

II. 1917–1919

III. From *Rewards of Wonder* (1919–1920)

IV. 1919–1922

V. September 1922–1925

VI. 1926 and after

INTRODUCTION

THE first selection of Ivor Gurney's poems was published in 1954, long enough ago for those who know his work to have decided what it is like. But nearly a quarter of a century later he was still being described, when a plaque to him was unveiled in Gloucester Cathedral, as a 'local' poet. It was well-meant – he was a local boy – but in the limiting sense of Edward Thomas's definition of poets 'whom we can connect with a district of England and often cannot sunder from it without harm', Gurney was not a local poet at all.

Yesterday Lost

What things I have missed today, I know very well,
But the seeing of them each new time is miracle.
Nothing between Bredon and Dursley has
Any day yesterday's precise unpraisèd grace.
The changed light, or curve changed mistily,
Coppice, now bold cut, yesterday's mystery.
A sense of mornings, once seen, forever gone,
Its own for ever: alive, dead, and my possession.

You do not have to know Bredon or Dursley to see what he is driving at. His Gloucestershire is real, of course, but it is also a region of the mind, The Good Place. He is sparing of topography and more interested in the seasons (especially autumn) and in sky-effects – clouds, dawn-lights, sunsets, even 'Novembery' lightlessness (he likes that too). If he is to be given a locality, he could with more justice be called a sky-poet.

But, like most poets, he is dependent on the particular and on being able to name it. After the war, when he could give the names of the places in France where he had served, his war poetry gains in immediacy. He had found wartime censorship more than usually cramping: 'forbidden names or dates without which the poets / are done for . . .' (from 'Jackson', an 'Appeal', not included here). His details – the Machonachie pickle, the shared fag, the noise of the cleaning-out of dixies – and his awareness that everything is happening in one place rather than another, at a certain hour, under a never-to-be-repeated pattern of sky, are what give these poems distinctiveness. Whereas the other war poets (Owen, Sassoon, and so on) reacted against the war rhetoric of their elders with indignation and tell us truths we ought to have guessed, Gurney gives us pictures we would not have imagined: the gentleness of his first reception in the front line (in two poems, both called 'First Time In'), the effect of a clarinet played in the trenches ('New Year's Eve' and 'Crucifix Corner'). It is the poetry of a particularized, not a generalized humanity, of the flesh and nerves rather than of the intellect. His precisions can be journalistic but he almost invariably looks up to notice the behaviour of the French sky. This widening of view after such narrowness of observation can be startling, putting the war itself in its place.*

The avoidance of predictable anger and the fastening upon the unexpected detail make Gurney himself present in his war poems, even when he is talking about someone else. For example, in 'The Silent One', which begins:

> Who died on the wires, and hung there, one of two –
> Who for his hours of life had chattered through
> Infinite lovely chatter of Bucks accent . . .

There is no mythologizing of the dead boy on the wires – surely the most appalling and demoralizing sight the troops on the Western Front had to endure – nor any attempt to shock. What is missed is his 'chatter': not loss of promise, ending of beauty and youth – grander conceptions which may come later – but the sudden cessation of the small inconsequences of life. That the chatter had the stamp of Buckinghamshire on it would have been as significant to the dead soldier as Gurney's Gloucestershire background was to him.

Then the poem, in a domestic fashion, goes on to describe how Gurney disobeyed an order, on the grounds of common sense, and apparently got away with it:

> Till the politest voice – a finicking accent, said:
> 'Do you think you might crawl through there: there's a hole'.
> Darkness, shot at: I smiled, as politely replied –
> 'I'm afraid not, Sir' . . .

* His interest in skies is one aspect of his difference from his 'Georgian' contemporaries, or he saw it so. In a rather cocky letter to the more successful Edmund Blunden, c.1920, he says, of Blunden's own poetry: 'Had you lived in Gloucestershire more than the general background of green leafage-stuff would seem to appear to me. The clouds here are terrific. I mean that you seem to write when [you] have become absorbed by lane-look. Here it would be different.'

'Finicking' is precise, and the exchange of politenesses comic. Already, quickly moving, impressionistic, this is not quite like any war poem one has read. But there is more surprise to come. Gurney tells us he kept flat under the bullets:

> And thought of music – and swore deep heart's deep oaths
> (Polite to God) . . .

That parenthesis could only have been written either by a man with no sense of the absurd (which we know from the previous lines, and from his letters, was certainly not the case with Gurney) or by a man who had risen above the absurd, who had lost all fear of being laughed at, had now no wish to appear sophisticated or knowing (although he was capable of appearing so) and who was in unembarrassed touch with the most childlike part of his nature.

So, at all events, I felt when I first read this poem, with its queer diction that matches the queer but precise content, an unpompous formality that controls shifts of tone and mood. Then, reading on among his other war poems and his agonized personal pieces, his exultations, praises, desperations, I found among his lyrics (which do sing) 'The High Hills':

> The high hills have a bitterness
> Now they are not known
> And memory is poor enough consolation
> For the soul hopeless gone.
> Up in the air there beech tangles wildly in the wind –
> That I can imagine
> But the speed, the swiftness, walking into clarity,
> Like last year's bryony are gone.

The tune matches the sense, is a part of the meaning, and that is rare. I began to wonder why I had not come across his work before. True, among the knowledgeable his name was sometimes mentioned; W. H. Auden had printed 'The High Hills' in his Commonplace book *A Certain World*; but where were the learned articles, biographies, generous selections in anthologies?

Then, as I learned more about Gurney*, I began to suspect that, apart from his own disinclination to compete, or pretend, several other things were working against him.

---

* The biographical omission was remedied in 1978 by Michael Hurd's *The Ordeal of Ivor Gurney* (OUP). There the story is told so well that I am able to be brief here; biographical details are largely drawn from Hurd's account.

First, he was acknowledged to be a musician, a composer of songs, of genius – and we always doubt whether a man can be good at two things. Second, he was mentally unbalanced: from about 1912, when he was twenty-two, he had been subject to mental breakdowns and in 1922 he was put in an asylum (where he wrote some of his best poems) for the last fifteen years of his life. So, Gurney was not only 'primarily' a musician (and a 'local' poet and an odd sort of war poet) he was a 'mad' poet too, and the combination of all these things had caused him to be shunted off into a siding.

But at least seventy out of every hundred poems included here show no sign of mental disturbance at all – unless to be a poet is to be in such a condition, which is possible, and certainly Gurney showed himself unsuited to the routines of 'ordinary' life. Also, where there are signs of unbalance, they are obvious; too many of his preoccupations crowd in at once and fall over each other: his sense of having been betrayed, his memories of his comrades in France, of Gloucestershire, of walks at night. The result, though seldom completely incoherent, is confused and painful. But these are also the themes of his best work and, right up to the end of his working life, he is capable of sudden, pictorial, simplicities.

Because there are so many interesting distractions on the way to a reading of Gurney's verse, my dearest wish would be for the reader to approach him first with no knowledge at all of his medical history. With a fate so dramatic and terrible this is hardly possible. But, so far as his poetry goes, by far the most extraordinary thing is that, apart from the occasional, terrible, shouts of indignation to God, there is hardly an event, certainly no fellow inmate, or attendant, from those last confined years, despite continuous writing, that is mentioned. It is as though, so far as the sources of his poetry are concerned, he simply ignores his situation. This surely should be a hint to the reader, at least at first, to do the same.

Ivor Bertie Gurney was born at 3 Queen Street, Gloucester, on 28 August 1890, the son of a tailor. A young clergyman, the Revd Alfred Cheesman, stood as godparent at his christening, and this was to have a significant effect on Gurney's life. As he grew, Cheesman took him under his protection, lending him books, walking and talking with him, and became the first of the surrogate parents Gurney was to acquire. So much so that he became a mystery to his

4

own family. In the words of his sister: 'The truth was, he did not seem to belong to us . . . He simply called on us briefly, and left again without a word!'*

He was educated, as a chorister, at King's School, Gloucester, and in 1911, encouraged and subsidized by Cheesman, won an Open Scholarship to the Royal College of Music. Marion Scott recorded her first glimpse of him at the College 'wearing a thick, dark blue Severn pilot's coat, more suggestive of an out-of-door life than the composition lesson with Sir Charles Stanford for which (by the manuscript tucked under his arm) he was clearly bound. But what struck me more was the look of latent force in him, the fine head with its profusion of light brown hair (not too well brushed!) and the eyes, behind their spectacles, were of mixed colouring – in Gurney's case hazel, grey, green and agate – which Erasmus once said was regarded by the English as denoting genius. "This", I said to myself, "must be the new Composition Scholar whom they call Schubert."' This is the Marion Scott who befriended him, arranged for his first poems to be published and who sent him books when he was in France. (It was F. W. Harvey, however, his Gloucester friend, who lent him Robert Bridges' *The Spirit of Man* in the trenches, with its selections from Whitman and Gerard Manley Hopkins. The latter has often been thought of as an influence on Gurney, but his initial reaction was unfavourable.)† Marion Scott plays a central part in the history of Gurney and his work. It was she who kept and transcribed his music and poetry for the rest of his life. That we have any Gurney at all is largely owing to her.

The impression he made at the College was of erratic brilliance. Hurd quotes Sir Charles Stanford: 'In later years Sir Charles declared that of all his pupils – Vaughan Williams, Ireland, Bliss and dozens more – Gurney was potentially "the biggest of them all. But [he added] he was the least teachable."'

In 1912 Gurney began to set poems to music, including five

* Hurd, op. cit. (as are most of the following references).

† 'My best friend went out on patrol some weeks back, and has never returned. I am glad to say that we accidentally met on that morning and he lent me R.B.'s 'Spirit of Man'. Mine for always I suppose now, unless that event occurs which dissolves such rights of ownership, or desire. For it is a good book, though very far below what it might be. Why all that Shelley, and Dixon, and Hopkins, or what's his name of the crazy, precious diction?' *Letter to Ethel Voynich, Sept? 1916* (F. W. Harvey was taken prisoner in August.)

5

Elizabethan lyrics. Of these Hurd, himself a musician, says: 'Gurney jumped in one bound from mere competence to mastery and genuine originality.' He adds that in his view the inspiration does not seem to be a musical one at all, but in direct response to the innocence and freedom of the poetry. So it is not surprising that about this time Gurney began to write verse himself. His Gloucestershire friends, John Haines and F. W. Harvey, wrote poetry, John Masefield had recently had a great success with *The Everlasting Mercy*: poetry was on one of its periodic upward swings.

At this time too came the first signs that the pendulum of his own moods could swing too violently. 'The Young Genius does not feel too well,' he wrote to Marion Scott, 'and his brain won't move as he wishes it to.' He fled from London, to Gloucestershire and his writing friends, where he talked, walked, wrote, smoked, starved himself (he was always poor) and afterwards compulsively ate cream buns. Then the Great War began.

He volunteered, was first turned down because of his eyesight, and then in 1915 was accepted. His letters of the time suggest how bad the previous period had been: 'It is a better way to die; with these men, in such a cause: than the end which seemed near me and was so desirable only just over two years ago.' That may be the self-dramatization of a talented young man; but it is enough to dispose of the idea that Gurney's subsequent mental illness was entirely owing to the war.

But many of his letters, quoted by Hurd, are playful, some funny. He shows himself a good critic: 'The Sonnet of R.B. you sent me, I do not like. It seems to me that Rupert Brooke would not have improved with age, would not have broadened; his manner had become a mannerism, both in rhythm and diction. I do not like it ... Great poets, great creators are not much influenced by immediate events: those must sink in to the very foundations and be absorbed.' That 'I do not like it' repeated: there is something formidable about Gurney. The poem he included with the letter, however, 'To the Poet Before Battle', does not show him practising what he preaches.

From France he sent back more poems. Marion Scott approached the firm of Sidgwick and Jackson. They were published under the title *Severn and Somme* in 1917 and went into a second edition. While he was in France he also composed five song-settings (one for his own 'Only the Wanderer') of which Hurd says 'four are undoubted masterpieces'.* Two were performed in England while he was in France.

In the same year he was wounded, not seriously enough for a 'blighty', then gassed, in uncertain circumstances, and at last sent home. After a spell in hospital he went on an easy training course, 'owing to slight indigestion presumably due to gas: wink, wink!'

He had survived. His poems had been published and were selling, his music was being performed; he was writing more poems, more music; there is even some evidence that he fell in love with one of his nurses, though it came to nothing; there is little sign in Gurney's work of any overt sexual drive. There are hints that he felt guilty that he was not in France, that he had let his comrades down, had somehow cheated ('wink, wink!'). Then, in March 1918, Marion Scott received a letter which began: 'Yesterday I felt and talked to (I am serious) the spirit of Beethoven.'

Once again, this might have been self-dramatization; the letter ends with humour, aimed at his boyhood Gloucester friend, the composer Herbert Howells: 'I could not get much about Howells off L. van B.; (the memory is faint) he was reluctant to speak; whether Howells is to die or not to develop I could not gather.' But things became more serious. There were suicide letters, and by June he was asking his superiors to put him in an asylum. In October 1918 he was discharged from the army and sent back to his alarmed family in Gloucester.

The next four years are a graph of mental disturbance and recovery. He went back to the Royal College for a time, to study under Vaughan Williams, but he was too restless, and took to wandering, occasionally sleeping on the Embankment or walking through the night back to Gloucester (he was justifiably proud of being a 'nightwalker'). Early in this period his second volume of poems, *War's Embers*†, was published, but he remained desperately short of cash. He had a small pension (twelve shillings a week) and friends helped, but they could not help enough. Like many men returned from France – and here the war surely does play its part – there is something inconsolable about him at this time. He worked as a church organist, cinema pianist, farm labourer, tax clerk, but noth-

* The four songs are settings of Masefield's 'By a Bierside', F. W. Harvey's 'In Flanders', his own 'Severn Meadows' (printed as 'Only the Wanderer'), and Raleigh's 'Even such is Time'. The exception Hurd makes is Yeats' 'The Fiddler of Dooney' ('amiable and fluent'), which he suspects is a re-working of earlier material.

† Sidgwick and Jackson, London, 1919.

ing lasted for long. Sometimes he settled for periods, with his aunt at Longford outside Gloucester, then in a farm cottage on the slopes of the Cotswolds under his beloved Crickley Hill ('Felling a Tree' gives some idea of his life there, and the hopes he had of it). 'What I Will Pay' shows the unbalanced regime he set himself: he seems to have decided, for instance, to go without sleep.

Friends rallied to him, Gloucestershire ones, influential London ones – Vaughan Williams, Walter de la Mare, J. C. Squire, and others – but nothing seemed to suffice.

Possibly this is because he was too preoccupied. During this time – 1919 to 1922 – sleepless or not, he was doing some of his best work in verse (he also wrote much music): 'Drachms and Scruples', 'Walking Song', 'Cotswold Ways', 'Water Colours', 'The Bohemians', 'Between the Boughs', 'The Silent One', 'The Lock Keeper', 'Longford Dawns', 'Time to Come', 'Yesterday Lost', 'The Hoe Scrapes Earth', 'The High Hills', 'Clay' – all belong to this period. So, as often happens in the story of Gurney, just when we begin to see pathos in his situation, and perhaps unconsciously to patronize him, he satisfactorily eludes us.

Worse than pathos was to come. In September 1922 he was committed to Barnwood House, in Gloucester, a private asylum for the insane. In December he was moved to the City of London Mental Hospital at Dartford, Kent. He never saw Gloucestershire again.

> I who was worker at dawn, who saw winter dawns even
> Walking from work, am stiffening, wasting in one
> Packed ward, where ceiling flat-white is for heaven,
> Electric-lamp bulbs for the night lights or great bright sun.
>
> If it were ever necessary or right to punish
> Me, why not labouring free in the open air –
> Or using for eighteen hours powers that do diminish
> By not using . . .

(from 'Memory')*

This is from a poem which becomes diffuse and is not included in this collection (he wrote several called 'Memory'), but is the only description of his physical surroundings that I have found among his papers. Apart from this brief picture he seems to have decided to live in the France and the Gloucestershire of his past; also in his reading.

* GA MS15 (49)

8

The behaviour which led his family to take the step in 1922 was described to me in conversation by his sister-in-law, Mrs Ronald Gurney. 'He started going to the Police Station every morning asking for a revolver because he wanted to shoot himself. In the end the police came and said we'd have to do something about him – and by that time it was either him or us – so we got a doctor and a magistrate here and when they came Ivor was as right as rain. They said, "We can't commit this man. There's nothing wrong with him." So Pop [Ronald Gurney] said, "You go into the next room, pretend to read the newspaper, and see what happens." They did this, and sure enough, within a few seconds, Ivor had crept up to one of them and said, "I say, old sport. You don't happen to have a revolver on you, do you? I want to shoot myself." – and that was that. They put him in Barnwood.'

It is possible to smile at the 'I say, old sport' without underestimating Gurney's suffering. But there is an odd vein of teasing humour in Gurney – it is seldom in his poems, which soon became unposed and intimate (he detested irony and uses it only once, in 'The Signallers') – but the teasing, mildly malicious, persisted in his dealings with the world. Marion Scott tells of visiting him in 1935. When she saw that he stared at a particularly fine sunset she exclaimed at it herself, and said, 'Isn't it fine?' 'I don't know about sunsets,' replied Gurney. 'I never see them now.' This, from such an eloquent lover of skies, must surely have been a jab at the faithful Miss Scott and the outside world she represented, which he considered had betrayed him. It was, perhaps justifiably, cruel. It could also of course, and more sombrely, have been true; that he could no longer 'see' in the way he once had.

He had not been betrayed by the world. It seems that many did everything they could. Whether modern medicine could have saved him, it is hard to say, but his disqualifications from ordinary life do not seem serious: they appear to have consisted of the habit of walking or working all night, eating irregularly or not at all, and of being generally unpredictable and demanding; also, of being unable to keep a job. There were, as well, delusions of being persecuted by electrical waves. A companion might have kept him in the world for longer, perhaps for the rest of his life. Even an injection of cash might have helped, for it was lack of it that caused him to be a burden to others who did not have much of it themselves. His family cannot be blamed (nor did he blame them in his long 'Appeals for Release'); he made life impossible for his brother, whom he nearly caused to become distracted himself. Besides, he knew that there was something wrong; a man who does not want something done for him – done *to* him – does not go round asking policemen and magistrates for revolvers.

In Barnwood – it must from the date have been among the first things he did – Gurney wrote a sheaf of poems. In one of these, 'There Is a Man', he tries to describe his mental condition: 'The pain is in thought, which will not freely range' – an echo of the letter ten years before. But another poem – and they have the appearance of being written hard upon each other – 'The Incense Bearers' is a technically clever untangling of a thought which is removed from his present circumstances. This is to be the pattern of his writing from now on. Apart from shouts of indignation ('To God') and the 'Appeals for Release' addressed to the Prime Minister, the Metropolitan Police, and so on, he writes on the whole as if he were free. That he kept on writing, and reading, is remarkable enough, but to do so with such disdain for his fate is heroic. 'But my blood, in its colour even, is known fighter':

> They have left me little indeed, how shall I best keep
> Memory from sliding content down to drugged sleep?
> But my blood, in its colour even, is known fighter.
> If I were hero for such things here would I make wars
> As love for dead things trodden under in January's stars,
>
> Or the gold trefoil itself spending in careless places
> Tiny graces like music's for its past exquisitenesses.
> Why war for huge domains of the planet's heights or plains?
> (Little they leave me.) It is a dream. Hardly my heart dares
> Tremble for glad leaf-drifts thundering under January's stars.

> ('*Memory*')

His unfailing visitor, Marion Scott, found seeing him almost unendurable: 'Ivor is so heart-breakingly sane in his insanity.' It was now that she left instructions for everything that he wrote, music and poetry, to be preserved and sent to her.

'Memory' shows the way Gurney's poems developed after his first two books. It is still traditional in shape, and Gurney always loved rhyme, but it is more direct. In a sense he consciously attempts to

abjure literature — 'He desiring books and I truth rather than the /
Writing continual' as he said of Southey ('To Gloucestershire').*
Whereas the early poems seem addressed to an audience, trying to
impress (as was natural in a young writer), the later Gurney is talking
to himself, to the air, and his relationship with the reader becomes
easier and more private. But there are plenty of indications of the
later Gurney in the first books. In *Severn and Somme* 'Pain' shows
that he was already better at indignation than self-pity and 'Only the
Wanderer' is almost pure music.

War's Embers did not mark a great advance. It contains humour
('Companion — North-East Dug-out') and touches a theme that re-
curs ('Old Martinmas Eve'): the hope for music to come to him,
'some most quiet tune', so that he can catch and express the moment;
then his regret, verbally musical, at its non-arrival. This poem is
more than usually reminiscent of Edward Thomas, whose prose
Gurney loved. If he had seen any poems of Thomas by this time,
which seems likely, he shows himself quicker, and readier for his
influence, than any of his English contemporaries. Also, in this
second book, Gurney attempts transcriptions of the ordinary speech
and slang of army life — dixies, whizzbangs, 'revally' and the like —
very jaunty, leading at least one reviewer to rebuke him for being too
colloquial. On the other hand, it also caused Edmund Blunden to say
of his war poems, 'to this day they express part of the Western Front
secret of fifty years ago with distinctive, intimate and imaginative
quickness.' However, it was perhaps not the kind of war poetry that
the public wanted. His third collection, titled in manuscript *Rewards
of Wonder*, was rejected.†

This is understandable because Gurney begins to sound original,
pressing music out of ordinary speech. With signs of the pressure too,
queer contortions and omissions which became a part of his manner.
They are intentional, as changes in his notebooks show, and are part
of his homage to his beloved Elizabethans, especially Shakespeare:
phrases like 'nerves soothed were so sore shaken' (the 'that' omitted)
have an Elizabethan ring about them. He also goes in for outrageous
rhymes:

---

* Appendix.

† Gurney probably refers to this rejection in an undated letter to Edmund Blunden:
'I hope you will not mind my sending you this stuff, in spite of the base word I am
proud. Sidgwick with some politeness has rejected it, but myself see [*sic*] thundering
good stuff there, beauty and a very good sense of form, and no swank.'

> ... fill full
> Those rolling tanks with chlorinated clay mixture
> And curse the mud with vain veritable vexture.

('Crucifix Corner')

Later he would carry the combination of slang and a sudden wider perspective as far as it could be carried – maybe further – but the risk he takes is exhilarating:

> True, the size of the rum ration was still a shocker
> But at last over Aubers the majesty of the dawn's veil swept.

('Serenade')

He served as a Private in the 2nd/5th Gloucestershire Regiment and his war is very much that of the private soldier: a cleaner business, humanly speaking, than that of someone with more responsibility. A conscripted Private's job in war is, rightly, to obey orders and stay alive, meanwhile making himself as comfortable as possible. In other words, to remain (unlike the Officer candidates in 'The Bohemians') triumphantly a civilian. Thus Gurney's account of his war contains stories of the scrounging of soft jobs (and guilt at this, for he was not, after all, an 'ordinary' Private), descriptions of the pleasure of having clean straw to lie on, a candle-stub to write letters by. He permits himself few large statements about the war, indeed it is possible that he barely took it seriously, and in this he would surely have been at one with his fellow Privates.* This is not to say that Gurney's war was 'funny' – any more than the Douanier Rousseau's picture of War as a grinning child on a horse crossing a landscape of severed limbs is funny. But Gurney can be allowed to describe his war for himself. (The nearest thing to his version, uncannily so, is in prose, in the opening pages of Ford Madox Ford's *No More Parades*, which is set in Gurney's part of the Front.)

Behind his lyric poetry the drive is a determination to celebrate the sacredness of the moment, to share sudden accesses of joy, and also to deplore its absence. The intricacies of human relations are not his subject: he attempts very little love-poetry, and when there are

---

* 'I did not intend this as a 'War Book' – it happens to be concerned with war. I should prefer it to be about a good kind of peace ... We find ourselves Privates in foot regiments. We search how we may see formal goodness in a life singularly inimical, hateful, to us.' David Jones, Preface to *In Parenthesis*, first published the year of Gurney's death.

people in his poems ('The Lock Keeper') they are seen with a rather abstract, lonely, passion of respect. He is concerned with personal epiphanies, the sense of enlargement suddenly granted, say, by the silhouettes of certain trees in certain lights; and with the idea of history, present, all around him. In a sense, therefore, his subject is himself, as he said in his delightful preface to *Severn and Somme*: 'I fear that those who buy the book (or even borrow), to get information about the Gloucesters, will be disappointed. Most of the book is concerned with a person named Myself, and the rest with my county, Gloucester, that whether I die or live stays always with me – being itself so beautiful, so full of memories; whose people are so good to be friends with, so easy-going and so frank.'

In some ways he is a consciously 'unpoetical' poet, refusing to enthuse about nightingales ('Three I heard once. . .'), preferring cabbages to 'that ink-proud lady the rose' ('The Garden'). In 'The Escape' he comes near to announcing a poetic:

> I believe in the increasing of life: whatever
> Leads to the seeing of small trifles,
> Real, beautiful, is good; and an act never
> Is worthier than in freeing spirit that stifles
> Under ingratitude's weight, nor is anything done
> Wiselier than the moving or breaking to sight
> Of a thing hidden under by custom – revealed,
> Fulfilled, used (sound-fashioned) any way out to delight:
> Trefoil – hedge sparrow – the stars on the edge at night.

'Wiselier' is typical Gurney. Such usages are not, I think, affectations. His occasional bathetic contrasts – the rum ration followed immediately by the majesty of the dawn in the extract from 'Serenade' already quoted – are also intentional and a representation of the mind's movement. The risks that he takes with his rhymes hold the poems together, and he usually carries the meaning on and through them, avoiding the jog-trot. He is always musical, sometimes unforgettably so, but his tunes are his own, and you never feel that he has allowed them to shape his thought. His faithfulness to his meaning is allowed to yield its own music.

He is the master of first lines. To go through his first lines in the archive (a list put together in the course of making this edition) is like reading one huge mysterious poem. No poet could live up to so many splendid beginnings: grandiloquent ones such as 'Darkness has cheating swiftness', 'What evil coil of fate has fastened me', 'Smudgy dawn scarfed with military colours'; and interestingly conversational ones, like 'One comes across the strangest things in walks'. (That is probably the single most important thing to say about Gurney: he is almost always interesting.) He is also capable of magnificent, poem-saving, last lines.

In between, there are sometimes flaws which are obvious: flat phrases, quirky ones, confusing syntax. These are often unfortunate later additions, but not always. He is a poet, on the whole, who should not be read line by line. His poems are more like jets of energy that hurry to their end. The bubbles, the hollow places, do not diminish the force of the jet if you allow yourself to be carried along with it. Even at his most contorted, his general meaning usually comes clear if we persist, not stopping, to the end; and individual obscurities clarify themselves when we go back. Gurney did however write some perfect poems (like 'The Songs I Had') – he is good at the short sprint, the poem expressed in two or three breaths.

But perfection of that kind is not what he was interested in. He is not a Georgian poet who 'broke down' but one who consciously though unprogrammatically broke away, and was, as far as he knew, on his own, fortified by his beloved Whitman. His subjects are conventional, but the intensity with which he sees and expresses them is not. He knew this, and one can sense his impatience with his more popular contemporaries because their matter – hedgerows, skies and so on – he considered peculiarly his own. So, 'free of useless fashions', he tries to go behind their verse, behind the verse of preceding centuries, back to his 'masters', the Elizabethans and Jacobeans, in much the same way as the Lake poets went back to the Ballads. The impatience is in his language, as though he wished to be as free as the Elizabethans in fashioning a new one. He wants a poetry composed on the nerves, 'a book that brings the clear / Spirit of him that wrote' ('To Long Island First'), and he hurls himself headlong, so that we feel 'The football rush of him', as he says in admiration of George Chapman. The result is, although Gurney tells us surprisingly little about himself, that we feel he has entirely opened his heart; there is nothing withheld, or prudent.

In fact the imprudence is so obvious that any fool could have warned him that it would end in tears. The tragedy is that it did. A tragedy for us as well as for him because it seems to imply what we must not believe: that it is not possible to live – sanely – with such intensity. Whereas his advice ('The New Poet') is entirely sane:

Let him say all men's thought nor sleep until
Some great thing he has fashioned of love inevitable.
For the rest, may he follow his happiness' true will.

Although I have been determined to help him escape the limiting tag
of 'local poet', Gurney's landscape is nevertheless such a special one
it is worth saying a few words about it.

The city of Gloucester retains a powerful personality. All sorts of
histories, Roman, Dane, and later, still lurk there. Gurney's birth-
place was set on top of the Roman wall, as has recently been
revealed, and under the house, unknown to him – but he would not
have been surprised – built into the wall, were shops of medieval
times and of the seventeenth century. Gloucester is a docks as well as
a county town; these are decayed now, but they still impart to the
streets a sense of the sea, of being in touch with distant places. You
can hear seagulls. In Gurney's day, the docks were busier; as a child
walking with his mother he saw American seamen, overheard them
talk, and dreamed of America for the rest of his life. But perhaps it is
the architecture that leaves the greatest mark on Gurney's vocabu-
lary, sometimes mysteriously so to a reader who does not know the
town. Perhaps in that sense only he is a local poet. The towers of the
cathedral, the towers and spires of other churches, St Nicholas, the
'two Maries' and so on, imposing yet homely, had, as Blunden
suggested in his Preface, much to do with Gurney's sense of form.
When he uses phrases like 'frame such squares and lights as these', or
'set square to form' – his poems are scattered with references to
framed squareness – it is surely these, the first buildings he saw, that
he is equating with a sense of rightness and order: 'Rest squares
reckonings Love set awry'. He says so himself in an unfinished
fragment in a notebook:

> The squareness of West Gloucester pleases me.
> The spires and square places and the supremacy
> Peter's Place has above that white-looked stretch,
> The river meadows . . .

(Peter's Place is the Cathedral.)

Gloucester has hills on one side, and the Severn River on the other,
where his father came from. An easy walk out of the town – across
the bridge at Over – and you are at Maisemore, 'sacred' Maisemore,
on the river; nearby are Ashleworth, Hartpury, Framilode, and

other places whose names are the litany Gurney recited in France and during the years he was out of sight of them in his asylum; sixty years later one can still see why.

As a boy, if he put his nose out of his front door, he saw, one way, the famous Cross of Gloucester – not a stone cross but the place where the four main streets have met since the foundation of the town – and if he looked the other way, down Barton Street, he saw, at the end of it (the effect is still theatrical) his mother's country, the green Cotswold Hills. It is an ideal imaginative landscape, poised between the past and a dreamed-of liberated future, between History and Paradise, for those are the roles the town and hills play in his verse. Gurney was not really a country boy, as his middle-class London friends thought. (Sometimes to Londoners anything outside their city is 'the country'!) He was a town boy, loving the town, but also dreaming of escape, and escape was within eye-shot. He had only to walk along his street for a couple of miles to the steep Portway and – 'One comes across the strangest things in walks' . . .

> Strange the large difference of up Cotswold ways:
> Birdlip climbs bold and treeless to a bend,
> Portway to dim wood-lengths without end,
> And Crickley goes to cliffs are the crown of days.
>
> ('*Cotswold Ways*')

In 1922, the poems show a darkening, although it is irregular. 'Sonnet: September 1922' is the most extraordinary and unforgettable. Within a few days of writing it, Gurney was in Barnwood House. There, his poems regain simplicity, which afterwards comes and goes. One of the earliest, for example, 'A Wish', probably inspired by something read in a newspaper, carries simplicity very far, but is deceptive. In it he suggests, in advance of his time, that the children of West Ham should be given what we would now call 'adventure playgrounds':

> Not crowded together, but with a plot of land,
> Where one might play and dig, and use spade or the hand
> In managing or shaping earth in such forms
> As please the sunny mind or keep out of harms
> The mind that's always good when let go its way
> (I think) so there's work enough in a happy day.

(Among Gurney's agonies during his confinement, listed in 'Appeal' after 'Appeal', is that he was not given work.) It is typical that he should say 'one might play' and not '*they* might play', and that he believes bare hands will serve for (his favourite ambitions) 'managing or shaping'. But the parenthesis '(I think)' is also revealing. Gurney's mind had been 'let go its way' because he had believed that the free mind is always good; now he is not sure, and with his usual honesty says so.

The asylum period contains many successes of different kinds: 'The Incense Bearers', 'On Somme', 'Hedger', 'The Mangel-Bury', 'The Dream', 'Varennes'; the variety of tone and style makes one wonder why he was where he was. The subjects are the same, with a new one added; outrage ('To God'). The lyrical touch is as sure, sometimes surer. He now inhabits the past, for as far as he is concerned he has no present:

> I march once more with hurt shoulders,
> And scent the air, a friend with soldiers.

('The Depths')

1925 must have been an unusually bad year, for he went back to old poems and tried to re-write them. It is a period from which an editor would like to rescue him. He even tried to re-write and add to *War's Embers*, and the changes confuse, belong to a different mood. But at the same time he also wrote 'Varennes', 'The Coin', and the formally adept 'Epitaph on a Young Child', as well as much music.

In 1926 he had one last extraordinary burst of poetic energy. All his writing and composing life he had passionately admired the Elizabethans and Jacobeans; indeed he showed signs of willing himself to become one: his notebooks contain verse addresses to Marston, Tourneur, Ben Jonson and so on, usually in the person of a contemporary. Now – and by the dates on some of the poems it seems to have been in September 1926 – he succeeds: the period suddenly speaks through his mouth, or rather, some timeless, classical utterance bursts out of him. The poems are not *pastiches*; they are more like acts of ventriloquism. Among confused poems of pain, with syntactical jumps difficult logically to follow ('I Read Now So', 'I Would Not Rest', 'December Evening'), poems which nevertheless contain their own 'rough power', he wrote dozens of clear, almost abstract lyrics. The ones that work are extraordinarily fluent; they hardly bear a correction in the MS and no preliminary drafts have been found. Gurney had been right when he said, earlier, 'Little now to learn'. He now ceases to hark back to the war.

It would be good to find them his best work. But, though some-times good, they seem bloodless compared to the previous work. It is as though the long struggle to remember, to live sanely, to celebrate his comrades, his native place, himself, went up in one quick flash, scattered, and that was the end.

He remembers the Severn floods and regrets he never celebrated the way they made the meadows especially fertile:

> I could have sung, but knew no fitting tunes
> (For all my lore) of the spread
> Of coloured sheets of the floods that ensure all June's
> Dark fan-grasses of the pretty head.

('*Traffic in Sheets*')

He says goodbye to the town of Gloucester, which he knows is changed:

> A dirty water drifts between crampt
> Borders, lies and goes past the shadow.
>
> In far ravines and in heights love delights in
> The trees will pity the haggard Half-Lady
> Of crystal-sprung Severn,
> The flowers beneath accuse angels betraying.

('*The Bridge*')

When one remembers his early passion for the town, that poem is possibly the saddest that he wrote. He was not beaten, but from this time on, so far as can be judged from the remaining manuscripts, he wrote mainly in prose, very variable in quality and coherence.

Over the years Marion Scott preserved the manuscripts and typed, or had typed, most of them. Occasionally she sent poems to magazines and several were printed in the 'twenties and 'thirties by J. C. Squire in *The London Mercury*. Squire also included Gurney in two antho-logies: *Selections from Modern Poets*, 1921 and 1924, and *Younger Poets of Today*, 1932. *Music and Letters* also published the oc-casional Gurney poem, as did the Royal College of Music magazine and the Gloucester Journal. This represents Gurney's publishing history of poems from 1919 to 1954.

Marion Scott prepared a selection, but there is no record of this having been sent to a publisher. Gurney's friend John Haines (friend, too, of Edward Thomas, W. H. Davies and many other poets) also made a (very good) selection, but the 1939 war came and the project was abandoned. Luckily for his verse, however, Gurney's music was still being performed and in 1920 the young composer Gerald Finzi had heard a performance of 'Sleep', Gurney's setting of a poem by Fletcher, composed in 1912. Finzi thought it the most beautiful thing of its kind he had come across, and made it his business to find out more about the composer. So began what was for him a lifelong effort to make Gurney better known and to have his manuscripts, of poetry as well as music, published. After Marion Scott, it is to Gerald Finzi and his wife Joy (neither of whom ever met Gurney) that we owe most.

Finzi, assisted by his friend the composer Howard Ferguson, at once ran up against an unexpected difficulty. Marion Scott, after her long guardianship, had become somewhat retentive of the manuscripts. She was also frequently unwell. This caused endless delays, but at last, in 1938, the long-projected issue of *Music and Letters*, devoted wholly to Gurney, was published. It contained some of his poems and enthusiastic tributes from Vaughan Williams, Walter de la Mare, J. C. Squire and others. Oxford University Press had also agreed to bring out two volumes of the songs. In 1937 Gurney was ill; 'proof copies of *Music and Letters* were rushed to him, but he was too weak to take the wrapping paper off the parcel and seemed not to understand what the articles signified. He was told about the songs but only murmured, "It is too late" . . .' A month later he died of tuberculosis.

The impression the tribute was intended to make was muffled by the anxieties of the time and by the outbreak of war. In 1945 Gerald Finzi began again, encountering more delaying tactics on the part of Marion Scott whom in moments of exasperation he took to calling 'Maid Marion'. He persisted, though he was under no illusion about the difficulties he would face if he were ever allowed to go through the jumbled boxes in her keeping. He had made a preliminary report in 1935. What he said then goes to the heart of the difficulty (and to the heart of a Gurney editor). He is talking of the music, but it is equally true of the poetry: 'The sorting has been even more difficult than I expected, chiefly because there is comparatively little one can really be sure is bad. Even the late 1925 asylum songs, though they get more and more involved (and at the same time more disintegrated, if you know what I mean) have a curious coherence, which makes it difficult to know whether they are really over the border. I think the eventual difficulty in "editing" the later Gurney may be great: a neat mind could smooth away the queernesses – like Rimsky-Korsakov with Mussorgsky – yet time and familiarity will probably show something not so mistaken after all, about the queer and odd things. However, there are some obviously incoherent things and a good many others of which one can say that it would be better for them not to be published.'* Gurney could hardly have fallen into better hands.

Finzi approached Edmund Blunden as a possible editor for the poems, on the face of it an ideal choice. Blunden had met Gurney (remembering him as a cheery fellow, playing the piano and singing) and had shared many of his wartime experiences. But there were practical difficulties: Blunden was in Hong Kong; Marion Scott died; the Gurney family claimed the manuscripts. At last, in 1954, Hutchinson published the *Poems of Ivor Gurney. Principally selected from unpublished manuscripts. With a memoir by Edmund Blunden.* From first to last it had taken Gerald Finzi more than thirty years.

Blunden's memoir, tentative, understanding, respectful, is a small masterpiece of its kind. But his selection of seventy-eight poems is eccentric. He has chosen on the whole the wilder, stranger, later poems, omitting most of the more approachable ones and the simpler lyrics. It is a relief to learn that he did this on purpose, as Gerald Finzi discovered when Blunden replied to a letter:

'You are right about shorter, more gracious pieces, but I hesitated over the degree of "finality" in the others, probably because I was a bit in disruption myself, or *was* it that I thought the book would do better on the rough power of the other sorts? Altogether, a *poet* is obvious all the way, and we should thank Gerald Finzi for insisting on his being "released".'†

Finzi enlarges on this: '[Blunden] deliberately avoided including much of the mellifluous Georgian work, for fear of antagonizing the present critical trend. I rather regretted this, but as it was only supposed to be a first selection, I can see his point.'

Thus Finzi, in 1935 fearful that 'a neat mind could smooth away the queernesses', had found twenty years later an editor who, himself out of tune with contemporary taste, was only too willing to rely on Gurney's 'rough power' to take him under and around and through what he understood to be the literary fortifications of the time . . .

* Hurd, op. cit., p. 184.
† Finzi–Blunden correspondence GA 51.

Blunden is soon writing: 'I'm afraid the book has not been reviewed much . . . Well, there haven't been many recent vols. of verse to my knowledge to come anywhere near this one for poetry at once traditional and original, and in the long run this must be recognized.' Three months later he wrote, with an air of conceding defeat: 'I've had one or two letters about Ivor's "Poems" but the bright boys don't appear, most of them, to have noticed their chance . . .'

After her husband's death in 1956 Joy Finzi continued with the task of collecting, sorting and typing Gurney's manuscripts. Anyone examining the archives comes upon her traces with relief. But to the outside world it was almost as though Blunden's edition had never been. W. H. Auden read it, and, as has been said, printed some Gurney in his published Commonplace book, *A Certain World* (1971). That was about all.

What went wrong? To some extent, surely, the indifference was because Blunden (and the reader) knew that Gurney was mentally ill. This made Blunden pass 'queernesses', of spelling, punctuation and phrasing, in typescript copies, that sometimes cast a blur over the whole poem. But reference back to a manuscript, where one exists, shows that for the most part these curiosities are not Gurney at all, but mistakes made by the many hands that typed the poems, or more serious misreadings.

During the 'sixties and early 'seventies, Leonard Clark fought for a further edition and in 1973 he printed (with Chatto & Windus – raising part of the money himself) a more catholic selection of 140 poems, omitting thirty-four of Blunden's. But to some extent he was in the same difficulty. When he did reproduce a poem printed by Blunden he naturally used Blunden's version, defective or not; so the mistakes were perpetuated. An editor faced with possibly incorrect typescripts (of poems by an unpredictable writer) is in a difficult position. Both Blunden and Clark are to be praised for not 'smoothing away queernesses'; they were not to know that most of these were not Gurney's.

I have been luckier. A box of MSS (now in the archive) was passed to me by Mrs Ronald Gurney, his sister-in-law, and is described in the Editorial Note to this edition. Checked now against manuscript, just a couple of examples will show how easy the many typing errors were to commit, and how unnecessarily baffling or peculiar they could make the poem. 'Tewkesbury' began, as printed by Blunden (though in this instance corrected by Clark):

> Some Dane looking out from the water-settlements,
> Of settlements there were, must have thought as I . . .

Gurney wrote '*If* settlements . . .'. He did not write:

> Sword shapes, wonder threat
> Brightening my first hopes . . .

('Old Tunes')

but 'wonder *thereat* . . .', and so on, almost everywhere. Whenever possible, then, all the texts in this edition are taken from manuscript.

Leonard Clark stands last in the roll of Gurney pioneers. Without him, Gurney might have foundered under the well-intentioned weighting of Blunden's selection.

Perhaps Gurney's time has now come. If we are, as we think we are, an age that admires honesty, it must be clear that there is seldom any striving for effect, any 'putting it on', in Gurney; none at all after 1920. He wrung the neck of his early elegance ('no swank'). What may have seemed naive and unpolished to his contemporaries has for us the stamp of sincerity. He says of his own poems ('As They Draw to a Close'):

> When you were launched there was small roughness in the touch of words,
> A woman's weapon, a boy's chatter, a thing for barter and loss:

And he goes on to claim, with justice, adopting the persona of Walt Whitman but surely talking about himself:

> But I have roughed the soul American or Yankee at least to truth and
>   instinct,
> And compacted the loose-drifting faiths and questions of men in a few
>   words.

Like Whitman, he was concerned with finding and touching the core of innocence in his own nature and he addressed himself to ours.

The last word should belong to Gerald Finzi, because of what he did for Gurney, and because anyone who has been through the material knows that what he says of it is true. He wrote to Blunden, probably after he had lamented the latter's omissions: 'Besides, I'm prejudiced. All his work, even the worst, seems to have (for me at any rate) the sense of heightened perception which makes art out of artifice.'

CHRONOLOGY

(Based on Michael Hurd's *The Ordeal of Ivor Gurney*, OUP 1978)

1890	28 August	Ivor Bertie Gurney born at 3 Queen Street, Gloucester. (Bertie a family surname.) Second of four children of David Gurney, a tailor (from Maisemore on the River Severn), and Florence Lugg (from Bisley in the Cotswold hills).
		Family move to shop premises at 19 Barton Street.
1900–06		In Gloucester Cathedral Choir and King's School.
1906–11		Articled pupil to Dr Brewer, Cathedral organist. Herbert Howells a fellow-student. Other friends include F. W. Harvey, John Haines, the Misses Hunt, his godfather, the Revd Alfred (later Canon) Cheesman.
1907		Tour of English cathedrals with Alfred Cheesman, taking matriculation examination at Durham.
1911		Scholarship to Royal College of Music, London.
1911–14		At RCM from autumn term 1911 to autumn 1914, with Sir Charles Stanford as tutor. Digs at Fulham; holidays at Gloucester.
		Meets Marion Scott (1877–1953): music historian, editor of RCM magazine.
		Composes 'Eliza' songs (Elizabethan settings), other piano and instrumental pieces.
1914	4 August	War declared. IG volunteers unsuccessfully.
1915	February	Volunteers again; drafted into 2nd/5th Gloucester Regiment ('B' Company).
		With battalion to Northampton, Chelmsford, Epping Forest. Writing verse. In army band.
1916	February	Training at Tidworth, Salisbury Plain.
	25 May	Gloucesters arrive at Le Havre, France, and march towards Flanders.
	May–October	In Laventie-Fauquissart sector (between Béthune and Armentières). In trenches with Welsh regiment at Riez Bailleul; billets at La Gorgue. (Richebourg, Neuve-Chapelle, Robecq, Gonnehem 'at rest'.)

	July	'In reserve' at Aubers Ridge.
		Many letters; MSS of poems and music sent to Marion Scott, who acts as his agent.
	October–December	Battalion moves south to Somme sector near Albert. Somme offensive front line (Grandcourt, Aveluy, Ovillers).
1917	January	Training at Varennes (between Albert and Doullens).
	February	Move south to Ablaincourt sector.
	March	Move east towards St Quentin, following German strategic withdrawal, to Caulincourt (near Vermand).
	6 April	(Good Friday) IG wounded in arm. In hospital at Rouen for six weeks.
		Edward Thomas killed at Arras (9 April).
	May–July	Back with regiment, transferred to Machine Guns. To Arras front; rest at Buire-au-Bois.
		Five of best songs composed during first half of this year. Two performed at RCM concert in London.
	July	Sidgwick & Jackson agree to publish *Severn and Somme* (original title *Strange Service*).
	31 July	Ypres offensive begins.
	August	Gloucesters move north to Ypres.
	September	IG in gas at St Julien, near Passchendaele. 'Blighty'. Sent to Bangour War Hospital, near Edinburgh. Meets Annie Drummond, a VAD. (Later poems dedicated to her as 'Hawthornden'.)
	October	*Severn and Somme* published (46 poems). Favourable reviews.
	November	At Seaton Delaval, Northumberland (Command Depot), on signalling course.
1918	February	In hospital, Newcastle-on-Tyne ('stomach trouble caused by gas').
		At Brancepeth Castle, Durham, training.
	May	Warrington Hospital.
	June	Seaton Delaval. Breakdown; suicide letters.
	July	St Albans, Napsbury Hospital.
	October	Discharged with 'deferred shell-shock' IG returns to Gloucester. Receives Army pension of 12s a week.
		War's Embers (58 poems) accepted by Sidgwick & Jackson. *Severn and Somme* reprinted.

	November	Walk in Black Mountains (Welsh Borders) with John Haines.
	December	In Cornwall staying with Mrs Voynich, novelist, (friend from RCM).
1918–22		Main years of music composition and poems. Takes various jobs unsuccessfully: organist, cinema pianist, tax clerk, in Cold Storage depot, on farm (Dryhill, Cold Slad, on Crickley Hill near Gloucester). Much walking, often at night.
1919	March	Margaret Hunt, early friend and patron, dies.
	May	David Gurney (father) dies.

War's Embers published. 'To His Love' chiefly praised by reviewers; some complaints of colloquialisms of style. New collection of poems, *Rewards of Wonder*, rejected by Sidgwick.

IG returns to RCM with Ralph Vaughan Williams as tutor. Lodgings in Earl's Court, but moves to High Wycombe staying with family of vicar of St Michael's. Organist at St Michael's Church.

1920		Five 'Eliza' songs published, and eight more; also piano preludes and other music accepted. Gerald Finzi hears 'Sleep'.
1921		Stays with aunt at Longford, near Gloucester. Later moves in with his brother Ronald.
1922		Increasing symptoms of mental disturbance; suicide threats to police, etc.
	September	Committed to asylum at Barnwood House, Gloucester.
	December	Moved to Stone House, Dartford, Kent (City of London Mental Hospital).
1922–6		Continual reading, and writing of poems, verse-autobiography and 'Appeals'. Over 1,000 MSS. Music composition also continues, but less intensely, except for 50 songs in 1925. Visited regularly and taken out by Marion Scott and other friends. Marion Scott ensures all possible MSS preserved.

During this time, a number of poems printed in magazines. Gerald Finzi, with Howard Ferguson, urges publication of songs and poems.

| 1923 | | Piano pieces published; and cycle of Housman settings (*Ludlow and Teme*) by Carnegie Collection of British Music. |

1926		Second Housman song-cycle (*The Western Playland*) published; and Edward Thomas settings (*Lights Out*), written 1918–22 with final song 1925.
1926–37		After 1926 fewer MSS surviving: chiefly prose essays, fictional letters, notes, 'Shakespeare' and 'Whitman' scripts, etc. Nothing dated later than 1933.
1932		Visit by Helen Thomas, described in RCM magazine, 1960.
1937		*Music and Letters* magazine symposium on Gurney decided. OUP agree to publish two volumes of songs.
	26 December	Ivor Gurney dies.
	31 December	Buried at Twigworth, near Gloucester. Service taken by Canon Cheesman, the Rector.
1938	January	*Music and Letters* symposium published. OUP publish 2 volumes of ten songs each. Two BBC programmes of Gurney's songs.
1940		Two violin/piano pieces published.
1953		OUP publish 3rd volume of ten songs.
		Hutchinson agree to publish new collection of poems.
	December	Marion Scott dies.
1954		*Poems by Ivor Gurney* – 78 mostly unpublished poems edited with introduction by Edmund Blunden (Hutchinson).
1956		Gerald Finzi dies; Joyce Finzi continues cataloguing of IG's work, and promotion of 4th volume of songs.
1959	December	OUP publish 4th volume of ten songs.
		Gurney MSS donated to Gloucester Public Library on permanent loan by Ronald Gurney (IG's brother).
1973		*Poems of Ivor Gurney* published with Edmund Blunden's introduction – about half of Blunden's previous selection with 97 previously uncollected poems, chosen by Leonard Clark (Chatto & Windus).
1978		*The Ordeal of Ivor Gurney*, biography by Michael Hurd (OUP).
1980		OUP publish 5th volume of 10 songs (ed. Michael Hurd).

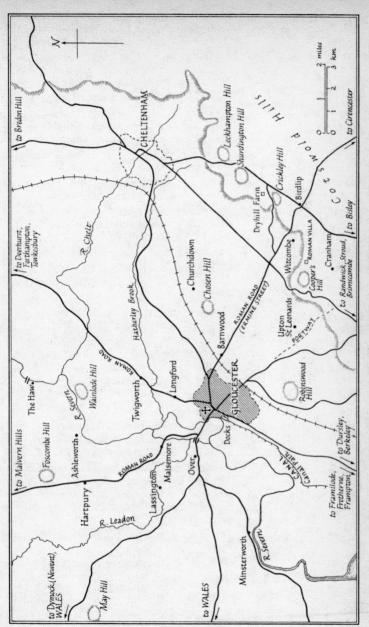

GURNEY'S GLOUCESTERSHIRE

GURNEY'S FRANCE, MAY 1916–SEPTEMBER 1917

I

From *Severn and Somme*
(1917)

To the Poet before Battle

Now, youth, the hour of thy dread passion comes;
Thy lovely things must all be laid away;
And thou, as others, must face the riven day
Unstirred by rattle of the rolling drums,
Or bugles' strident cry. When mere noise numbs
The sense of being, the fear-sick soul doth sway,
Remember thy great craft's honour, that they may say
Nothing in shame of poets. Then the crumbs
Of praise the little versemen joyed to take
Shall be forgotten; then they must know we are,
For all our skill in words, equal in might
And strong of mettle as those we honoured; make
The name of poet terrible in just war,
And like a crown of honour upon the fight.

Strange Service

Little did I dream, England, that you bore me
Under the Cotswold hills beside the water meadows,
To do you dreadful service, here, beyond your borders
And your enfolding seas.

I was a dreamer ever, and bound to your dear service,
Meditating deep, I thought on your secret beauty,
As through a child's face one may see the clear spirit
Miraculously shining.

Your hills not only hills, but friends of mine and kindly,
Your tiny knolls and orchards hidden beside the river
Muddy and strongly-flowing, with shy and tiny streamlets
Safe in its bosom.

Now these are memories only, and your skies and rushy sky-pools
Fragile mirrors easily broken by moving airs . . .
In my deep heart for ever goes on your daily being,
And uses consecrate.

Think on me too, O Mother, who wrest my soul to serve you
In strange and fearful ways beyond your encircling waters;
None but you can know my heart, its tears and sacrifice;
None, but you, repay.

The Mother

We scar the earth with dreadful engin'ry;
She takes us to her bosom at the last;
Hiding our hate with love, who cannot see
Of any child the faults; and holds us fast.
We'll wait in quiet till our passion's past.

Bach and the Sentry

Watching the dark my spirit rose in flood
    On that most dearest Prelude of my delight.
The low-lying mist lifted its hood,
    The October stars showed nobly in clear night.

When I return, and to real music-making,
    And play that Prelude, how will it happen then?
Shall I feel as I felt, a sentry hardly waking,
    With a dull sense of No Man's Land again?

Song and Pain

Out of my sorrow have I made these songs,
    Out of my sorrow;
Though somewhat of the making's eager pain
    From joy did borrow.

Some day, I trust, God's purpose of pain for me
    Shall be complete,
And then – to enter in the House of Joy . . .
    Prepare, my feet.

Song

Only the wanderer
    Knows England's graces,
Or can anew see clear
    Familiar faces.

And who loves joy as he
    That dwells in shadows?
Do not forget me quite,
    O Severn meadows.

Ballad of the Three Spectres

As I went up by Ovillers
    In mud and water cold to the knee,
There went three jeering, fleering spectres,
    That walked abreast and talked of me.

The first said, 'Here's a right brave soldier
    That walks the dark unfearingly;
Soon he'll come back on a fine stretcher,
    And laughing for a nice Blighty.'

The second, 'Read his face, old comrade,
    No kind of lucky chance I see;
One day he'll freeze in mud to the marrow,
    Then look his last on Picardie.'

Though bitter the word of these first twain
    Curses the third spat venomously;
'He'll stay untouched till the war's last dawning
    Then live one hour of agony.'

Liars the first two were. Behold me
    At sloping arms by one – two – three;
Waiting the time I shall discover
    Whether the third spake verity.

Time and the Soldier

How slow you move, old Time;
    Walk a bit faster!
Old fool, I'm not your slave . . .
    Beauty's my master!

You hold me for a space . . .
    What are you, Time?
A ghost, a thing of thought,
    An easy rhyme.

Some day I shall again,
    For all your scheming,
See Severn valley clouds
    Like banners streaming.

And walk in Cranham lanes,
    By Maisemore go . . .
But, fool, decrepit fool,
    You are SO SLOW!!!

After-Glow

(To F. W. Harvey)

Out of the smoke and dust of the little room
With tea-talk loud and laughter of happy boys,
I passed into the dusk. Suddenly the noise
Ceased with a shock, left me alone in the gloom,
To wonder at the miracle hanging high
Tangled in twigs, the silver crescent clear.
Time passed from mind. Time died; and then we were
Once more at home together, you and I.

The elms with arms of love wrapped us in shade
Who watched the ecstatic west with one desire,
One soul uprapt; and still another fire
Consumed us, and our joy yet greater made:
That Bach should sing for us, mix us in one
The joy of firelight and the sunken sun.

Praise

O friends of mine, if men mock at my name,
Say 'Children loved him.'
Since by that word you will have far removed him
From any bitter shame.

Song of Pain and Beauty

(To M. M. S.)

O may these days of pain,
    These wasted-seeming days,
Somewhere reflower again
    With scent and savour of praise.
Draw out of memory all bitterness
    Of night with Thy sun's rays.

And strengthen Thou in me
    The love of men here found,
And eager charity,
    That, out of difficult ground,
Spring like flowers in barren deserts, or
    Like light, or a lovely sound.

A simpler heart than mine
    Might have seen beauty clear
Where I could see no sign
    Of Thee, but only fear.
Strengthen me, make me to see Thy beauty always
    In every happening here.

Requiem

Pour out your light, O stars, and do not hold
    Your loveliest shining from earth's outworn shell –
Pure and cold your radiance, pure and cold
    My dead friend's face as well.

Pain

Pain, pain continual; pain unending;
Hard even to the roughest, but to those
Hungry for beauty . . . Not the wisest knows,
Nor most pitiful-hearted, what the wending
Of one hour's way meant. Grey monotony lending
Weight to the grey skies, grey mud where goes
An army of grey bedrenched scarecrows in rows
Careless at last of cruellest Fate-sending.
Seeing the pitiful eyes of men foredone,
Or horses shot, too tired merely to stir,
Dying in shell-holes both, slain by the mud.
Men broken, shrieking even to hear a gun.
Till pain grinds down, or lethargy numbs her,
The amazed heart cries angrily out on God.

Servitude

If it were not for England, who would bear
This heavy servitude one moment more?
To keep a brothel, sweep and wash the floor
Of filthiest hovels were noble to compare
With this brass-cleaning life. Now here, now there
Harried in foolishness, scanned curiously o'er
By fools made brazen by conceit, and store
Of antique witticisms thin and bare.

Only the love of comrades sweetens all,
Whose laughing spirit will not be outdone.
As night-watching men wait for the sun
To hearten them, so wait I on such boys
As neither brass nor Hell-fire may appal,
Nor guns, nor sergeant-major's bluster and noise.

From *War's Embers*
(1919)

To His Love

He's gone, and all our plans
  Are useless indeed.
We'll walk no more on Cotswold
  Where the sheep feed
  Quietly and take no heed.

His body that was so quick
  Is not as you
Knew it, on Severn river
  Under the blue
  Driving our small boat through.

You would not know him now . . .
  But still he died
Nobly, so cover him over
  With violets of pride
  Purple from Severn side.

Cover him, cover him soon!
  And with thick-set
Masses of memoried flowers –
  Hide that red wet
  Thing I must somehow forget.

De Profundis

If only this fear would leave me I could dream of Crickley Hill
  And a hundred thousand thoughts of home would visit my
    heart in sleep;
But here the peace is shattered all day by the devil's will,
  And the guns bark night-long to spoil the velvet silence deep.

O who could think that once we drank in quiet inns and cool
  And saw brown oxen trooping the dry sands to slake
Their thirst at the river flowing, or plunged in a silver pool
  To shake the sleepy drowse off before well awake?

We are stale here, we are covered body and soul and mind
 With mire of the trenches, close clinging and foul,
We have left our old inheritance, our Paradise behind,
 And clarity is lost to us and cleanness of soul.

O blow here, you dusk-airs and breaths of half-light,
 And comfort despairs of your darlings that long
Night and day for sound of your bells, or a sight
 Of your tree-bordered lanes, land of blossom and song.

Autumn will be here soon, but the road of coloured leaves
 Is not for us, the up and down highway where go
Earth's pilgrims to wonder where Malvern upheaves
 That blue-emerald splendour under great clouds of snow.

Some day we'll fill in trenches, level the land and turn
 Once more joyful faces to the country where trees
Bear thickly for good drink, where strong sunsets burn
 Huge bonfires of glory – O God, send us peace!

Hard it is for men of moors or fens to endure
 Exile and hardship, or the northland grey-drear;
But we of the rich plain of sweet airs and pure,
 Oh! Death would take so much from us, how should we not
 fear?

Turmut-Hoeing

I straightened my back from turmut-hoeing
 And saw, with suddenly opened eyes,
Tall trees, a meadow ripe for mowing,
 And azure June's cloud-circled skies.

Below, the earth was beautiful
 Of touch and colour, fair each weed,
But Heaven's high beauty held me still,
 Only of music had I need.

And the white-clad girl at the old farm,
  Who smiled and looked across at me,
Dumb was held by that strong charm
  Of cloud-ships sailing a foamless sea.

Ypres – Minsterworth

(To F.W.H.)

Thick lie in Gloucester orchards now
  Apples the Severn wind
With rough play tore from the tossing
  Branches, and left behind
Leaves strewn on pastures, blown in hedges,
  And by the roadway lined.

And I lie leagues on leagues afar
  To think how that wind made
Great shoutings in the wide chimney,
  A noise of cannonade –
Of how the proud elms by the signpost
  The tempest's will obeyed –

To think how in some German prison
  A boy lies with whom
I might have taken joy full-hearted
  Hearing the great boom
Of autumn, watching the fire, talking
  Of books in the half gloom.

O wind of Ypres and of Severn
  Riot there also, and tell
Of comrades safe returned, home-keeping
  Music and autumn smell.
Comfort blow him and friendly greeting,
  Hearten him, wish him well!

Old Martinmas Eve

The moon, one tree, one star.
Still meadows far,
Enwreathed and scarfed by phantom lines of white.
November's night
Of all her nights, I thought, and turned to see
Again that moon and star-supporting tree.
If some most quiet tune had spoken then;
Some silver thread of sound; a core within
That sea-deep silentness, I had not known
Ever such joy in peace, but sound was none –
Nor should be till birds roused to find the dawn.

Companion – North-East Dug-out

He talked of Africa,
   That fat and easy man.
I'd but to say a word,
   And straight the tales began.

And when I'd wish to read,
   That man would not disclose
A thought of harm, but sleep;
   Hard-breathing through his nose.

Then when I'd wish to hear
   More tales of Africa,
'Twas but to wake him up,
   And but a word to say

To press the button, and
   Keep quiet; nothing more;
For tales of stretching veldt,
   Kaffir and sullen Boer.

O what a lovely friend!
  O quiet easy life!
I wonder if his sister
  Would care to be my wife. . . .

The Poplar

(To Micky)

A tall slim poplar
  That dances in
A hidden corner
  Of the old garden,
What is it in you
  Makes communion
With this wind of autumn,
  The clouds, the sun?

You must be lonely
  Amidst round trees
With their matron-figures
  And stubborn knees,
Casting hard glances
  Of keen despite
On the lone girl that dances
  Silvery white.

But you are dearer
  To sky and earth
Than lime-trees, plane-trees
  Of meaner birth.
Your sweet shy beauty
  Dearer to us
Than tree-folk, worthy,
  Censorious.

The Battalion is now On Rest

(To 'La Comtesse')

Walking the village street, to watch the stars and find
Some peace like the old peace, some soothe for soul and mind;
The noise of laughter strikes me as I move on my way
Towards England – westward – and the last glow of day.

And here is the end of houses. I turn on my heel,
And stay where those voices a moment made me feel
As I were on Cotswold, with nothing else to do
Than stare at the old houses, to taste the night-dew;

To answer friendly greetings from rough voices kind . . .
Oh, one may try for ever to be calm and resigned,
A red blind at evening sets the poor heart on fire –
Or a child's face, a sunset – with the old hot desire.

Photographs

(To Two Scots Lads)

Lying in dug-outs, joking idly, wearily;
    Watching the candle guttering in the draught;
Hearing the great shells go high over us, eerily
    Singing; how often have I turned over, and laughed

With pity and pride, photographs of all colours,
    All sizes, subjects: khaki brothers in France;
Or mothers' faces worn with countless dolours;
    Or girls whose eyes were challenging and must dance,

Though in a picture only, a common cheap
    Ill-taken card; and children – frozen, some
(Babies) waiting on Dicky-bird to peep
    Out of the handkerchief that is his home

(But he's so shy!). And some with bright looks, calling
   Delight across the miles of land and sea,
That not the dread of barrage suddenly falling
   Could quite blot out – not mud nor lethargy.

Smiles and triumphant careless laughter. O
   The pain of them, wide Earth's most sacred things!
Lying in dug-outs, hearing the great shells slow
   Sailing mile-high, the heart mounts higher and sings.

But once – O why did he keep that bitter token
   Of a dead Love? – that boy, who, suddenly moved,
Showed me, his eyes wet, his low talk broken,
   A girl who better had not been beloved.

II

1917–1919

The Old City – Gloucester

Who says 'Gloucester' sees a tall
Fair fashioned shape of stone arise,
That changes with the changing skies
From joy to gloom funereal,
Then quick again to joy; and sees
Those four most ancient ways come in
To mix their folk and dust and din
With the keen scent of the sea-breeze.
Here Rome held sway for centuries;
Here Tom Jones slept,
Here Rufus kept
His court, and here was Domesday born,
Here Hooper, Bishop, burnt in scorn
While Mary watched his agonies.
Time out of mind these things were dreams,
Mere tales, not touching the quick sense,
Yet walking Gloucester history seems
A living thing and an intense.
For here and now I see the strength
In passing faces, that held at bay
Proud Rupert in an arrogant day
Till Essex' train-bands came at length,
And king's power passed like mist away.
Courage and wisdom that made good
Each tiny freedom, and withstood
The cunning or the strength of great
Unscrupulous lords; and here, elate,
The spirit that sprang to height again
When Philip would conquer the wide Main
And England, and her tigerish queen.
Here countenances of antique grace
And beautiful smiling comedy-look
That Shakespeare saw in his own place
And loved and fashioned into a book.
Beauty of sweet-blood generations
The strength of nations
Hear the passion-list of a fervent lover:
The view from Over,

Westgate Street at night, great light, deep shadows,
The Severn meadows,
The surprising, the enormous Severn Plain
So wide, so fair
From Crickley seen or Cooper's, my dear lane
That holds all lane-delightfulnesses there
(O Maisemore's darling way!)
Framilode, Frampton, Dymock, Minsterworth. . .
You are the flower of villages in all earth!
Whatever those may say
That have been cursed with an unlucky birth
Poor blinded multitudes
That far from happy woods,
Like these, in towns and hovels make their stay.
If one must die for England, Fate has given
Generously indeed, for we have known
Before our time, the air and skies of Heaven
And Beauty more than common have been shown,
And with our last fight fought, our last strife striven
We shall enter unsurprised into our own.

To the Prussians of England

When I remember plain heroic strength
And shining virtue shown by Ypres pools,
Then read the blither written by knaves for fools
In praise of English soldiers lying at length,
Who purely dream what England shall be made
Gloriously new, free of the old stains
By us, who pay the price that must be paid,
Will freeze all winter over Ypres plains.
Our silly dreams of peace you put aside
And brotherhood of man, for you will see
An armed mistress, braggart of the tide,
Her children slaves, under your mastery.
We'll have a word there too, and forge a knife,
Will cut the cancer threatens England's life.

Above Ashleworth

O does some blind fool now stand on my hill
To see how Ashleworth nestles by the river?
Where eyes and heart and soul may drink their fill.

The Cotswolds stand out eastward as if never
A curve of them the hand of Time might change,
Beauty sleeps most confidently for ever.

The blind fool stands, his dull eyes free to range
Endlessly almost, and finds no word to say:
Not that the sense of wonder is too strange

Too great for speech. Naught touches him; the day
Blows its glad trumpets, breathes rich-odoured breath;
Glory after glory passes away

(And I'm in France!). He looks, and sees beneath
The clouds in steady Severn silver and grey
But dead he is, and comfortable in death.

Memory, Let All Slip

Memory, let all slip save what is sweet
Of Ypres plains.
Keep only autumn sunlight and the fleet
Clouds after rains,

Blue sky and mellow distance softly blue;
These only hold
Lest I my pangèd grave must share with you.
Else dead. Else cold.

Song

My heart makes songs on lonely roads
To comfort me while you are away
And strives with lovely sounding words
Its crowded tenderness to say.

Yet I am glad that Love has come
To bind me fast, and try my worth
For Love's a powerful lord and gives
His friends dominion over the earth.

I walk deserted ways and see
Against the forward dark your face
Pale glimmering against the dark;
Your face I see with pride, with pain
So that, one turn, I did desire
Never to see that face again.

Song of Urgency

Sing in me now you words
That she may know
What love is quick in me,
O come not slow!

Nor cold to me, but run
Molten, fiercely hot
Before Time carelessly
Make me forgot,

Or dull of image in
My dear Love's mind.
You words of power, of flame
Hasten, be kind!

Excursion

They turned the village band on us
Who sat with desperate calm of face
To meet the sound, storm clamorous.
They turned the village band on us

And manners failed. Without a fuss
We vanished in a black disgrace.
They turned the village band on us
Who sat with desperate calm of face.

Crickley Hill

The orchis, trefoil, harebells nod all day,
High above Gloucester and the Severn Plain.
Few come there, where the curlew ever and again
Cries faintly, and no traveller makes stay,
Since steep the road is,
And the villages
Hidden by hedges wonderful in May.

At Buire-au-Bois a soldier wandering
The lanes at evening talked with me and told
Of gardens summer blessed, of early spring
In tiny orchards, the uncounted gold
Strewn in green meadows,
Clear-cut shadows
Black on the dust and grey stone mellow and old.

But these were things I knew, and carelessly
Heard, while in thought I went with friends on roads
White in the sun and wandered far to see
The scented hay come homeward in warm loads.
Hardly I heeded him;
While coloured dim
Evening brought stars and lights in small abodes.

When on a sudden, 'Crickley' he said. How I started
At that old darling name of home! and turned,
Fell into a torrent of words warm-hearted
Till clear above the stars of summer burned
In velvety smooth skies.
We shared memories,
And the old raptures from each other learned.

O sudden steep! O hill towering above!
Chasm from the road falling suddenly away!
Sure no two men talked of you with more love
Than we that tender-coloured ending of day.
(O tears! Keen pride in you!)
Feeling the soft dew,
Walking in thought another Roman way.

You hills of home, woodlands, white roads and inns
That star and line our darling land, still keep
Memory of us; for when first day begins
We think of you and dream in the first sleep
Of you and yours –
Trees, bare rock, flowers
Daring the blast on Crickley's distant steep.

O Tree of Pride

O Tree of pride,
Before your green to gold and orange fade,
And scarce one single leaf of summer's shade
Remains to hide
Robin or wren,
Give me one song of all your songs, that men
May take your beauty winter's fire beside.

For memory passes
Of even the loveliest things, bravest in show;
The mind to beauty most alert not know
How the August grasses
Waved, by December's
Glow, unless he see deep in the embers
The poet's dream, gathered from cold print's spaces.

Equal Mistress

Most tiny daisies are
Not anything
Less dear than the great star,
Riding the west afar,
To their mistress Spring.

Jupiter, the Pleiades
To her equal
With celandine and cress,
Stone-crop, freckled pagles
And bird's-eye small.

Since in her heart of love
No rank is there
Nor degree aught; hers is
The most willing service
And free of care.

Violets, stars, birds
Wait on her smile; all
Too soon must autumn come,
Sheaves, fruit be carried home,
And the leaves fall.

Crocus Ring

O show to me a crocus ring
That dances round a bush of green,
And I will make a lovely thing
To match the magic seen.

And swift the words should run to place,
The rhyming fall inevitable,
The crocus come to show its face
In sound set well.

Children should read with bright-eyed wonder
And long to dance as flowers do,
Or fairies, in and out and under
Brambles and dew.

Clap hands and call for country going.
But O how false does memory
Play with a golden circlet growing
Round a March tree!

North Woolwich

Hellene memories taunting of the bright
Morning of new Time amongst tall derricks
And floating chimney pots with empty tackle

Drawn by fierce asp-things slowly out of sight.
For Sappho's easy happy mirth the cackle
Brittle that's not of help to odes or lyrics.

Houses like long Iliadian lines stretch on
And railing shadows bar a recognizable
Of-no-man-questioned earth, whose chemistry

To Marathon or Sparta kin must be.
The vault of air as stable
As on Olympus ringed with careless vines
Or where Ithaca seaward green inclines.

Speed is here, for bread is still to fetch;
And cunning, for milk spills from any vessel;
The turnstile is through-gone without wrestle.

But filled is every ditch
No boys to show that smoothly running muscle.
Gaol waits for them would face without a stitch
Heaven's nakedness, those feet are black as pitch
Should gleam on gold sands white or in stadium lines.
Can Aphrodite bless so evil dwelling
Or Mercury have heed to Canning Town?
Nay, rather, for that ugly, that evil smelling
Township, a Christ from Heaven must come down,
Pitiful and comradely, with tender signs,
And warm the tea, and shield a chap from fines.
A foreman carpenter, not yet full-grown.

The Companions

On uplands bleak and bare to wind
Beneath a maze of stars one strode.
Phantoms of fear haunted the road,
Mocking my footsteps close behind.

Till Heaven blew clear of cloud, showed each
Most tiny baby-star as fine
As any king's jewel, Orion
Triumphed through tracery of beech.

So unafraid the tramp went on
Past dusky rut and pool alight,
With Heaven's chief wonder of night,
Jupiter close companion.

And in no mood of pride, courteous,
Light-hearted as with a king's friend
He went with me till journey's end
His courtiers Mars and Regulus.

My door reached, gladly had I paid
With stammered thanks his courtesy,
And theirs, but ne'er a star could see
Of all Heaven's ordered cavalcade.
Pools inky-black, unbottomed shade. . .
Fine snow drove west and blinded me.

Michaelmas

The autumn rooms of green and bronze
Are swept with cleanest airs today.
Large air puffs jostle little ones –
Not quarrelsome nor yet in play.

And in the valley bonfires spread
A blue enchantment on the day.
No spoil, no flaw! How good that spring
Is lengths of calendar away.

London Dawn

Dawn comes up on London
And night's undone.
Stars are routed
And street lamps outed,
Sodden great clouds begin to sail again
Like all-night anchored galleons to the main
From careful shallows to the far-withdrawn
Wide outer seas of sky.
Sleepers above river change their pain,
Lockhart's shows lively up Blackfriars Lane.
Motors dash by
With 'Mirrors', 'Mails', 'Telegraphs', what not?
South shore of Thames on London shows a blot
And first careful coffee-stall is withdrawn.
Only the poet strolls about at ease
Wondering what mortal thing his soul may please,
And spitting at the drains, while Paul's as ever
Is mighty and a king of sky and river,
And cares no more, Much-Father, for this one
Broke child, although a poet-born and clever,
Than any spit-kid of seven million
Must drudge all day until his earning's done.
A huffler has her red sails just a-quiver;
Sun's very near now and the tide's a-run.

Tobacco

When tobacco came, when Raleigh did first bring in
The unfabled herb, the plant of peace, the king
Of comfort-bringers, then indeed new hope
Came to the host of poets – with new scope,
New range of power, since henceforth one might sit
Midnight-on and still further, while the war of wit
More kindly became and coloured till dawn came in
Piercing shutter-chinks with pale daylight thin.

Raleigh he knew, but could not the impossible
War of swift steel and hurtled bronze foretell,
Nor the imaginary hurt on body's vessel;
Nor how tobacco then would steady disastered
Nerves, courage by grey terror almost mastered.
Gloucester men, half a day or more, would hide
Five cigarettes and matches well inside
Their breasts, the one thing unsodden, while despair
Dripped incessantly without interest from the air;
Or go supperless
The better next day's tobacco taste to bless.
Wonder at fogs, stars, posts till headaches came,
Those chief of trouble-comforts still the same.
Watch Verey lights, sandbags, grasses, rifle-sights, mud –
Crampt in uncouth postures men crouched or stood –
A Woodbine breakfast inspiriting the blood.

Or in those caves of dug-outs, men taking lazily
Smoke in luxuriously, of Woodbines easily.
For one stroke forgiving Fate and its so mazily
Self-tangled knots. Easing the strained back,
Somehow or other slipping unseen from the rack
Into tobacco scent, or savour or look;
The divine virtue of some contenting book
Multiplying; or in the sunniest quiet resting
Loll into restlessness or sleepy jesting.
Tobacco truly taken, neat, as a Thing.
Tobacco tasted exactly; in waves or ring
Noted; tobacco blown to the wind, or watched
Melt into ether's farthest smother unmatched.
Keen sentries whiffing surreptitiously,
Sly fatigue parties hidden from scrutiny,
Last breath favours begged desperately.

Over all the breath of the airy vapour is known,
Life's curtain rises on it and Death's trembles down.
Heroism has taken it for sufficient crown.

When I think of the Ark slapping hopeless waters –
Of Aeneas' sailors cursed with unclean hunger –
Of Irus and his scorn, or the legions Germanicus
Met, and was nearly scotted by whose anger,
I know, I realize, and am driven to pity
By sunscorched eternal days of Babylon City
And any unsoothed restless greedy clamour,
As hunger for Empire, any use of war's hammer.
Tea and tobacco after decent labour
Would bring again England of pipe and tabor
Merry England again after four centuries,
Of dawn-rising and late-talking and go-as-you-please.

Above Maisemore

O, lovely City! All the valley blue
Covers thee like a garment of soft art,
Harbour of peace, haven for contented and high heart,
Desire is satisfied, sorrow finds salve in you.
No marble nor gold mosque gleams out from thee,
Thy sober usual beauty shows as one
Yet drawn together by dominion
Of Peter's Abbey ruling quietly,
The ages' friend of Cotswold and the sun.
Not loudest music is the sweetest, nor
The highest statue most noble seen.
Distant is dim azure over pasture green
And like the Promised Land your sight from far.
Sober and glorious City of the plain,
A thousand years stay so, and stay again.

When from the Curve

When from the curve of the wood's edge does grow
Power, and that spreads to envelope me –
Wrapped up in sense of meeting tree and plough
I feel tiny song stir tremblingly
And deep; the many birth-pangs separate
Taking most full of joy, for soon shall come
The kindling, the beating at Heaven gate
The flood of tide that bears strongly home.

Then under the skies I make my vows
Myself to purify and fit my heart
For the inhabiting of the high House
Of Song, that dwells high and clean apart.
The fire, the flood, the soaring, these the three
That merged are power of song and prophesy.

There Was Such Beauty

There was such beauty in the dappled valley
As hurt the sight, as stabbed the heart to tears.
The gathered loveliness of all the years
Hovered thereover, it seemed, eternally
Set for men's joy. Town, tower, trees, river
Under a royal azure sky for ever
Up-piled with snowy towering bulks of cloud:
A herald-day of spring more wonderful
Than her true own. Trumpets cried aloud
In sky, earth, blood; no beast, no clod so dull
But the power felt of the day, and of the giver
Was glad for life, humble at once and proud.
Kyrie Eleison, and Gloria,
Credo, Jubilate, Magnificat:
The whole world gathered strength to praise the day.

If I Walked Straight Slap

If I walked straight slap
Headlong down the road
Toward the two-wood gap
Should I hit that cloud?

Advice

Why do you not steer straight, my love, she cried:
The wind makes steady your way, favours the tide:
The boat obeys the helm, were you now to steer
Courageous, our troubles and doubts would vanish here.

And cassia and pearls would pack your hold,
And your returning act crown manifold
Our upward course, and not a thing to desire. . .
The rudder swang in the tide, and we beached in the mire.

March

My boat moves and I with her delighting,
Feeling the water slide past, and watching white fashion
Of water, as she moves faster ever more whitening;
Till up at the white sail in that great sky heightening
Of fine cloth spread against azure and cloud commotion
My face looks, and there is joy in the eyes that asking
Fulfilment of the heart's true and golden passion
(Long dimmed) now gets hold of a truth and an action. . .
The ears take the sound of Severn water dashing.
The great spirit remembers Ulysses with his courage lighting
Before the danger of sea water, in a rocky passion
Of surges – and over Barrow comes the wind I've been waiting.

III

From *Rewards of Wonder*
(collected 1919–1920)

First Time In

After the dread tales and red yarns of the Line
Anything might have come to us; but the divine
Afterglow brought us up to a Welsh colony
Hiding in sandbag ditches, whispering consolatory
Soft foreign things. Then we were taken in
To low huts candle-lit, shaded close by slitten
Oilsheets, and there the boys gave us kind welcome,
So that we looked out as from the edge of home.
Sang us Welsh things, and changed all former notions
To human hopeful things. And the next day's guns
Nor any line-pangs ever quite could blot out
That strangely beautiful entry to war's rout;
Candles they gave us, precious and shared over-rations –
Ulysses found little more in his wanderings without doubt.
'David of the White Rock', the 'Slumber Song' so soft, and that
Beautiful tune to which roguish words by Welsh pit boys
Are sung – but never more beautiful than there under the
    guns' noise.

La Gorgue

The long night, the short sleep, and La Gorgue to wander,
So be the Fates were kind and our Commander;
With a mill, and still canal, and like-Stroudway bridges.
One looks back on these as Time's truest riches
Which were so short an escape, so perilous a joy
Since fatigues, weather, line trouble or any whimsical ploy
Division might hatch out would have finished peace.

There was a house there, (I tell the noted thing)
The kindest woman kept, and an unending string
Of privates as wasps to sugar went in and out.
Friendliness sanctified all there without doubt,
As lovely as the mill above the still green
Canal where the dark fishes went almost unseen.
B Company had come down from Tilleloy
Lousy, thirsty, avid of any employ

Of peace; and this woman in leanest times had plotted
A miracle to amaze the army-witted.
And this was café-au-lait as princes know it,
And fasting, and poor-struck; dead but not to show it.
A drink of edicts, dooms, a height of tales.
Heat, cream, coffee; the maker tries and fails,
The poet too, where such thirst such mate had.
A campaign thing that makes remembrance sad.

There was light there, too, in the clear North French way.
It blessed the room, and bread, and the mistress giver,
The husband for his wife's sake, and both for a day
Were blessed by many soldiers tired however;
A mark in Time, a Peace, a Making-delay.

June Night

Clouds die out in June where the sun drops –
The skies are clear as water when the sand stops
In flood time, settles; and the winds have settled now.
Stars as bright sand-grains remain, and the still flow
Of the high heavens like deep sea water not hides
Them, as the course of the Heavens nobly, strongly glides.
There are the hour's tides, the sky's and the eternal tides
Over the dark day's tides.
But for all my worship of these, I shall go in to studies
Of music or verse or Elizabethans – in my labour's plans,
See lamp light – make notes and verse – read noble words
     sufficient.
Only to come out when the thought will not move to its bent.
Longford dark worshipping upwards to the dim sky,
I, dazed a little; till walking, moving easily and lonelily
I come to the brook meadow with its line of elm trees,
The small bridge that has dignity and its own heart's place,
To turn there, and be glad that night wide is come
All men asleep save I, in my loved, never-so-loved, town,
And my friends asleep; while I work and my honour and
     clear eyes keep
Waiting for the dawn as first mark – and more clouds
     of high June.

Blighty

It seemed that it were well to kiss first earth
On landing, having traversed the narrow seas,
And grasp so little, tenderly, of this field of birth.
France having trodden and lain on, travelled bending the knees.
And having shed blood, known heart for her and last nerve freeze,
Proved body past heart, and soul past (so we thought) any worth.
For what so dear a thing as the first homecoming,
The seeing smoke pillar aloft from the home dwellings;
Sign of travel ended, lifted awhile the dooming
Sentence of exile; homecoming, right of tale-tellings?
But mud is on our fate after so long acquaintance,
We find of England the first gate without Romance;
Blue paved wharfs with dock-policemen and civic decency,
Trains and restrictions, order and politeness and directions,
Motion by black and white, guided ever about-ways
And staleness with petrol-dust distinguishing days.
A grim faced black-garbed mother efficient and busy
Set upon housework, worn-minded and fantasy-free,
A work-house matron, forgetting her old birth friend – the sea.

The Bargain

For two grains of wheat grown on Waltheof's field
To the Abbot of Stare, the Mill of Knuts Weald
Should be to Waltheof he and heirs for ever.
Nine hundred years passed, and the weir baulked endeavour,
Water banked up in the old February manner,
Though never Hugo passed there with bright banner.
Now Waltheof's field grew no more lovely grain,
A brick kiln stood there and blazed at the clay's pain,
Rubbish heaped there and waste paper wind scattered,
Two grains of wheat were all ever that mattered.
What easier thing than to sow a handful of corn?
Scratched earth in spring, a scatter, and stalks were born
From the waste, the weedy corner of side's path.
Tenure held, money was made there and the field felt death

Sinking deeper, the bowels of it taken far
To be villas, schools, churches freaked perpendicular,
And lovely soil made rough, square, money-bringing
Saleable bricks. Water came, the black moorhens flinging
Frightened courses; reeds, sedges stood up in small woods,
The last island of clay vanished, and lonelier moods
Possessed the pit now, mere and most melancholy.
Town Council had no poetry and decided ceremoniously
That the rubbish there (surely) as elsewhere might be voided.
(Five pounds a year and two grains wheat was cheap.)
Waltheof's field will become a rubbish heap.
Villas will stand there and look polite; with folk polite
Where sedges stood for the wind's play and poet-delight,
But Severn will be sorry and it can never be right.

Songs Come to the Mind

Songs come to the mind –
Other men's songs
Or one's own, when something is kind
And remembers not any wrongs.

Swift cleaving paths in air
On a bicycle, or slow
Wandering and wondering where
One's purposes may go.

Songs come and are taken, written,
Snatched from the momentary
Accidents of light, shape, spirit meeting
For one light second spirit, unbelievably.

That Centre of Old

Is it only Cotswold that holds the glamour
Memory felt of England in the gun-stammer –
Thud, smack, belch of war – and kept virtue by?
I do not know, but only that, most unhappy,
The hills are to me what to happy I
They were in Somme muckage-baths and east of Laventie
When hunger made one worthy to absorb the sky –
Look, or play fancy-tricks with small cloudlets high:
Count them – or dare not count – love and let go by.
Now as ever Cotswold rewards the mere being and seeing
As truly as
Ever in the relief of knowing mere being
In the still space
At a strafe end grateful for silence and body's grace
(Whole body – and after hell's hammering and clamouring).
Then memory purified made rewarding shapes
Of all that spirit runs towards in escapes,
And Cooper's Hill showed plain almost as experience.
Soft winter mornings of kind innocence, high June's
Girl's air of untouched purity, and on Cooper's Hill
Or autumn Cranham with its boom of colour . . .
Not anyway does ever Cotswold's fail – her dear blue long
      dark slope fail –
Of the imagining promise in full exile.

Possessions

France has victory, England yet firm shall stay,
But what shall please the wind now the trees are away
War took on Witcombe steep?
It breathes there, and wonders at old roarings
October time at all lights; and the new clearings
For memory are like to weep.

War need not cut down trees, three hundred miles over seas,
Children of those the Romans saw – lovely trunk and great-
  sail trees!
Not on Cranham, not on Cooper's of camps;
Friend to the great October stars – and the July sky lamps.

Billet

O, but the racked clear tired strained frames we had!
Tumbling in the new billet on to straw bed,
Dead asleep in eye shutting. Waking as sudden
To a golden and azure roof, a golden ratcheted
Lovely web of blue seen and blue shut, and cobwebs and tiles,
And grey wood dusty with time. June's girlish kindest smiles.
Rest at last and no danger for another week, a seven-day week.
But one Private took on himself a Company's heart to speak,
'I wish to bloody hell I was just going to Brewery – surely
To work all day (in Stroud) and be free at tea-time – allowed
Resting when one wanted, and a joke in season,
To change clothes and take a girl to Horsepool's turning,
Or drink a pint at "Travellers Rest", and find no cloud.
Then God and man and war and Gloucestershire would have
  a reason,
But I get no good in France, getting killed, cleaning off mud.'
He spoke the heart of all of us – the hidden thought burning,
  unturning.

The Soaking

The rain has come, and the earth must be very glad
Of its moisture, and the made roads all dust clad;
It lets a friendly veil down on the lucent dark,
And not of any bright ground thing shows any spark.

Tomorrow's grey morning will show cow-parsley,
Hung all with shining drops, and the river will be
Duller because of the all soddenness of things,
Till the skylark breaks his reluctance, hangs shaking, and sings.

I Saw England – July Night

She was a village
Of lovely knowledge
The high roads left her aside, she was forlorn, a maid –
Water ran there, dusk hid her, she climbed four-wayed.
Brown-golden windows showed last folk not yet asleep;
Water ran, was a centre of silence deep,
Fathomless deeps of pricked sky, almost fathomless
Hallowed an upward gaze in pale satin of blue.
And I was happy indeed, of mind, soul, body even
Having got given
A sign undoubtful of a dear England few
Doubt, not many have seen,
That Will Squele he knew and so was shriven.
Home of Twelfth Night – Edward Thomas by Arras fallen,
Borrow and Hardy, Sussex tales out of Roman heights
    callen.
No madrigals or field-songs to my all reverent whim;
Till I got back I was dumb.

First March

It was first marching, hardly we had settled yet
To think of England, or escaped body pain –
Flat country going leaves but small chance for
The mind to escape to any resort but its vain
Own circling greyness and stain.
First halt, second halt, and then to spoiled country again.
There were unknown kilometres to march, one must settle
To play chess or talk home-talk or think as might happen.
After three weeks of February frost few were in fettle,
Barely frostbite the most of us had escapen.
To move, then to go onward, at least to be moved.
Myself had revived and then dulled down, it was I
Who stared for body-ease at the grey sky
And watched in grind of pain the monotony
Of grit road metal slide underneath by.
To get there being the one way not to die.

Suddenly a road's turn brought the sweet unexpected
Balm. Snowdrops bloomed in a ruined garden neglected:
Roman the road as of Birdlip we were on the verge,
And this west country thing so from chaos to emerge.
One gracious touch the whole wilderness corrected.

What I Will Pay

What I will pay to my God is that I will not sleep between
   sheets,
Neither take rest unwanted, but work till the first small bird
   fleets
Past my window, to take rest then (new power); and to take it
   walking,
To be of first flowers a friend – and to noble tree-trunks talking.
Resting so, without ever closing the eyes or at all
Ceasing from work till need or gratitude gives the word, and my
   soul.
To praise God in sound or words – and to follow masters,
Beethoven, Bach, Jonson – keeping any safe, clear from disasters.
To watch trees and stone, others asleep, and see them alone,
There to learn truth and beauty – and be holier – then be gone.
To keep strict thought – to honour, and have no envy;
To honour water of a morning, and to lave my clean fair body.
Tea and tobacco and my masters, the Elizabethans and Bach my
   food,
Drink when I would – to have Carlyle his thought of good, and
   by wood
Stone, iron, earth, air, water, to keep thoughts all steady to ages,
To start day at dawn's wind, and write fair on strict thought-
   pages.
These prices to have paid were enough for Shakespeare or
   Borrow,
Their God, or of Homer – and might Gloucestershire guard from
   all sorrow.

Thoughts on Beethoven

Beethoven, I wronged thee undernoting thus
Thy dignity and worth; the overplus
Of one quartett almost would our book overweigh –
Almost chosen out at random from your own day.
You have our great Ben's mastery and a freer
Carriage of method, spice of the open air . . .
Which he, our greatest builder, had not so:
Not as his own at least but acquirèd-to.
May no false fashion put thy true fame away
As in Vienna, when wantons laid all away
Thy work Homeric for a soft southern zephyr,
And heroes were no other than as day's heifer
Sacrificed on the altar of world's praise,
The amusement or brittle heightening of drab days.

Whereas thy sinewed strength is by Aeschylus,
Homer, Ben Jonson, Shakespeare, and a pillar of us.
Master. Such are our memories which do never betray
Our own makings, thou so generous in thy great-heart way.

Laventie

One would remember still
Meadows and low hill
Laventie was, as to the line and elm row
Growing through green strength wounded, as home elms grow.
Shimmer of summer there and blue autumn mists
Seen from trench-ditch winding in mazy twists.
The Australian gunners in close flowery hiding
Cunning found out at last, and smashed in the unspeakable lists.
And the guns in the smashed wood thumping and griding.

The letters written there, and received there,
Books, cakes, cigarettes in a parish of famine,
And leaks in rainy times with general all-damning.
The crater, and carrying of gas cylinders on two sticks
(Pain past comparison and far past right agony gone),
Strained hopelessly of heart and frame at first fix.

Café-au-lait in dug-outs on Tommies' cookers,
Cursed minniewerfs, thirst in eighteen-hour summer.
The Australian miners clayed, and the being afraid
Before strafes, sultry August dusk time than death dumber –
And the cooler hush after the strafe, and the long night wait –
The relief of first dawn, the crawling out to look at it,
Wonder divine of dawn, man hesitating before Heaven's gate.
(Though not on Cooper's where music fire took at it.
Though not as at Framilode beauty where body did shake at it)
Yet the dawn with aeroplanes crawling high at Heaven's gate
Lovely aerial beetles of wonderful scintillate
Strangest interest, and puffs of soft purest white –
Seeking light, dispersing colouring for fancy's delight.
Of Machonachie, Paxton, Tickler and Gloucester's Stephens;
Fray Bentos, Spiller and Baker, odds and evens
Of trench food, but the everlasting clean craving
For bread, the pure thing, blessèd beyond saving.
Canteen disappointments, and the keen boy braving
Bullets or such for grouse roused surprisingly through
(Halfway) Stand-to.
And the shell nearly blunted my razor at shaving;
Tilleloy, Fauquissart, Neuve Chapelle, and mud like glue.
But Laventie, most of all, I think is to soldiers
The town itself with plane trees, and small-spa air;
And vin, rouge-blanc, chocolat, citron, grenadine:
One might buy in small delectable cafés there.
The broken church, and vegetable fields bare;
Neat French market-town look so clean,
And the clarity, amiability of North French air.

*

Like water flowing beneath the dark plough and high Heaven,
Music's delight to please the poet pack-marching there.

The Touchstone – Watching Malvern

What Malvern is the day is, and its touchstone –
Grey velvet, or moon-marked; rich, or bare as bone;
One looks towards Malvern and is made one with the whole;
The world swings round him as the Bear to the Pole.

Men have crossed seas to know how Paul's tops Fleet,
That as music has rapt them in the mere street,
While none or few care how the curved giants stand,
(Those upheaved strengths!) on the meadow and plough-land.

Glimmering Dusk

Glimmering dusk above the moist plough and the
Silence of trees' heaviness under low grey sky
Are some comfort for the mind gone soft in lethargy;
White road dark with pools, but growing soon to dry;
But the mind complains 'This indeed is beauty enough
And comfort, but itself not enough cure for sorrows,
Nor equal weight for good things and fine stuff
Of thought snatched ruthlessly by thieves best under harrows'.
But the soul would not be denied; comfort from the night
Gathered, the mind unwilling, hope past all thought of
        matters
Of right anger – and the body only spoke of its plight
That a kind law makes dust of at last and scatters.
No notice the soul took – it desired God with all friendly might.
The leaves, not sodden, moved on trees with winter patters.

New Year's Eve

Aveluy and New Year's Eve, and the time as tender
As if green buds grew. In the low west a slender
Streak of last orange. Guns mostly deadest still.
And a noise of limbers near coming down the hill.

Nothing doing, nothing doing, and a screed to write,
Candles enough for books, a sleepy delight
In the warm dug-out, day ended. Nine hours to the light.
There now and then now, one nestled down snug.
A head is enough to read by, and cover up with a rug.
Electric. Clarinet sang of 'A Hundred Pipers'
And hush awe mystery vanished like tapers
Of tobacco smoke, there was great hilarity then!
Breath, and a queer tube, magicked sorrow from men.
The North, and all Scott called me – Ballads and Burns again!
Enough! I got up and lit (the last little bit
But one) of candle and poked the remaining fire,
Got some blaze into the cold; sat, wrote verse there . . .
(Or music). The 'hundred pipers' had called so plain
('And a'') and for three hours stuck it and worked as best
Drippings, and cold, and misery would let desire.

Crucifix Corner

There was a water dump there and regimental
Carts came every day to line up and fill full
Those rolling tanks with chlorinated clay mixture
And curse the mud with vain veritable vexture.
Aveluy across the valley, billets, shacks, ruins.
With time and time a crump there to mark doings.
On New Year's Eve the marsh gloomed tremulous
With rosy mist still holding so marvellous
Sunglow; the air smelt home; the time breathed home –
Noel not put away; New Year's Eve not yet come.
All things said 'Severn', the air was of those dusk meadows –
Transport rattled somewhere in southern shadows,
Stars that were not strange ruled the lit tranquil sky,
Arched far and high.

What should break that but gun-noise or Last Trump?
Neither broke it. Suddenly at a light jump
Clarinet sang into 'Hundred Pipers and a''
Aveluy's pipers answered with pipers' true call
'Happy we've been a'-tegether' when nothing, nothing
Stayed of war-weariness or winter-loathing.

Cracker with stockings hung in the quaint Heavens
Orion and the seven stars comical at odds and evens –
Gaiety split discipline in sixes or sevens –
Hunger mixed strangely with magical leavens.
It was as if Cinderella had opened the Ball
And music put aside the time's saddened clothing.
It was as if Sir Walter were company again
In the late night – 'Antiquary' or 'Midlothian' –
Or 'Redgauntlet' bringing Solway clear to the mind.
After music, and a day of walking or making
To return to music, or to read the starred dark dawn-blind.

Darkness Has Cheating Swiftness

Darkness has cheating swiftness
When the eyes rove,
Opens and shuts in long avenues
That thought cannot prove.

Darkness shuts in and closes;
There are three ghosts
Different in one clump of hedge roses
And a threat in posts

Until one tops the road crest,
Turns, sees the city lie
Long stretched out in bright sparkles of gratefullest
Homecalling array.

Half Dead

Half dead with sheer tiredness, wakened quick at night
With dysentery pangs, going blind among dim sleepers
And dazed into half dark, illness had its spite.
Head cleared, eyes saw; pangs and ill body-creepers

Stilled with the cold – the cold bringing me sane –
See there was Witcombe Steep as it were, but no beeches
    there.
Yet still clear flames of stars over the crest bare,
Mysterious glowing on the cloths of heaven.
Sirius or Mars or Argo's stars, and high the Sisters – the
    Pleiads – those seven.

Best turn in, fatigue party out at seven . . .
What though beauty was – I had been Cranham's walks . . .
Dark was the billet after that seeing of rare
Gold stars, stumbling among the still forms to my lair.
Still were the stars bright – my sick mind hung on them even.

But long after, in solitary day walking, I recalled
Caulaincourt's Mausoleum and the stars March midnight
    called;
On the east horizon's dim loveliest shape upheld.
To mix with music in my thought and forget sickness –
To drown sorrow deep that on me was then masterless –
Hunger and weak body and tired of needed sleep.
For Argo or Sirius in the east skies or for Regulus.

Daily – Old Tale

If one's heart is broken twenty times a day,
What easier thing than to fling the bits away,
But still one gathers fragments, and looks for wire,
Or patches it up like some old bicycle tyre.

Bicycle tyres fare hardly on roads, but the heart
Has an easier time than rubber, they sheathe a cart
With iron; so lumbering and slow my mind must be made,
To bother the heart and to teach things and learn it its trade.

The Poet Walking

I saw people
Thronging the streets
Where the Eastway with the old
Roman Wall meets –
But none though of old
Gloucester blood brought,
Loved so the City
As I – the poet unthought.
And I exulted there
To think that but one
Of all that City
Had pride or equity
Enough for the marvelling
At street and stone,
Or the age of Briton,
Dane, Roman, Elizabethan –
One grateful one – true child of that dear City – one worthy one.

Near Vermand

Lying flat on my belly shivering in clutch-frost,
There was time to watch the stars, we had dug in:
Looking eastward over the low ridge; March scurried its blast
At our senses, no use either dying or struggling.
Low woods to left – (Cotswold her spinnies if ever) –
Showed through snow flurries and the clearer star weather,
And nothing but chill and wonder lived in mind; nothing
But loathing and fine beauty, and wet loathed clothing.
Here were thoughts. Cold smothering and fire-desiring,
A day to follow like this or in the digging or wiring.

*

Worry in snow flurry and lying flat, flesh the earth loathing.
I was the forward sentry and would be relieved
In a quarter or so, but nothing more better than to crouch
Low in the scraped holes and to have frozen and rocky couch –
To be by desperate home thoughts clutched at, and heart-grieved.
Was I ever there – a lit warm room and Bach, to search out sacred
Meaning; and to find no luck; and to take love as believed?

After War

One got peace of heart at last, the dark march over,
And the straps slipped, the warmth felt under roof's low cover,
Lying slack the body, let sink in straw giving;
And some sweetness, a great sweetness felt in mere living,
And to come to this haven after sorefooted weeks,
The dark barn roof, and the glows and the wedges and streaks;
Letters from home, dry warmth and still sure rest taken
Sweet to the chilled frame, nerves soothed were so sore shaken.

Brimscombe

One lucky hour in middle of my tiredness
I came under the pines of the sheer steep
And saw the stars like steady candles gleam
Above and through them; Brimscombe wrapped (past life) in
    sleep:
Such body weariness and bad ugliness
Had gone before, such tiredness to come on me;
This perfect moment had such pure clemency
That it my memory has all coloured since,
Forgetting the blackness and pain so driven hence.
And the naked uplands from even bramble free,
That ringed-in hour of pines, stars and dark eminence.
Wonder of men had walked there, and old Romance.
(The thing we looked for in our fear of France.)

Riez Bailleul

Riez Bailleul in blue tea-time
Called back the Severn lanes, the roads
Where the small ash leaves lie, and floods
Of hawthorn leaves turned with night's rime.
No Severn though, nor great valley clouds . . .

Now, in the thought, comparisons
Go with those here-and-theres and fancy
Sees on the china firelight dancy,
The wall lit where the sofa runs.
A dear light like Sirius or spring sun's.

But the trench thoughts will not go, tomorrow
Up to the line, and no straw laid
Soft for the body, and long nights' dread,
Lightless, all common human sorrow.
Unploughed the grown field once was furrow.

Meanwhile soft azure, and fall's emerald
Lovely the road makes, a softness clings
Of colour and texture of light; there rings
Metal, as it were, in air; and the called
Of twilight, dim stars of the dome, appear.

There's dusk here; west hedgerows show thin;
In billets there's sound of packs reset,
Tea finished; the dixies dried of the wet.
Some walk, some write, and the cards begin.
Stars gather in heaven and the pools drown in.

First Time In

The Captain addressed us. Afterglow grew deeper,
Like England, like the west country, and stars grew thicker.
In silence we left the billet, we found the hard roadway
In single file, jangling (silent) and on the grey
Chipped road, moaned over ever by snipers' shots.
Got shelter in the first trench; and the thud of boots
On duck-board wood from grate on rough road stone it changed.
(Verey lights showed ghastly, and a machine-gun ranged.)
Sentry here and there. How the trench wound now! Wires
Hindered, thistles pricked, but few guns spat their fires.
Upward a little . . . wider a little, the reserve line reached.
Tin hat shapes, dark body shapes and faces as bleached.

85

And the heart's beat: 'Here men are maimed and shot
 through, hit through;
Here iron and lead rain, sandbags rent in two;
And the honours are earned. The stuff of tales is woven.'
Here were whispers of encouragement, about the cloven
Trenches faces showed and west soft somethings were said.
Lucky were signallers who (intellectual) strangely had
Some local independence in line danger, but
In training or on Rest were from honour shut.
Bundling over sky lines to clear trench digging –
On the Plain scorn went with tapping and flag wagging
Directions. And then one took us courteously
Where a sheet lifted, and gold light cautiously
Streamed from an oilsheet slitted vertical into
Half-light of May. We entered, took stranger-view
Of life as lived in the line, the line of war and daily
Papers, despatches, brave-soldier talks, the really, really
Truly line, and these the heroes of story.

Never were quieter folk in teaparty history.
Never in 'Cranford', Trollope, even. And, as it were, home
Closed round us. They told us lore, how and when did come
Minnewerfers and grenades from over there east;
The pleasant and unpleasant habits of the beast
That crafted and tore Europe. What line-mending was
When guns centred and dug-outs rocked in a haze
And hearing was difficult – (wires cut) – all necessary
Common-sense workmanlike cautions of salutary
Wisdom – the mechanic day-lore of modern war-making,
Calm thought discovered in mind and body shaking.
The whole craft and business of bad occasion.
Talk turned personal, and to borders of two nations
Gone out; Cotswold's Black Mountain edges against august
August after-sun's glow, and air a lit dust
With motes and streams of gold. Wales her soul visible
Against all power west Heaven ever could flood full.
And of songs – the 'Slumber Song', and the soft Chant
So beautiful to which Rabelaisian songs were meant
Of South and North Wales; and 'David of the White Rock':
What an evening! What a first time, what a shock

86

So rare of home-pleasure beyond measure
And always to time's ending surely a treasure.

*

Since after-war so surely hurt, disappointed men
Who looked for the golden Age to come friendly again.
With inn evenings of meetings in warm glows,
Talk: coal and wood fire uttering rosy shows
With beer and 'Widdicombe Fair' and five mile homeward –
Moonlight lying thick on frost spangled fleet foot sward,
And owl crying out every short while his one evil word.

At any rate, disputeless the romantic evening was –
The night, the midnight; next day Fritz strafed at us,
And I lay belly upward to wonder: when – but useless.

Canadians

We marched, and saw a company of Canadians,
Their coats weighed eighty pounds at least, we saw them
Faces infinitely grimed in, with almost dead hands
Bent, slouching downwards to billets comfortless and dim.
Cave dwellers last of tribes they seemed, and a pity
Even from us just relieved, much as they were, left us.
Lord, what a land of desolation, what iniquity
Of mere being, of what youth that country bereft us;
Plagues of evil lay in Death's Valley, we also
Had forded that up to the thighs in chill mud,
Gone for five days then any sign of life glow,
As the notched stumps or the grey clouds we stood
Dead past death from first hour and the needed mood
Of level pain shifting continually to and fro.
Saskatchewan, Ontario, Jack London ran in
My own mind; what in others? these men who finely
Perhaps had chosen danger for reckless and fine,
Fate had sent for suffering and dwelling obscenely
Vermin-eaten, fed beastly, in vile ditches meanly.

87

IV

1919–1922

Drachms and Scruples

Misery weighed by drachms and scruples
Is but scrawls on a vain page.
To cruel masters are we pupils,
Escape comes careless with old age.

O why were stars so set in Heaven
To desire greedily as gluttons do,
Or children trinkets – May death make even
So rough an evil as we go through.

April Gale

The wind frightens my dog, but I bathe in it,
Sound, rush, scent of the spring fields.

My dog's hairs are blown like feathers askew,
My coat's a demon, torturing like life.

Personages

Beauty and bright fame go not together, I
Bought oranges today from Queen Deirdre.
Apollo hewed the beech, I stood and watched
A ghost of wonder weaving while one thatched;
A pattern of lithe movements all a wonder;
An axe one farmer dealt like Zeus his thunder,
But no harm came save splinters on the dog.
Rosalind milks brown Jerseys Brimscombe way,
With careless royal air born of the first breath
And stealthy air-stirrings of breaking day.
Young gods a-many hew stubborn at their log,
Strong labours shows the breed plain underneath,
And goddesses a-many near . . .

Compensations

Spring larch should set the body shaking
In masterless pleasure,
But virtue lies in a square making –
The making pleasure.
True, the poet's true place is in that high wood,
And his gaze on it,
But work has a bent, and some grey sort of good.
Worship, or a sonnet?

April – Dull Afternoon

The sun for all his pride dims out and dies.
Afternoon sees not one
Of all those flames that lit the primrose lamps
At winter's hest fordone,

Like music eager curving or narrowing
From here to there. Strange how no mist can dull
Wholly the silver edge of April song
Though the air's a blanket weighing on like wool.

Silver Birch

A silver birch dances at my window.
The faint clouds dimly seen
On the sloped azure are easy to be scattered
When full day's wind sweeps clean.

Call to walk comes as of true nature,
Easy should the body move.
And poetry comes after eight miles' seeking,
Mere right out of mere love.

The Garden

The ordered curly and plain cabbages
Are all set out like school-children in rows;
In six short weeks shall these no longer please,
For with that ink-proud lady the rose, pleasure goes.

I cannot think what moved the poet men
So to write panegyrics of that foolish
Simpleton – while wild rose as fresh again
Lives, and the drowsed cabbages keep soil coolish.

Tobacco Plant

We wondered at the tobacco plants there in France
And hung on the rafters brown where our bacon hangs
Sunny in the clear light autumn wind a-dance;
Or to be looked at upwards in its dry ranks,
But the wonder more when in cold nights fumes arose
From the hidden bags, and the frost a moment grew less.

'What! you love smoking, indeed?' he said, and I
Spoke with love of Virginia and Egypt, but not a
Good word for tobacco issue wherever given
And the talk passed to my love of the dear French heaven,
Her people, her soldiers, her books, music and lovely land.
Speaking broken French he could hardly easily understand,
Until I spoke of Daudet, whose book I loved
And of Ronsard, Molière, others, the *Journals* that proved
Friendly enough in that news-lacking and forlorn land.
Talking of all my love, all, in forlorn exile.

Till, looking up in the comfort of that fire-warm room
I saw the tobacco plants – brown leaves on the beams
Reminding gratitude of tobacco's never-ending boon,
Happy to see the leaf, after the smoked thing in gleams
Whirling white puffs contented to the ceiling's gloom.
And thank the gods for one thing in these damned extremes,
And his man's friendliness so good to have, and lost so soon.

Mist on Meadows

Mist lies heavy on English meadows
As ever on Ypres, but the friendliness
Here is greater in full field and hedge shadows,
And there is less menace and no dreadfulness
As when the Verey lights went up to show the land stark.
Dreadful green light baring the ruined trees,
Stakes, pools, lostness, better hidden dreadful in dark
And not ever reminding of these other fields
Where tall dock and clover is, and this sweet grass yields
For that poisoned, where the cattle hoof makes mark,
And the river mist drifts slowly along the leas.

*

But they honour not – and salute not those boys who saw a
    terror
Of waste, endured horror, and were not fearer
Before the barrages like Heaven's anger wanton known –
Feared not and saw great earth spouts in terror thrown,
But could not guess, but could not guess, alas!
How England should take as common their vast endurance
And let them be but boys having served time overseas.

The Awakening

In the white painted dark lobby
The rosy firelight is thrown,
And the mat is still moisted with fresh mud
As I work at my task alone.

The murmuring of the kettle soothes me –
As those above sleep on still.
I love that dear winter-reflection . . .
Gone truant from loving too well.

Walking Song

The miles go sliding by
Under my steady feet,
That mark a leisurely
And still unbroken beat,
Through coppices that hear
Awhile, then lie as still
As though no traveller
Ever had climbed their hill.

My comrades are the small
Or dumb or singing birds,
Squirrels, field-things all
And placid drowsing herds.
Companions that I must
Greet for a while, then leave
Scattering the forward dust
From dawn to late of eve.

Cotswold Ways

One comes across the strangest things in walks:
Fragments of Abbey tithe-barns fixed in modern
And Dutch-sort houses where the water baulks
Weired up, and brick kilns broken among fern,
Old troughs, great stone cisterns bishops might have blessed
Ceremonially, and worthy mounting-stones;
Black timber in red brick, queerly placed
Where Hill stone was looked for – and a manor's bones
Spied in the frame of some wisteria'd house
And mill-falls and sedge pools and Saxon faces;
Stream-sources happened upon in unlikely places,
And Roman-looking hills of small degree
And the surprise of dignity of poplars
At a road end, or the white Cotswold scars,

Or sheets spread white against the hazel tree.
Strange the large difference of up-Cotswold ways;
Birdlip climbs bold and treeless to a bend,
Portway to dim wood-lengths without end,
And Crickley goes to cliffs are the crown of days.

Quiet Talk

Tree-talk is breathing quietly today
Of coming autumn and the staleness over –
Pause of high summer when the year's at stay,
And the wind's sick that now moves like a lover.

On valley ridges where our beeches cluster
Or changing ashes guarding slopes of plough,
He goes now sure of heart, now with a fluster
Of teasing purpose. Night shall find him grow

To dark strength and a cruel spoiling will.
First he will baffle streams and dull their bright,
Cower and threaten both about the hill –
Before their death trees have their full delight.

Water Colours

The trembling water glimpsed through dark tangle
Of late-month April's delicatest thorn,
One moment put the cuckoo-flower to scorn
Where its head hangs by sedges, Severn bank-full.
But dark water has a hundred fires on it;
As the sky changes it changes and ranges through
Sky colours and thorn colours, and more would do,
Were not the blossom truth so quick on it,
And beauty brief in action as first dew.

Generations

The ploughed field and the fallow field
They sang a prudent song to me:
We bide all year and take our yield
Or barrenness as case may be.

What time or tide may bring to pass
Is nothing of our reckoning,
Power was before our making was
That had in brooding thought its spring.

We bide our fate as best betides
What ends the tale may prove the first.
Stars know as truly of their guides
As we the truth of best or worst.

Going Out at Dawn

Strange to see that usual dark road paven wet
With shallow dim reflecting rain pools looking
To north, where light all night stayed and dawn braving yet
Capella hung, above dark elms unshaking, no silence breaking.
And still to dawn night's ugliness owed no debt.
About eleven from the touch of the drear raining,
I had gone in to Shakespeare and my own writing,
Seen the lovely lamplight in golden shining,
And resolved to move no more till dawn made whitening
Between the shutter-chinks, or by the door-mat.
Yet here at five, an hour before day was alive . . .
Behold me walking to where great elm trees drip
Melancholy slow streams of rainwater, on the too wet
Traveller, to pass them, watching, and then return.
Writing Sonata or Quartett with a candle dip.

Possessions

Sand has the ants, clay ferny weeds for play
But what shall please the wind now the trees are away
War took on Witcombe steep?
It breathes there, and wonders at old night roarings;
October time at all lights, and the new clearings
For memory are like to weep.
It was right for the beeches to stand over Witcombe reaches,
Until the wind roared and softened and died to sleep.

Changes

Villas are set up where the sheepfolds were,
And plate glass impudent stares at the sun,
For byres and stack-boards threshing for ever is done,
New things are there, shining new-fangled gear.

Peasants and willow pattern went together,
And whiskers with the white road suited well.
Now there's a mixtured hotch-potch bad to tell,
'Twill lame the mare, turn cream, and spoil the weather.

When I Am Covered

When I am covered with the dust of peace
And but the rain to moist my senseless clay,
Will there be one regret left in that ill ease

One sentimental fib of light and day –
A grief for hillside and the beaten trees?
Better to leave them, utterly to go away.

When every tiny pang of love is counterpiece
To shadowed woe of huge weight and the stay
For yet another torment ere release

Better to lie and be forgotten aye.
In death his rose-leaves never is a crease.
Rest squares reckonings love set awry.

Leckhampton Chimney Has Fallen Down

Leckhampton chimney has fallen down,
The birds of Crickley have cried it – it is known in the town,
The cliffs have changed. What will come next to that line
Watcher of west England, now that landmark has fallen.

Severn has changed course, it is known by Barrow;
Malvern may heave up in other lines by tomorrow,
But Maisemore Hill stable and rounded shall stay –
And strawberry flowers found surprise on Christmas Day.

Cleeve will front sunset, Birdlip shall have its road
Flung angled and noble on its breast broad.
Many things shall stay, but the stone chimney,
Leckhampton's mark has fallen, like a stick or a tree.

The Change

Gone bare the fields now, and the starlings gather,
Whirr above stubble and soft changing hedges.
Changed the season chord too, F major or minor,
The gnats sing thin in clouds above the sedges.

And there is nothing proud now, not disconsolate,
Nothing youthful save where dark crocus flings
Summer's last challenge toward winter's merciless
Cohort, for whom the robin alone sings.

Fields for a while longer, then, O soul,
A curtained room close shut against the rime –
Where shall float music, voice or violin's
Denial passionate of the frozen time.

Stars Sliding

The stars are sliding wanton through trees,
The sky is sliding steady over all.
Great Bear to Gemini will lose his place
And Cygnus over world's brink slip and fall.

Follow-my-Leader's not so bad a game.
But were it leap-frog: O to see the shoots
And tracks of glory; Scorpions and Swans tame
And Argo swarmed with Bulls and other brutes.

Of Grandcourt

Through miles of mud we travelled, and by sick valleys –
The Valley of Death at last – most evil alleys,
To Grandcourt trenches reserve – and the hell's name it did
    deserve.
Rain there was – tired and weak I was, glad for an end.
But one spoke to me – one I liked well as friend,
'Let's volunteer for the Front Line – many others won't.
I'll volunteer, it's better being there than here.'
But I had seen too many ditches and stood too long
Feeling my feet freeze, and my shoulders ache with the
    strong
Pull of equipment, and too much use of pain and strain.
Beside, he was Lance Corporal and might be full Corporal
Before the next straw resting might come again,
Before the next billet should hum with talk and song.
Stars looked as well from second as from first line holes.

There were fatigues for change, and a thought less danger —
But five or six there were followed Army with their souls
Took five days dripping rain without let or finish again —
With dysentery and bodies of heroic ghouls.
Till at last their hearts feared nothing of the brazen anger,
(Perhaps of death little) but once more again to drop on straw
    bed-serving,
And to have heaven of dry feeling after the damps and fouls.

Between the Boughs

Between the boughs the stars showed numberless
And the leaves were
As wonderful in blackness as those brightnesses
Hung in high air.

Two lovers in that whispering silence, what
Should fright our peace?
The aloofness, the dread of starry majesties,
The night-stilled trees.

Rainy Midnight

Long shines the line of wet lamps dark in gleaming,
The trees so still felt yet as strength not used,
February chills April, the cattle are housed,
And night's grief from the higher things comes streaming.

The traffic is all gone, the elver-fishers gone
To string their lights 'long Severn like a wet Fair.
If it were fine the elvers would swim clear;
Clothes sodden, the out-of-work stay on.

The Silent One

Who died on the wires, and hung there, one of two –
Who for his hours of life had chattered through
Infinite lovely chatter of Bucks accent:
Yet faced unbroken wires; stepped over, and went
A noble fool, faithful to his stripes – and ended.
But I weak, hungry, and willing only for the chance
Of line – to fight in the line, lay down under unbroken
Wires, and saw the flashes and kept unshaken,
Till the politest voice – a finicking accent, said:
'Do you think you might crawl through there: there's a hole.'
Darkness, shot at: I smiled, as politely replied –
'I'm afraid not, Sir.' There was no hole no way to be seen
Nothing but chance of death, after tearing of clothes.
Kept flat, and watched the darkness, hearing bullets whizzing –
And thought of music – and swore deep heart's deep oaths
(Polite to God) and retreated and came on again,
Again retreated – and a second time faced the screen.

The Telegraph Post

The Telegraph post stands and is a foil
To the high and the dim sky,
Hardly aware of the ribbon of roadway
That's checked by it and then goes by.

But the poles on the edge of the rises out westward
Are symbol for all lonely travel –
A strange distance of untold futures,
Significances hard to unravel.

Fragment

Dewy are the stars against their dark cloth
And infinitely far that star Capella
That calls to poetry. Dark are the roads now
Running northward, the hill-mass its fellow.

No one walks. String Quartett fills northwest space

The Lock Keeper

Men delight to praise men; and to edge
A little further off from death the memory
Of any noted or bright personality
Is still a luck and poet's privilege.
And so the man who goes in my dark mind
With sand and broad waters and general kind
Of fish-and-fox-and-bird lore, and walking lank;
Knowledge of net and rod and rib and shank,
Might well stretch out my mind to be a frame –
A picture of a worthy without name.
You might see him at morning by the lock-gates,
Or busy in the warehouse on a multitude
Of boat fittings, net fittings; copper, iron, wood,
Then later digging, furious, electric
Under the apple boughs, with a short stick,
Burnt black long ages, of pipe between set teeth,
His eyes gone flaming on the work beneath –
He up-and-down working like a marionette.
Back set, eyes set, wrists; and the work self-set.

His afternoon was action but all nebulous
Trailed over four miles country, tentaculous
Of coalmen, farmers, fishermen his friends,
And duties without beginnings and without ends.
There was talk with equals, there were birds and fish to
    observe,
Stuff for a hundred thoughts on the canal's curves,

A world of sight – and back in time for tea;
Or the tide's change, his care, or a barge to let free.
The lowering of the waters, the quick inflow,
The trouble and the turmoil; characteristic row
Of exits or of river entrances;
With old (how old?) cries of the straining crews,
(Norse, Phoenician, Norse, British? immemorial use.)
Tins would float shining at three-quarter tide
Midstream his line of fire, never far wide –
Dimples of water showed his aim a guide,
And ringed the sunset colours with bright ripples.

Later, tide being past violence, the gates known safe,
He would leave his station, lock warehouse and half
Conscious of tiredness now, moving lankly and slow,
Would go in a dark time like some phantom or wraith,
Most like a woodsman in full summer glow.
There he was not known to me, but as hearers know
Outside the blue door facing the canal path;
Two hours or three hours of talk; as the fishers know
Or sailors, or poachers, or wandering men know talk.

Poverty or closing time would bring him again.
On the cinder path outside would be heard his slow walk.
It had a width, that Severn chimney-corner,
A dignity and largeness which should make grave
Each word or cadence uttered or let fall, save
When the damp wind in garden shrubs was mourner.
It would have needed one far less sick than I
To have questioned, to have pried each vein of his wide
    lore.
One should be stable, and be able for wide views,
Have knowledge, and skilled manage of questions use
When the captain is met, the capable in use,
The pictured mind, the skilled one, the hawk-eyed one;
The deft-handed, quick-moving, the touch-commanded one.
Man and element and animal comprehending
And all-paralleling one. His knowledge transcending
Books, from long vain searches of dull fact.
Conviction needing instant change to act.

The nights of winter netting birds in hedges;
The stalking wild-duck by down-river sedges:
The tricks of sailing; fashions of salmon-netting:
Cunning of practice, the finding, doing, the getting –
Wisdom of every various season or light –
Fish running, tide running, plant learning and bird flight.

Short cuts, and watercress beds, and all snaring touches,
Angling and line laying and wild beast brushes;
Badgers, stoats, foxes, the few snakes, care of ferrets,
Exactly known and judged of on their merits.
Bee-swarming, wasp-exterminating and bird-stuffing.

There was nothing he did not know; there was nothing,
        nothing.

Some men are best seen in the full day shine,
Some in half-light or the dark star-light fine:
But he, close in the deep chimney-corner, seen
Shadow and bright flare, saturnine and lean;
Clouded with smoke, wrapped round with cloak of
        thought,
He gave more of desert to me – more than I ought –
Who was more used to book-poring than bright life.

One had seen half-height covering the stretched sand
With purpose, insistent, creeping-up with silver band,
But dark determined, making wide on and sure.

So behind talk flowed the true spirit – to endure,
To perceive, to manage, to be skilled to excel, to
        comprehend;

A net of craft of eye, heart, kenning and hand.
Thousand-threaded tentaculous intellect
Not easy on a new thing to be wrecked –
Since cautious with ableness, and circumspect
In courage, his mind moved to a new stand,
And only with full wisdom used that hand.

Months of firelight and lamplight of night-times; before-bed
Revelations; a time of learning and little said
On my part, since the Master he was so wise –
Easy the lesson; while the grave night-winds' sighs
At window or up chimney incessant moaning
For dead daylight or for music or fishermen dead.
Dark river voice below heard and lock's overflow.

Longford Dawns

Of course not all the watchers of the dawn
See Severn mists like forced-march mists withdrawn;
London has darkness changing into light
With just one quarter-hour of any weight.

Casual and common is the wonder grown –
Time's duty to lift light's curtain up and down.
But here Time is caught up clear in Eternity,
And draws as breathless life as you or me.

London

Clear lamps and dim stars,
Worry of heart-ache,
Are poor things should make
A consolation for the trees and bars
Of cloud on stars,
That men in western meadows stay awake
And fight with sleep for, till the strong dawn wake.

Brown Earth Look

The youth burning couch grass is as tired
As muscle has right to bear and keeps work on
The brown earth slopes from the potato field to the wired
Sheep enclosure; and hidden high and white the sun.

Brown the sense of things, the light smoke blows across
The field face, light blue wisps of sweet bitter reek
Dear to the Roman perhaps, so old seems the dross
Burning of root, grass, wheat, so near, easy to seek.

Old is the land, a thousand generations
Have tilled there, sought with bright sweat the stuff of its
    bread.
Here one comes for the sense of fine books, revelations
Of beauty in usualty, found as well of heart as of head.

And all the tales of far Europe that come on one,
The sense of myriads tending the needings of life,
Are more to one than the near memory of battle gun.
Peace with its sorrow blots out the agonies of strife.

Time to Come

They will walk there, the sons of our great-grandsons and
Will know no reason for the old love of the land.
There will be no tiny bent-browed houses in the
Twilight to watch, nor small shops of multi-miscellany.
The respectable and red-brick will rule all,
With green-paint railings outside the front door wall,
And children will not play skip-games in the gutter,
Nor dust fly furious in hot valour of footer;
Queerness and untidiness will be smoothed out
As any steam-roller tactful, and there'll be no doubt
About the dustbins or the colour of curtains,
No talking at the doors, no ten o'clock flirtings,

And Nicholas will look as strange as any
Goddess ungarmented in that staid company,
With lovely attitude of fixèd grace,
But naked and embarrassed in the red brick place.

We see her well, and should have great thanksgiving,
Living in sight and form of more than common living.
She is a City still and the centuries drape her yet;
Something in the air or light cannot or will not forget
The past ages of her, and the toil which made her,
The courage of her, the army that made not afraid her,

And a shapely fullness of being drawn maybe from the air
Crystal or mellow about her or above her ever:
Record of desire apparent of dreamer or striver,
And still the house between the Cotswolds bare
And the Welsh wars; mistress of the widening river.

Midnight

There is no sound within the cottage now,
But my pen and the sound of long rain
Heavy and musical, I must think again
To find so sweet a noise, and cannot anyhow.

The soothingness and deep-toned tinkle, soft
Happenings of night, in pain there's nothing better
Save tobacco, or long most-looked-for letter . . .
The different roof-sounds – house, shed, loft and scullery.

Saturday's Comings

The horses of day plunge and are restrained,
Dawn broadens to quarter height, and the meadow mists
Drift like gauze veilings, the roadway ingrained
With traffic marks shows so. Saturday enters the lists

To show like a panorama – cattle brought in
And dapper farmers bargaining in white spats;
Cross crowded, bookstalls past paupers' resisting
And as ever the Cathedral masterfully blessing the flats.

Song

O were there anything by half
As fair as promise true
We should not change for any strange
Or violent fancy new.

But since the cheats are only real
And truths like vapours fade,
Our best advance is toward black fancies
Blind groping in dark shade.

Behind the Line

I suppose France this morning is as white as here
High white clouds veiling the sun, and the mere
Cabbage fields and potato plants lovely to see,
Back behind at Robecq there with the day free.

In the estaminets I suppose the air as cool, and the floor
Grateful dark red; the beer and the different store
Of citron, grenadine, red wine as surely delectable
As in Nineteen Sixteen; with the round stains on the dark table.

Journals Français tell the same news and the queer
Black printed columns give news, but no longer the fear
Of shrapnel or any evil metal torments.
High white morning as here one is sure is on France.

We Who Praise Poets

We who praise poets with our labouring pen
And justify ourselves with laud of men,
Have not the right to call our own our own,
Being but the groundsprouts from those great trees
    grown.
The crafted art, the smooth curve, and surety
Come not of nature till the apprentice free
Of trouble with his tools, and cobwebbed cuts,
Spies out a path his own and casts his plots.
Then looking back on four-square edifices
And wind-and-weather-standing tall houses
He stakes a court, and tries his unpaid hand,
Begins a life whose salt is arid sand,
Whose bread of cactus comes, whose wine is clear
Being bitter water from fount all too near.
Happy if after toil he grow to worth
And praise of complete men of earlier birth,
Of happier pen and more steel-propertied
Nerves: of the able and the mighty dead.

Yesterday Lost

What things I have missed today, I know very well,
But the seeing of them each new time is miracle.
Nothing between Bredon and Dursley has
Any day yesterday's precise unpraisèd grace.
The changed light, or curve changed mistily,
Coppice, now bold cut, yesterday's mystery.
A sense of mornings, once seen, for ever gone,
Its own for ever: alive, dead, and my possession.

On the Night

On the night there are shown dim few stars timorous
And light is smothered in a cloak of fear.
Are these hills out? Then night has brooded there
Of dark things till they were no more for us.

Gone are the strict falls, there is no skyline boundary,
The stars are not resting or coming to rest.
What will dawn show? A land breathing calm of breast,
Or a frightened rook-wheeling plain once bed of the sea?

Robecq Again

Robecq had straw and a comfortable tavern
Where men might their sinews feel slowly recovering
From the march-strain, and there was autumn's translucence
In the calm air and a tang of the earth and its essence.
A girl served wine there with natural dignity
Moving as any princess from care free,
And the North French air bathed crystal the flat land
With cabbages and tobacco plants and varied culture spanned,
Beautiful with moist clarity of autumn's breath.
Lovely with the year's turning to leafless death
Robecq, the dark town at night with estaminets lit,
The outside roads with poplars, plane trees on it,
Huge dark barn with candles throwing warning flares,
Glooms steady and shifting pierced with cold flowing airs,
With dumb peace at last and a wrapping from cares.

Towards Lillers

In October marching, taking the sweet air,
Packs riding lightly, and homethoughts soft coming,
'This is right marching, we are even glad to be here,
Or very glad?' But looking upward to dark smoke foaming,
Chimneys on the clear crest, no more shades for roaming,
Smoke covering sooty what man's heart holds dear,
Lillers we approached, a quench for thirsty frames,
And looked once more between houses and at queer names
Of estaminets, longed for cool wine or cold beer.
This was war; we understood; moving and shifting about;
To stand or be withstood in the mixèd rout
Of fight to come after this. But that was a good dream
Of justice or strength-test with steel tool a gleam
Made to the hand. But barb-wire lay to the front,
Tiny aeroplanes circled as ever their wont
High over the two ditches of heart-sick men;
The times scientific, as evil as ever again.
October lovely bathing with sweet air the plain.

*

Gone outward to the east and the new skies
Are aeroplanes, and flat there as tiny as bright
As insects wonderful coloured after the night
Emerging lovely as ever into the new day's
First coolness and lucent gratefulness
Of the absorbing wide prayer of middle sight.
Men clean their rifles insentient at that delight;
Wonder increases as fast as the night dies.

Now up to the high above aeroplanes go
Swift bitter smoke puffs and spiteful flames,
None knows the pilots, none guesses at their names,
They fly unthought courses of common danger,
Honour rides on the frame with them through that anger,
As the heroes of Marathon their renown we know.

The Hoe Scrapes Earth

The hoe scrapes earth as fine in grain as sand,
I like the swirl of it and the swing in the hand
Of the lithe hoe so clever at craft and grace,
And the friendliness, the clear freedom of the place.

And the green hairs of the wheat on sandy brown.
The draw of eyes toward the coloured town,
The lark ascending slow to a roof of cloud
That cries for the voice of poetry to cry aloud.

Schubert

Made the song as a slow movement
Of Beethoven, probably,
Took ordinary good health technique
Of Beethoven and used it against words,
When his mind was probably not up
To sustained flight or creative power.

The creation of the song is his great
Achievement, but there is at least
The 'Rosamunde Overture' and
'Unfinished Symphony' the 'Quartett
In D Minor', and as one says, the
'Quintett in C' which looks to have
Very good texture.

His work probably stands in fair
Relation to Burns, he having the same
Grip and peasant thought, but
Much more beauty. The
Amount of dull Schubert is vast.

Imitation

The door stands open
　　Light is golden on the wall
Tea-time is content within there
　　Five o'clock winds call

Of summer and the hot breath
　　Is cooled of soaked air,
Afternoon rests after its strain,
　　Time moves steadier

To a smooth going
　　And flowing. Cottagers take
Content in thought of rested
　　Strain, the evening's new lake

Of gold is looked for. Meanwhile
　　The Jubilee pictures are noted,
The blue and white china,
　　And past summers are quoted.

Cottagers are happier now
　　Than any perhaps
Of the townsfolk, tired
　　Decent at hours' lapse.

Seeing as of right the true
　　Texture of rare living
Azure had into nature, green
　　Tasted, thanked of giving.

All common loveliest,
　　Trifles apprehended,
Possessed, put aside then
　　Garden calls, tea's ended.

*

While they must walk the Broadway
Dusty, torrid with the town sun,
And not knowing anything save
The day's doing, the week done.

Old Dreams

Once I had dreamed of return to a sunlit land,
Of summer and firelight winter with inns to visit,
But here are tangles of fate one does not understand,
And as for rest or true ease, where is it or what is it?

With criss-cross purposes and spoilt threads of life,
Perverse pathways, the savour of life is gone.
What have I then with crumbling wood or glowing coals,
Or a four-hours' walking, to work, through a setting sun?

Looking Out

First for the hanging curtain –
Next for the breeze –
That hangs in the light wind waving,
Comfort in these –

Familiar things, gone out
From the preoccupied
And too-busy present-mind
To some deep inside.

But in old days
How were present the sighted
Everyday things the mind
Infinitely delighted.

And all the rewards, O where
Are they misted, withered,
All into time's waste heap
Taken-up, gathered.

Poem

Horror follows horror within me
There is a chill fear
Of the storm that does deafen and din me
And rage horribly near.

What black things had the human
Race in store, what mind could view?
Good guard the hour that is coming,
Mankind safe, honour bring through.

East Wind

Cool air moves there up on Cotswold edge,
By Crickley's bastion or the Shurdington wedge,
Grey grass rustles, the harebells dance and the east
Wind has no good influences on the cattle at feast.

Naked land-slides show, away down hill mist-shades cover
The land where South-West once moved high like a lover,
With colour and boy's glory and breath of renewal:
That also, that valley, for this dry air is a fuel.

But the great steeps keep one in right hoping still,
Mighty the upstanding curving of the golden-crowned hill
Crickley, where scabious and serious thistle nods,
And there is good hiding place for the old gods.

The Escape

I believe in the increasing of life: whatever
Leads to the seeing of small trifles,
Real, beautiful, is good; and an act never
Is worthier than in freeing spirit that stifles
Under ingratitude's weight, nor is anything done
Wiselier than the moving or breaking to sight
Of a thing hidden under by custom – revealed,
Fulfilled, used (sound-fashioned) any way out to delight:
Trefoil – hedge sparrow – the stars on the edge at night.

On Foscombe Hill

O exquisite
And talking water, are you not more glad
To be sole daughter and one comfort bright
Of this small hill lone-guarding its delight,
Than unconsidered to be
Some waif of Cotswold or the Malvern height?
Your name a speck of glory in so many.
You are the silver of a dreaming mound
That likes the quiet way of thought and sound,
Moists tussocks with a sunken influence,
Collects and runs one way down to farm yard
Sheds, house, standing up there by soft sward,
Green of thorn, green of sorrel and age-old heath
Of South-West's lovely breath.

Autumn's Flame

Autumn sent a flame
Up from the rough
Seven-ages field for proof
Of her fine fame
On Cotswold in clear year-fall.

No music is there, no tongue
To tell the complete
Wonder surpassing great
Of the firs' shape outflung
Against Cotswold edge at the year-fall.

Up There

On Cotswold edge there is a field and that
Grows thick with corn and speedwell and the mat
Of thistles, of the tall kind; Rome lived there,
Some hurt centurion got his grant or tenure,
Built farm with fowls and pigsties and wood-piles,
Waited for service custom between whiles.
The farmer ploughs up coins in the wet-earth-time,
He sees them on the topple of crests gleam,
Or run down furrow; and halts and does let them lie
Like a small black island in brown immensity,
Till his wonder is ceased, and his great hand picks up the
    penny.
Red pottery easy discovered, no searching needed . . .
One wonders what farms were like, no searching needed,
As now the single kite hovering still
By the coppice there, level with the flat of the hill.

The Sea Borders

Well I know though I have not seen how the white edges
Of the sea make fury now by Devon or Maryland –
What grand spirit batters uselessly against old Brittany,
Or against Hebrides with black granite wedges
Of rock. And all the writers who ever have written the
Annals of seafaring will tell me little more
Of how the water at a huge ship's onset surges
Than my own little boat's prow sailing Severn recklessly.
(But O those great three-masters of the past ages!)

Tales told in the foc'sle, or hauling hand over hand
Hauling on ropes, the companionship in close quarters –
The lovely shocks of beauty of the noises of broken waters . . .
These I have known, not because writers made tales to
　　command
My shame and glory, and terror all clear to me.
Not because my life has had soldiership and greatest labour of
　　body . . .
Not because only I have been all men's all women's friend.
But because I musician have wrestled with the stuff in making,
And wrought a square thing out of my stubborn mind –
And gathered a huge surge of spirit as the great barriers bind
The whole Atlantic at them by Devon or west Ireland.

The Dearness of Common Things

The dearness of common things,
Beech wood, tea, plate shelves,
And the whole family of crockery,
Woodaxes, blades, helves.

Ivory milk, earth's coffee,
The white face of books
And the touch, feel, smell of paper,
Latin's lovely looks.

Earth fine to handle,
The touch of clouds
When the imagined arm leaps out to caress
Grey worsted or wool clouds.

Wool, rope, cloth, old pipes
Gone warped in service
And the one herb of tobacco,
The herb of grace, the censer weed
Of blue whorls, finger-traced curves
The touch of sight how strange and marvellous
To any blind man pierced through his opaque,
When concrete objects grow.

Friendly Are Meadows

Friendly are meadows when the sun's gone in
And no bright colour spoils the broad green of grey,
And one's eyes rest looking to far Cotswold away
Under cloud ceilings whorled and most largely fashioned
With seventeenth-century curves of the tombstone way.
A day of softnesses, of comfort of no din, not passioned.
Sorrel makes rusty rest for the eyes, and the worn path,
Brave elms, and stiles, willows by dyked deep water-run –
North French general look, and a sort of bath
Of freshness – a light wrap of comfortableness
Over one's being, a sense as of music begun;
A slow gradual symphony of worthiness, fulfilledness.
But this is Cotswold, Severn: when these go stale
Then the all-universal and wide decree shall fail
Of world's binding, and earth's dust apart be loosed,
And man's worship of all grey comforts be abused,
To mere wonder at lightning and torrentous strong flying hail.

Andromeda over Tewkesbury

Andromeda over Tewkesbury in state
Has taken place with calm and lucent mien,
I think the dark houses there have been
A hundred times so set, but not so great.
Square tower, carved upward by the laboured thought,
The imagined bare concept, how must that soften
Now to the ivory glow and pride unsought –
Queenly Andromeda not so exalted often.

The Bare Line of the Hill

The bare line of the hill
Shows Roman and
A sense of Rome hangs still
Over the land.

So that one looks to see
Steel gleam, to hear
Voice outflung suddenly
Of the challenger.

Yet boom of the may-fly
The loudest thing
Is of all under the sky
Of the wide evening.

And the thing metal most
The pond's last sheen
Willow shadow crossed
But still keen.

How long, how long before
The ploughland lose
Sense of that old power?
The winds, the dews

Of twice ten hundred years
Have dimmed no jot
Of Roman thought there, fears,
Triumphs unforgot.

Has Caesar any thought
In his new place, of lands
Far west, where cohorts fought,
Watched at his commands?

Carausius, Maximus,
Is all let slip, then why
Does Rome inherit thus
Dominate memory

So royally that Here
And Now are nothing known?
The regal and austere
Mantle of Rome is thrown

As of old – about the walls
Of hills and the farm – the fields.
Scabious guards the steeps,
Trefoil the slopes yield.

Had I a Song

Had I a song
I would sing it here
Four lined square shaped
Utterance dear

But since I have none,
Well, regret in verse
Before the power's gone
Might be worse, might be worse.

Quiet Fireshine

Quiet is fireshine when the light is gone,
The kettle's steam is comfort and the low song.
Now all the day's business stills down and is done
To watch them seems but right; nothing at all is wrong.

Save the dark thoughts within most bitter with
Disappointment, mere pain; gnawing at heart's peace.
The heavy heart so ponderous once was lithe
Travelling the hill slope easy at light's pace.

Quiet is fireshine, and the mind would soak
Years ago, after football, in drowse of light.
Now the slack body is sick and a bitter joke
To a soul too sick for dreams at fall of night.

The High Hills

The high hills have a bitterness
Now they are not known
And memory is poor enough consolation
For the soul hopeless gone.
Up in the air there beech tangles wildly in the wind —
That I can imagine
But the speed, the swiftness, walking into clarity,
Like last year's bryony are gone.

Old Thought

Autumn, that name of creeper falling and tea-time loving,
Was once for me the thought of high Cotswold noon-air,
And the earth smell, turning brambles, and half-cirrus
      moving,
Mixed with the love of body and travel of good turf there.

O up in height, O snatcht up, O swiftly going,
Common to beechwood, breathing was loving, the yet
Unknown Crickley Cliffs trumpeted, set music on glowing
In my mind. White Cotswold, wine scarlet woods and leaf
      wreckage wet.

Kettle Song

The worry and low murmur
Of the black kettle are set
Against my unquiet achings
And vanish, so strong is the fret.

Such tangles and evil-skeined fibres
Of living so matted are grown
That water-song is hardly noticed
For all its past comfortings known.

Hedges

'Bread and cheese' grow wild in the green time,
Children laugh and pick it, and I make my rhyme
For mere pleasure of seeing that so subtle play
Of arms and various legs going every, any way.

And they turn and laugh for the unexpensiveness
Of country grocery and are pleased no less
Than hedge sparrows. Lessons will be easier taken,
For this gipsy chaffering, the hedge plucked and shaken.

When March Blows

When March blows, and Monday's linen is shown
On the gooseberry bushes, and the worried washer alone
Fights at the soaked stuff, meres and the rutted pools
Mirror the wool-pack clouds and shine clearer than jewels.

And the children throw stones in them, spoil mirrors and clouds.
The worry of washing over, the worry of foods
Brings tea-time; March quietens as the trouble dies.
The washing is brought in under wind-swept clear infinite skies.

All Souls' Day 1921

The smell of earth there in the coloured plain;
The bell tolling summons through colour and soft
Mist of clear air, and other land memories again.
These were of All Souls' Day indeed, and the loft
Of farmstead should have scented with sweet apples plain.

The shrine there, Tuscan of look at corners round
Would have persuaded any to some acquiescent
Admiring of that faith grown in with the ground,
The earth itself, with first worship grown-in and blent
Centred with hollow iron, in dark sound.

And the autumn darkness good, as if Autumn had cast
By purple crocus and trefoil a brooding shade.
Not now the tea-time comfort to expect at last.
No end of clean-walked body in rest laid,
The times were not of making, but swift terrible waste.

*

But, O, the worship that hurt my heart with fear . . .
Going into Merville's church, and seeing the bowed
Supplicating women with souls crying dark-deep to where
God might pity France again, and lift off the plague's cloud . . .
And the mothers of the dead by Robecq under bright poplar.

Sonnet to J. S. Bach's Memory

Honoured Sebastian, that to many men
Has been the speaker of their deep honour –
You that have kept makers in fine manner
Beyond any, save Shakespeare – here again
One writes to praise thee; and for thy Christian
Greatness, thy nobleness of strict banner,
Of grey metal, of truth of love's demeanour –
Page on page with the look and life of stone –

Europe gives thanks ennobling, Sebastian,
When her heart touches thy praise. It is her own
Hard and age-old virtue, out of prayer grown.
The aisles that fill with thunder, the height that thrills,
Most to thy name respond. And it is predestined
That by thy chief gratitude men will make miracles.

Song

Past my window dawn and
    Through the open shutters thrown
Pass the birds the first awaking,
    And the light wind peace breaking.

Now the ink will dry on pen
    And the paper take no more
Thoughts of beauty from the far
    Night, or remembered day of men,
Cotswold breaking the dark or standing
    Brave as the sun, with white scar.

Now my footsteps shall go light
    By the fence and bridge till white
The farm show, that till now had glimmered,
    In the trees July had summered.

Kilns

Severn has kilns set all along her banks
Where the thin reeds grow and rushes in ranks;
And the carts tip rubbish there from the town;
It thunders and raises white smoke and goes down.
I think some of those kilns are very old,
An age is on those small meres, and could unfold

Tales of the many tenders of kilns and tales
Of the diggers and earth delvers of those square weals
Or oblong, of Severn bank. And all the flowers
June ever imagined stand and fulfil June's hours.
I think of the countless slabs gone out from all of them;
Farmhouse, cottage, loved of generations of men,
Fronting day as equal, or in dusk shining dim;
Of the Dane-folk curious of the sticky worthy stuff;
Kneading, and crumbling till the whim wearied enough.
Of the queer bricks unlearned hands must have made;
Spoiling clay, wasting wood, working out the war's trade;
With one hand the clear eyes fending, keeping in shade
Fierce fire that grazes and melts with its regardings rough.
Or the plays children had of Dane-Saxon breed,
Chasing round the square kilns with devil-may-care
Headlong roughness of heedless body-reckless speed;
Grazing knees and knuckles to disaster there.
Of the creeping close to parents when November azure
Melancholy made company, and stillness, new pleasure,
And the wonder of fire kept the small boys to stay sure.

And the helping of fathers build well of the new brick,
The delight in handling over thin and thick – the youthful
    critic.

Of the Normans, how they liked kilns, that thrust to endure
Endless abbeys and strong chapels up in the air,
And Domesday questioners who worried the too evasive
Owner as to tales and days' work to a story unplausive,
As to the fuels used, and the men there and the hours, the
    wage hours.

George Chapman – The Iliad

The football rush of him, and that country knowledge,
That pluck driving through work, endless that wearying
    courage,
Still unwearying. Still face on: and the wide heaven taking
At one glance in at his eye: O that set on shaking

Keats, and new wonder brought fresh from mortal power.
That first hand still, and in sad heart-break hour
The voice of David brought once again to say
What joy what grief on man Time's heavy hand doth lay.
Homer's re-bringer, and of joy that great map-man,
Friend of great makers: scholar, mixed-minded doer, George
  Chapman.

The Cloud

One could not see or think, the heat overcame one,
With a dazzle of square road to challenge and blind one,
No water was there, cow-parsley the only flower
Of all May's garland this torrid before-summer hour,
And but one ploughman to break ten miles of solitariness.
No water, water to drink, stare at, the lovely clean grained one.

Where like a falcon on prey, shadow flung downward
Solid as gun-metal, the eyes sprang sunward
To salute the silver radiance of an Atlantic high
Prince of vapour required of the retinue
Continual changing of the outer-sea's flooding sun.
Cloud royal, born called and ordered to domination,
Spring called him out of his tent in the azure of pleasure,
He girt his nobleness – and in slow pace went onward
A true monarch of air chosen to service and station,
And directed on duties of patrolling the considered blue.
But what his course required being fulfilled, what fancy
Of beyond-imagination did his power escape to
With raiment of blown silver . . .

Early Spring Dawn

Long shines the thin light of the day to north-east,
The line of blue faint known and the leaping to white;
The meadows lighten, mists lessen, but light is increased,
The sun soon will appear, and dance, leaping with light.

Now milkers hear faint through dreams first cockerel crow,
Faint yet arousing thought, soon must the milk pails be flowing.
Gone out the level sheets of mists, and see, the west row
Of elms are black on the meadow edge. Day's wind is blowing.

Tewkesbury

Some Dane looking out from the water-settlements,
 If settlements there were, must have thought as I,
 'Square stone should fill that bit of lower sky.
Were I a king and had my influence,
Farms should go up for this, flames make terror go high.
But I would set my name in high eminence.'
Forthampton walking, thinking and looking to Tewkesbury,
Where a cricketer was born and a battle raged desperate,
And mustard grew, and Stratford boys early or late
 May have come, and rivers, green Avon, brown Severn, meet.
And Norman Milo set a seal on the plain –
'Here man rules; his works to be found here;
Acknowledges supremacy, his strengths to be in vain;
And gathers by a sign the broad meadows in round here.'

What is best of England, going quick from beauty,
Is manifest, the slow spirit going straight on,
The dark intention corrected by eyes that see,
The somehow getting there, the last conception
Bettered, and something of one's own spirit outshown;
Grown as oaks grow, done as hard things are done.

On a Two-Hundredth Birthday

Of worthy towns worthy should be Messenger
Of News that's food to heart of Everyman,
The curious of his kind. And on this birthday,
This twice a hundred mark of age and honour,
Well do we salute 'Journal' of Land's fame;
That's gossip to our region villages,
And Record to the Merchant with his lad,
Art's Table and the Tale of Sport and Stage.
Those country folk that stare to see the queer
Rough-textured first-of-kind, have often taken
Their whole week's thought from 'Journal's' gathering-in,
Severn and Vale alike, and known our England,
Europe, the wider world, from that respected
Close-ordered print; and we in hacked-up Flanders
Read Sunday School, Fairs, football-scores alike.
(Raikes, that kind-thoughted, gay man, had laughed,
We sitting there in drips of rain to ponder
On small home businesses, so mired and chill.)
Well to the sober, beautiful city serves
This grave news-printing, old in praise as years,
Looked for at week-ends; worthy of that first
Director, whom in London surprised one sees
Smile from the dun wall on the curious.

But he, could return be, having heard the presses
And thunderous printing, seen and grasped so much,
By fumbling questions groping near the truth,
Would yet have asked what thought the townsfolk had,
This 'Journal', how it stood yet in their minds;
And, answered, should indeed be well content.

Towns are not often lucky in their print-sheets;
But this, the Roman City, has for servant
A Teller wise of grave news-currency.

Clay

The clay our mothers feed us with is taken
To be the tie and case of the bright spirit,
It is washed and dressed and hindered and does inherit
A thousand vermin cares are of all Time's making.
The clay does enter, does possess us and we have then
A thousand clayey consequences, known
By the hurt and hinders of action, and the left undone
Adventurous things which salt the lives of men.
That clay has cased the fibre and tied the limb
Nor yet that entail shall we put away
Till the clay wrap us affectionately in clay
And the adhesive marl film the bright eyeglance dim.

Wandering Thoughts

Lonely people had best wander in blue halls
Walled up and down with glory of rich fire
Where the azure curtain rounds its power and falls
Plenteously from the rafters gyre on gyre.
And the fleet clouds fleece the wide coverture
Swift messengers of the Atlantic broodings
To increase to broad gloom and ubiquitous cloudings
When the shamed beeches mumble in dark desire
Having stilled so long in chaste thought under the moon
So quietly and steadfastly light pouring down
And Saturn no longer grieves for his old crown.

Larches

Larches are most fitting small red hills
That rise like swollen ant-heaps likeably
And modest before big things like near Malvern
Or Cotswold's further early Italian

Blue arrangement; unassuming as the
Cowslips, celandines, buglewort and daisies
That trinket out the green swerves like a child's game.
O never so careless or lavish as here.
I thought, 'You beauty! I must rise soon one dawn time
And ride to see the first beam strike on you
Of gold or ruddy recognisance over
Crickley level or Bredon sloping down.
I must play tunes like Burns, or sing like David,
A saying-out of what the hill leaves unexprest,
The tale or song that lives in it, and is sole,
A round red thing, green upright things of flame'.
It is May, and the conceited cuckoo toots and whoos his name.

Near Vermand

A park there, with a stream running, deep up-and-down
Banks sliding with green face, and young trees running hither
And thither in the small valley, up to the smooth crown
Of the steep; and we with full packs, weak with hunger,
Thought of the present labour with dull anger.
The copse was like a Cranham copse with scythèd curve –
In a month violets would bloom, but no Birdlip swerve
Meet our eyes – Roman – backs turned to that far west
Where April is pattern of living not merely guest.
And we were in forced marches after an enemy pressed
Through snowstorms and such, seeking an end to this ending.
But an order took us on, we were led, brought to the four
Ways of Vermand, at the station place, turned east to more
Digging, but new wood-searching, and new good war tricks,
With Germans seen actually, and private bivouacs
(Rain-spoilt) and March stars spoiled with grey cloudy racks.

The Bronze Sounding

In the old days autumn would clang a gong
Of colour between Cranham and the Birdlip curve,
Hollow brass sustained the woods' noble swerve
And the air itself stood against music as crystal strong.
So it may be so still, but the body now
No longer takes in distance as slow thought.
Old man's beard may be tangled in black hedges caught,
But the body hurt, spirit is hindered and slow,
And evil hurts me past my maker's right.

February Dawn

Rooks flew across the sky, bright February watched
Their steady course straight on, like an etcher's line scratched.
The dark brown or tawny earth breathed incense up,
I guessed there were hidden daisies, hoped the first buttercup.

The tunes of all the county, old-fashioned and my own
Wilful, wanton, careless, thronged in my mind, alone.
The sight of earth and rooks made passion rise in my blood.
Far gleamed Cotswold. Near ran Severn. A god's mood.

Save that I knew no high things would amaze day-fall
I had prayed heaven to kill me at that time most to fulfil
My dreams for ever. But looked on to a west bright at five,
Scarred by rooks in purpose; and the late trees in strife.

Moments

I think the loathed minutes one by one
That tear and then go past are little worth
Save nearer to the blindness to the sun
They bring me, and the farewell to all earth

Save to that six-foot-length I must lie in
Sodden with mud, and not to grieve again
Because high autumn goes beyond my pen
And snow lies inexprest in the deep lane.

Remembrances

Faces are seen sometimes that stay with one
Longer than any sight of hill-scar or sun;
A fitting to the mood, a sight strict in tune
With the moment, and the poetry is seized and done.

Across Europe rumour of Helen came
To Outer Hebrides, she is a test and a fame
For beauty in the sandy and tided isles.
Atlantic has framed beauty from the Greekish wiles.

What mixed blood runs to what distinction here;
Garrison settlements and Dane colonies steer
No strict course in British or Danish towns.
Heroes' blood not wholly in common drowns.

Early Winter

I love chrysanthemums and winter jasmine,
Clustering lichened walls a century old;
That in my western ways when days draw in,
Grow in the farm gardens in the first cold.
Strange foreigners should prove
So homely to my love.

For all the age that lies upon this land
Seems to call out for things native, things like
Britain knew, when the tongue talked soft, and
Not yet Rome from the far Gaul might strike.
Yet here Japan
Has flowered, as after plan.

The Valley Farm

Ages ago the waters covered here
And took delight of dayspring as a mirror;
Hundreds of tiny spikes and threads of light.
But now the spikes are hawthorn, and the hedges
Are foamed like ocean's crests, and peace waits here
Deeper than middle South Sea, or the Fortunate
Or Fabled Islands. And blue wood-smoke rising
Foretells smooth weather and the airs of peace.
Even the woodchopper swinging bright
His lithe and noble weapon in the sun
Moves with such grace peace works an act through him;
Those echoes thud and leave a deeper peace.
If war should come here only then might one
Regret water receding, and earth left
To bear man's grain and use his mind of order,
Working to frame such squares and lights as these.

Winter Has Clouds

Winter has clouds like other seasons
But having their own currents and other reasons
Than spring whose boyish glory spends out all
His fantasy at one glory and is mendical.
Winter keeps high pale skies and cirrus wisps,
Winter puts pressed-flower clouds out and all over sky clasps
A frozen expressionless dull steely cloak of cloud
Under which no brave bird complains aloud:
A toothache sky, a cruelty without frost
Of the Enyopean dry salt plains of terror vast.

The Dark Tree

Strange that the dark tree, the unblossomed apple
Should show so much the princess of this orchard,
Whose clear shadows equal the pear's dappled,
And patterns black for cloudy the smooth sward.
The light-bearing tree should far surpass
This slim and winter-garmented young slut,
That's never watched her dark fire in the glass,
Nor wondered vainly till her eyelids shut.
The Cinderella of unjealous kin
Who watch their sister till her time comes in.

Felling a Tree

The surge of spirit that goes with using an axe,
The first heat – and calming down till the stiff back's
Unease passed, and the hot moisture came on body.
There under banks of Dane and Roman with the golden
Imperial coloured flower, whose name is lost to me –
Hewing the trunk desperately with upward strokes;
Seeing the chips fly – (it was at shoulder height, the trunk)

The green go, and the white appear –
Who should have been making music, but this had to be done
To earn a cottage shelter, and milk, and a little bread:
To right a body, beautiful as water and honour could make one –
And like the soldier lithe of body in the foremost rank
I stood there, muscle stiff, free of arm, working out fear.
Glad it was the ash tree's hardness not of the oaks', of the iron
    oak.
Sweat dripped from me – but there was no stay and the echoing
    bank
Sent back sharp sounds of hacking and of true straight woodcraft.
Some Roman from the pinewood caught memory and laughed.
Hit, crack and false aim, echoed from the amphitheatre
Of what was Rome before Romulus drew shoulder of Remus
Nearer his own – or Fabius won his salvation of victories.
In resting I thought of the hidden farm and Rome's hidden mild
    yoke
Still on the Gloucester heart strong after love's fill of centuries,
For all the happy, or the quiet, Severn or Leadon streams.
Pondered on music's deep truth, poetry's form or metre,
Rested – and took a thought and struck onward again,
Who had frozen by Chaulnes out of all caring of pain –
Learnt Roman fortitude at Laventie or Ypres,
Saw bright edge bury dull in the beautiful wood,
Touched splinters so wonderful – half through and soon to come
    down
From that ledge of rock under harebell, the yellow flower – the
    pinewood's crown.
Four inches more – and I should hear the crash and great thunder
Of an ash Crickley had loved for a century, and kept her own.
Thoughts of soldier and musician gathered to me
The desire of conquest ran in my blood, went through me –
There was a battle in my spirit and my blood shared it,
Maisemore – and Gloucester – bred me, and Cotswold reared it,
This great tree standing nobly in the July's day full light
Nearly to fall – my courage broke – and gathered – my breath
    feared it,
My heart – and again I struck, again the splinters and steel glinters

Dazzled my eyes – and the pain and the desperation and near
victory
Carried me onwards – there were exultations and mockings
sunward
Sheer courage, as of boat sailings in equinoctial unsafe squalls,
Stiffened my virtue, and the thing was done. No. Dropped my
body,
The axe dropped – for a minute, taking breath, and gathering
the greedy
Courage – looking for rest to the farm and grey loose-piled walls,
Rising like Troilus to the first word of 'Ready',
The last desperate onslaught – took the two inches of too steady
Trunk – on the rock edge it lurched, threatening my labouring life
(Nearly on me). Like Trafalgar's own sails imperiously moving to
defeat
Across the wide sky unexpected glided and the high bank's pines
and fell straight
Lower and lower till the crashing of the fellow trees made strife.
The thud of earth, and the full tree lying low in state,
With all its glory of life and sap quick in the veins . . .
Such beauty, for the farm fires and heat against chilly rains,
Golden glows in the kitchen from what a century made great . . .

The axe fell from my hand, and I was proud of my hand,
Crickley forgave, for her nobleness, the common fate of trees
As noble or more noble, the oak, the elm that is treacherous,
But dear for her cherishing to this beloved and this rocky land.
Over above all the world there, in a tired glory swerved there,
To a fall, the tree that for long had watched Wales glow strong,
Seen Severn, and farm, and Brecon, Black Mountains times
without reckon.
And tomorrow would be fuel for the bright kitchen – for brown
tea, against cold night.

The Noble Wars of Troy

That was not of Laventie or the ditch of Grandcourt,
But King's School football, and the sail taut by Rudfords farm
    court –
I knew it walking Portway hard so the blood sang tunes,
My eyes searching shadows, and the better of light than the
    moon's.

Water – I bathed with water – Earth – I have dug earth where
Salisbury Plain fulls to Stonehenge in a level clear.
Air? It was my comrade, like light, or music.
Leadon, or Longford, the Cairn – those have known me – my step.

Bathed in October's Severn, muddied with Picardy –
Kissed by the June wind on high Cooper's looking to Severn Sea;
Beloved child of the ploughland and the grassy fallows –
There was no gift Briton or Roman denied me of love that all
    hallows.

Hector I knew of Southwark and of Buckle's pages –
Wrestled with Chapman, and took eternal golden wages.
Troilus in the January night wondering at Orion and never
Able to understand half such a wonder of high beauty – not ever.
My friends of Greece or Rome, Cotswold, my two thousand
    years' home.

The County's Bastion

What looks far Bredon had, words to make said
Nothing are wanting, but will not square to place
Fall, the poet is hurt, of tears are his bread,
And takes his words, as pangs, as untold mischance.

But azure and noble, like the thought of Rome,
Show under clear after-dawn – soft like love's thought
Bredon after night working showed from the home
I had, where Rome loved me – and to strict work brought:

Bredon, and Nottingham Hill, Cleeve, Crickley and those
Sudden with new beauty, day after unlooked-for day.
The poet might weep to have such thoughts, but well knows
Earth's poetry calls his pen, nothing his own of poetry
Save God he follow, in simple spirit, till his lamp light goes.

Roads – Those Roads

Roads are sometimes the true symbolical
Representations of movement in the fate of man.
One goes from Severn of tales and sees Wales
A wall against England as since time began.

Hawthorn and poplar call to mind the different people
That ruled and had shaping of this land at their periods.
One goes from the Abbey to the smaller steeples,
There made worthy, and by tithe-barns, and all by roads.

Daylight colours grey them, they are stained blue by the
     April
Skies on their pools and summer makes carpet of dust
Fit for the royal; autumn smothers all with colour
Blown clean away by the withering cruel winter's gust.

Roads are home-coming and a hope of desire reached,
(There is the orange window at the curve of the dark way),
Whether by winter white frozen or by summer bleached,
Roads are the right pride of man and his anxiety.

Strange Hells

There are strange hells within the minds war made
Not so often, not so humiliatingly afraid
As one would have expected – the racket and fear guns made.
One hell the Gloucester soldiers they quite put out:
Their first bombardment, when in combined black shout

Of fury, guns aligned, they ducked lower their heads
And sang with diaphragms fixed beyond all dreads,
That tin and stretched-wire tinkle, that blither of tune:
'Après la guerre fini', till hell all had come down,
Twelve-inch, six-inch, and eighteen pounders hammering
    hell's thunders.

Where are they now, on state-doles, or showing shop-patterns
Or walking town to town sore in borrowed tatterns
Or begged. Some civic routine one never learns.
The heart burns – but has to keep out of face how heart burns.

The Songs I Had

The songs I had are withered
Or vanished clean,
Yet there are bright tracks
Where I have been,

And there grow flowers
For others' delight.
Think well, O singer,
Soon comes night.

From the Meadows – The Abbey

What sorrow raised you mighty, for I have forgotten joy
And know only sufficient black urge of pain,
Upon the fair thing standing up there in light promising rain,
Mask above meadows.

Severn has made flat for boy
And baby-tending girl-slip, such grass floors smooth.
Pain struck you out I am sure, from beauty denied –
A longed-for image of birth-grace by the waters a-slide,
The hills beneath, ruling the valley with maiden's truth.
Sternness in winter; spring's joy and October's ruth,
Miles away quickening pilgrims into new stride.

O, but there's many a poem from happier men
To come to you. Silence. Watch out and wonder again.

Looking Up There

'Hans Andersen', said the fir-tree
By the Roman farm buried,
And the flame worthy the hill-slope
Into heaven seemed carried.

But the earth below with its coarse stuff
And reality and plain look,
Is better than other men's tales, and enough
To turn thoughts from any book.

*

How hard beauty hurts men with commonness and
    pangs and starts them!

Townshend

Townshend? I knew him well, queer ways he had.
Fond of plays, fond of books, and of Roman talk,
Campments, marches, *pila*, and a mix of relics
Found by western folk in a casual walk.
A quick man in his talk, with eyes always sad.
Kind? Yes, and honourer of poets and actor folk.

Chettle and Heywood . . . but most Jonson he loved.
Angry with London for neglect that so evil proved
Who lived two years with him and was great labourer
As 'Cataline' and many other things to which he was moved
Showed; he read much Latin, and was proud of Greek.
Townshend would leave him whole days alone in his house
And go to Surrey or Buckingham and take delight,
Or watch Danbury changing in the March light,
Knowing Jonson labouring like the great son he was
Of Solway and of Westminster – O, maker, maker,
Given of all the gods to anything but grace.
And kind as all the apprentices knew and scholars;
A talker with battle honours till dawn whitened the curtains,
With many honourers, and many many enemies, and followers.

There's one said to me 'I love his face,
But if he smites me flat for a false Greek quantity,
And drinks a quart where I should be trembler and shaker,
It must be said, "I love him". He does me disgrace
And I shall pay him back for the sight of posterity
For all great "Cataline" and "Alchemist" its high play,
Unless he loves me more or I have greater charity.'

Smudgy Dawn

Smudgy dawn scarfed with military colours
Northward, and flowing wider like slow sea water,
Woke in lilac and elm and almost among garden flowers.
Birds a multitude; increasing as it made lighter.
Nothing but I moved by railings there; slept sweeter
Than kings the country folk in thatch or slate shade.
Peace had the grey west, fleece clouds sure in its power –
Out on much-Severn I thought waves readied for laughter,
And the fire-swinger promised behind the elm-pillars
A day worthy such beginning to come after.
To the room then to work with such hopes as may
Come to the faithful night worker, in west country's July.

143

Thomas Heywood

Thomas Heywood wrote his clerk's page each night,
Some guess, with a wary eye on it from winter's half-light
Or summer's thicker gold. But others must wonder
How such a slap-dash impulse could be so kept under
By willing mere putting-off. Where are his tavern scenes,
His gold-lit fire-embraced pictures of autumn dusk,
London quarrels, heath days where bowls played, inns and
    the rest
Most prolific Heywood kept shut in his deep breast?
Head for gallery writing, hand put to his wine
Or fruit, Heywood the actor, friend of gentlemen fine.
Two hundred plays; that main finger, that clear writing
Would fate have given him for smooth-tune-inditing?
What desperate shifts drove him at whiles Lucrece
Must show, that horror clowned at, that hell's jest so easy.

Lovely Playthings

Dawn brings lovely playthings to the mind,
But sunset fights and goes down in battle blind.
The banners of dawn spread over in mystery,
But nightfall ends a boast and a pageantry.

After the halt of dawn comes the slow moving of
Time, till the sun's hidden rush and the day is admitted.
Sunset dies out in a smother of something like love,
With dew and the elm-hung stars and owl outcries half-witted.

Schubert

The loved one, in the great fiery mood, the not-asking mood;
After a century still the greatly loved one;
But the true Celt in him wholly was undone
By his fate: storms tossed him half out of his good.
One reads and loves the story of his short stay:
Early rising, Beethoven-following and the rest
(Only the peasant wants our liking, quick maker, the guest
Of beer-drinkings); he the player of pipes, of first day
The lover, and of stars; true one, faithfullest and shyest.
One holds him but as part of what was to be,
Square shaper, bender of metal, happy in task.
The known figure in Vienna grows comradely
With five continents, and but great honour to ask.

*

Would death take all too soon what was of Europe's own?
(Although lacking the greatness of the high maker's starkness.)
Yes, indeed, like Keats, Shelley, and the divine Mozart
Death cared no more for him or us than to break heart
With rape-of-beauty — hiding for ever under darkness,
Mind of the 'Erl-King' and the east wind's hurt sighing;
The Unfinished Symphony — and a hundred things more of pride
Or natural truth. Since Marlowe or perhaps John Fountain died
Perhaps the world suffered never so — heart had not such denying.

By Severn

If England, her spirit lives anywhere
It is by Severn, by hawthorns and grand willows
Earth heaves up twice a hundred feet in air
And ruddy clay-falls scooped out to the weedy shallows.
There in the brakes of May spring has her chambers,
Robing-rooms of hawthorn, cowslip, cuckoo flower —
Wonder complete changes for each square joy's hour,
Past thought miracles are there and beyond numbers.

If for the drab atmospheres and managed lighting
In London town, Oriana's playwrights had
Wainlode her theatre and then coppice-clad
Hill for her ground of sauntering and idle waiting,
Why, then I think, our chiefest glory of pride
(The Elizabethans of Thames, south and northern side)
Would nothing of its meeding be denied,
And her sons praises from England's mouth again be outcried.

The Not-Returning

Never comes now the through-and-through clear
Tiredness of body on crisp straw down laid,
Nor the tired thing said
Content before the clean sleep close the eyes,
Or ever resistless rise
Pictures of far country westward, westward out of the sight
    of the eyes.
Never more delight comes of the roof dark lit
With under-candle flicker nor rich gloom on it,
The limned faces and moving hands shuffling the cards,
The clear conscience, the free mind moving towards
Poetry, friends, the old earthly rewards.
No more they come. No more.
Only the restless searching, the bitter labour,
The going out to watch stars, stumbling blind through the
    difficult door.

What Evil Coil

What evil coil of fate has fastened me
Who cannot move to sight, whose bread is sight,
And in nothing has more bare delight
Than dawn or the violet or the winter tree.
Stuck-in-the-mud – blinkered-up, roped for the fair.

What use to vessel breath that lengthens pain?
O but the empty joys of wasted air
That blow on Crickley and whimper wanting me!

Swift and Slow

Death swooped suddenly on men in Flanders
There were no tweedledees or handy-danders
The skull was cleft, the life went out from it
And glory in a family tale was set.
But here, having escaped the steely showers
Endured through panged intolerable hours
The expensive and much determined doom,
Find slow death in the loved street and bookish room.
Liver and bowels congested to devil's pitch
For a pittance or sake of benefit, what matters which?
Life witch-like seen as Dürer saw, the detested witch.

Looking There

Out to the glow my eyes look from the writing place,
What glow there is is good after the blank and the ache
Of thinking, in fields gone empty up into space;
And the wish for peace, the look for contentment's sake.
But I look for some past through the dear flames and remember
What thoughts were once known in bitter frost – and
Loveliest light looked for in a coming December
Firelight, and after bright frost across the dark land.

*

Which after fulfilled in a longing for one companion,
Time gave for one minute, and snatched with a blackguard
    hand.
But there is no help in thinking past the deepest ache
Of heart, and empty is desire when the reach is far too far.
Tears cannot help the solitary one, the forgetting one, the self-
    blinding one.
So if my thoughts hurt, I must leave my writing and go where
Stars and dusk may comfort my lost-souled despair,
And if not she, at least my master Beethoven.
Are there not many ways for the heart to escape in loving?
And is the blood to be bright for one thought alone?
One quarter hour of moving and I shall forget all this.
If not, Ben Jonson: and the great surge and sway
Of 'Cataline' shall me safe from the dangerous way
Of thinking of too much beauty by an evil snatcht
From one humble as David or as proud as Whitman,
Or glad as Pippa seeing the wide heavens unlatch . . .
Misery drowns in many ways and I take this
To hurt a heart with making past remembrance – and to get
    work done.

When the Body Might Free

When the body might free, and there was use in walking,
In October time – crystal air-time and free words were talking
In my mind with light tunes and bright streams ran free;
When the earth smelt, leaves shone and air and cloud had glee;

Then there was salt in life but now none is known
To me who cannot go either where the white is blown
Of the grass, or scarlet willow-herb of past memory.
Nothing is sweet to thinking, nothing from life free.

In the Old Time

In the old time when September's stubble gleamed
And as the content of all folk-writing seemed
The true consolation for all woes, I made
Music out of stubbornness and was glad.
But now the pen writes words, and the brain is content,
Fates haggle for me, the body has its bent,
And only theological and ethical discussions
Continue like a toothache, from black hidden dread.

Sonnet – September 1922

Fierce indignation is best understood by those
Who have time or no fear, or a hope in its real good.
One loses it with a filed soul or in sentimental mood.
Anger is gone with sunset, or flows as flows
The water in easy mill-runs; the earth that ploughs
Forgets protestation in its turning, the rood
Prepares, considers, fulfils; and the poppy's blood
Makes old the old changing of the headland's brows.

But the toad under the harrow toadiness
Is known to forget, and even the butterfly
Has doubts of wisdom when that clanking thing goes by
And's not distressed. A twisted thing keeps still –
That thing easier twisted than a grocer's bill –
And no history of November keeps the guy.

V

September 1922–1925

There Is a Man

There is a man who has swept or rubbed a floor
This morning crying in the Most Holy Name
Of God for pity, and has not been able to claim
A moment's respite, that for one hour, or more.
But can the not-conceiving heart outside
Believe the atmosphere that hangs so heavy
And clouds the torment. Afterwards in the leavy
And fresher air other torments may abide,
Or pass; and new pain; but this memory
Will not pass, it is too bad and the grinding
Remains, and what is better is the finding
Of any ease from working or changing free
Words between words, and cadences in change.
But the pain is in thought, which will not freely range.

The Incense Bearers

Toward the sun the drenched May-hedges lift
White rounded masses like still ocean-drift,
And day fills with heavy scent of that gift.

There is no escaping that full current of thick
Incense; one walks, suddenly one comes quick
Into a flood of odour there, aromatic,

Not English; for cleaner, sweeter, is the hot scent that
Is given from hedges, solitary flowers, not
In mass, but lonely odours that scarcely float.

But the incense bearers, soakers of sun's full
Powerfulness, give out floods unchecked, wonderful
Utterance almost, which makes no poet grateful,

Since his love is for single things rarely found,
Or hardly: violets blooming in remote ground,
One colour, one fragrance, like one uncompanied sound

Struck upon silence, nothing looked-for. Hung
As from gold wires this May incense is swung,
Heavy of odour, the drenched meadows among.

There Have Been Anguishes

There have been anguishes
In the different poetries
Where the man's mind cries
Out on God's deep mercies.
None has denied them,
They are of old time
And a faded rhyme
No living one does condemn.

But half my suffering,
Told out in pencil or
Ink as night came, before
Justice or witan-ring,
Would not gain redress
For its strange seeming.
And a true deeming
Lacked of its witness.

Vain is the use of the mind,
Almost the soul halts here,
Consumed with black fear,
Black fear of a pain-blind
Nature, that craves ending
To such bad being,
Or truly to be seeing
At least the use and mending.

Riez Bailleul

Behind the line there mending reserve posts, looking
On the cabbage fields with other men carefully tending
    cooking;
Hearing the boiling; and being sick of body and heart,
Too sick for anything but hoping that all might depart –
We back in England again, and white roads to walk on,
Eastwards to hill-steeps, or see meadows good to go talk on.
Grey Flanders sky over all and a heaviness felt
On the sense that no working or dreaming would any way
    melt . . .
This is not happy thought, but a glimpse most strangely
Forced from the past, to hide this pain and work myself free
From present things. The parapet, the grey look-out, the
    making
Of a peasantry, by dread war, harried and set on shaking;
A hundred things of age, and of carefulness,
Spoiling; a farmer's treasure perhaps soon a wilderness.

Old Times

Out in the morning
For a speed of thought I went,
And a clear thought of scorning
For homekeeping; while downward bent
Grass blades with dewdrops
Heavy on those delicate
Sword shapes, wonder thereat
Brightening my first hopes.

A four hours' tramping
With brisk blood flowing,
And life worth knowing
For all that something
Which let happiness then –
Sometimes, not always,
Breath-on-mirror of days –
And all now gone, since when?

The Shame

If the pain I suffer were of the Devil enemy of man
It might pass, might be proper, but from man's self, O the
    black shame
Of torture, when, as some think, so easy were the plan
Of kind life; but this is dreadfulness beyond name.

Each minute packed with a badness beyond words,
The brain, the mind tortured as blind stones would do,
What help in life? None. Hope is that death affords
A shelter in some shade beyond pain's come-through.

What help? Who tortures? and why? Why not grant death
Which ends all, as some hope, and that Romans would think
An expiation complete: offence ended with breath.
And self killing as good a deed as ever were drink.

To God

Why have you made life so intolerable
And set me between four walls, where I am able
Not to escape meals without prayer, for that is possible
Only by annoying an attendant. And tonight a sensual
Hell has been put on me, so that all has deserted me
And I am merely crying and trembling in heart
For death, and cannot get it. And gone out is part
Of sanity. And there is dreadful hell within me.
And nothing helps. Forced meals there have been and electricity
And weakening of sanity by influence
That's dreadful to endure. And there is Orders
And I am praying for death, death, death,
And dreadful is the indrawing or out-breathing of breath
Because of the intolerable insults put on my whole soul,
Of the soul loathed, loathed, loathed of the soul.
Gone out every bright thing from my mind.
All lost that ever God himself designed.
Not half can be written of cruelty of man, on man,
Not often such evil guessed as between man and man.

On Somme

Suddenly into the still air burst thudding
And thudding, and cold fear possessed me all,
On the grey slopes there, where winter in sullen brooding
Hung between height and depth of the ugly fall
Of Heaven to earth; and the thudding was illness' own.
But still a hope I kept that were we there going over,
I in the line, I should not fail, but take recover
From others' courage, and not as coward be known.
No flame we saw, the noise and the dread alone
Was battle to us; men were enduring there such
And such things, in wire tangled, to shatters blown.
Courage kept, but ready to vanish at first touch.
Fear, but just held. Poets were luckier once
In the hot fray swallowed and some magnificence.

After 'The Penny Whistle'

The heels hammered out in the frosty roadway
A rhythm long time not known
To a body and soul in long torment managed –
Winter and swiftness gone.

But at the Front there was such desiring,
Such hope in the going again,
With the telegraph wires singing frosty in January
Under stars friendly to men.

Those heels must stay still there, deep in frost mud,
While the imagination sought
To be back there, out of the agony, with shelter
To look to; and glowing fire caught

In bars of iron, with tea-kettle steaming,
And after a soak of blaze
And sauntering, preparing, music to be making
Of lovely lost unhappy days.

The Golden Age

Who walked in dawns to find the fitting word,
Who watched the twilight till all faded dim;
The men of Cadiz or of Flores heard –
Poets and songmen, all who walked with them.

Not as a later, polite, truly gentlemanly
Time that was set on cold forms and outside look
Would have praises – conduct of cold-blooded unfree
Life, that was forced in channels, like a clayey brook.

O for some force to swing us back there to some
Natural moving towards life's love, or that glow
In the word to be glow in the State, that golden age come
Again, men working freely as nature might show,
And a people honouring stage-scenes lit bright with fine sound
On a free soil, England happy, honoured and joy-crowned.

The Interview

Death I have often faced
In the damp trench – or poisoned waste:
Shell or shot, gas or flying steel, bayonet –
But only once by one bullet my arm was wet
With blood. Death faced me there, Death it was that I faced.
But now by no means may it come to me.
Mercy of Death noways vouchsafed to pain.
Were but those times of battle to come again!

Or even boat-sailing, danger on a mimic inland sea!
Death moaning, Death flying, shrieking in air.
Desiring its mark sufficient everywhere – everywhere.
Interview enough. But now I can not get near
Such challenge or dear enmity; pain more than fear
Oppresses me – would that might come again!
Death in the narrow trench . . . or wide in the fields.
Death in the Reserve, where the earth wild beautiful
    flowers yields.
Death met – outfaced – but here – not to be got.
Prayed for, truly desired, obtainèd not –
A lot past dreadfulness, an unhuman lot.
For never Man was meant to be denied chance
Of ending pain past strength – O for France! for France!
Death walked freely; one might be sought of him
Or seek, in twilight or first light of morning dim.
Death dreadful that scared the cheeks of blood;
Took friends, spoilt any happy true-human mood;
Shrieked in the near air – threatened from up on high.
Dreadful, dreadful. But not to be come by
Now, confined – no Interview is ever here.
And worse than Death is known in the spirit of fear.
Death is a thing desired, never to be had at all –
Spirit for Death cries, nothing hears; nothing granted here. O
If Mercy would but hear the cry of the spirit grow
From waking till Death seems far beyond a right,
And dark is the spirit has all right to be bright.
Death is not here, save mercy grant it. When
Was cruelty such known last among like-and-like men?
An Interview? It is cried for – and not known –
Not found. Death absent what thing is truly man's own?
Beaten down continually, continually beaten clean down.

A Wish

I would hope for the children of West Ham
Wooden-frame houses square, with some-sort stuff
Crammed in to keep the wind away that's rough,
And rain; in summer cool, in cold comfortable enough.
Easily destroyed – and pretty enough, and yet tough.
Instead of brick and mortar tiled houses of no
Special appearance or attractive show.
Not crowded together, but with a plot of land,
Where one might play and dig, and use spade or the hand
In managing or shaping earth in such forms
As please the sunny mind or keep out of harms
The mind that's always good when let go its way
(I think) so there's work enough in a happy day.

Not brick and tile, but wood, thatch, walls of mixed
Material, and buildings in plain strength fixed.
Likeable, good to live in, easily pulled
Down, and in winter with warm ruddy light filled –
In summer with cool air; O better this sort of shelter –
And villages on the land set helter-skelter
On hillsides, dotted on plains – than the too exact
Straight streets of modern times, that strait and strict
And formal keep man's spirit within bounds,
Where too dull duties keep in monotonous rounds.

These villages to make for these towns of today –
O haste – and England shall be happy with the May
Or meadow-reach to watch, miles to see and away.

Hazlitt

Hazlitt, also, tea-drinker and joyous walker,
To him we give thanks and are grateful that
He saw Shakespeare as man, not as over-great
Above the comprehending of reader and talker.

In swift English writing of Hamlet and those
Live-moving figures of poetry and high wit
He cast new wholesome light on the sense that writ
And a love that with friendship is instinct and glows.
Never more need of brave minds than in setting free
This figure of Time for friendship and not for fear:
Shakespeare, companier of men that were lively here
And walked happy in thought in an England Merry.
So to Hazlitt thanks, and a clear thought of gratitude,
For his speaking in words so plain our Shakespeare's mood.

Hedger

To me the A Major Concerto has been dearer
Than ever before, because I saw one weave
Wonderful patterns of bright green, never clearer
Of April; whose hand nothing at all did deceive
Of laying right
The stakes of bright
Green lopped-off spear-shaped, and stuck notched, crooked-up;
Wonder was quickened at workman's craftsmanship
But clumsy were the efforts of my stiff body
To help him in the laying of bramble, ready
Of mind, but clumsy of muscle in helping; rip
Of clothes unheeded, torn hands. And his quick moving
Was never broken by any danger, his loving
Use of the bill or scythe was most deft, and clear –
Had my piano-playing or counterpoint
Been so without fear
Then indeed fame had been mine of most bright outshining;
But never had I known singer or piano-player
So quick and sure in movement as this hedge-layer
This gap-mender, of quiet courage unhastening.

Memory

They have left me little indeed, how shall I best keep
Memory from sliding content down to drugged sleep?
But my blood, in its colour even, is known fighter.
If I were hero for such things here would I make wars
As love for dead things trodden under in January's stars,

Or the gold trefoil itself spending in careless places
Tiny graces like music's for its past exquisitenesses.
Why war for huge domains of the planet's heights or plains?
(Little they leave me.) It is a dream. Hardly my heart dares
Tremble for glad leaf-drifts thundering under January's stars.

Song

I had a girl's fancies
At the pools –
And azure at chances
In the rut holes
Minded me of Maisemore,
And Gloucester men
Beside me made sure
All faithfulness again.

The man's desiring
Of great making
Was denied, and breaking
To the heart, much-caring –
Only the light thoughts
Of the poet's range
Stayed in that war's plights.
Only, soul did not change.

So, to the admiration
Of the rough high virtues
Of common marching
Soldiers, and textures

Of russet noblenesses,
My mind was turned.
But where are such verses
That in my heart burned?

The Mangel-Bury

It was after war; Edward Thomas had fallen at Arras –
I was walking by Gloucester musing on such things
As fill his verse with goodness; it was February; the long
　　house
Straw-thatched of the mangels stretched two wide wings;
And looked as part of the earth heaped up by dead soldiers
In the most fitting place – along the hedge's yet-bare lines.
West spring breathed there early, that none foreign divines.
Across the flat country the rattling of the cart sounded;
Heavy of wood, jingling of iron; as he neared me I waited
For the chance perhaps of heaving at those great rounded
Ruddy or orange things – and right to be rolled and hefted
By a body like mine, soldier still, and clean from water.
Silent he assented; till the cart was drifted
High with those creatures, so right in size and matter.
We threw with our bodies swinging, blood in my ears
　　singing;
His was the thick-set sort of farmer, but well-built –
Perhaps, long before, his blood's name ruled all,
Watched all things for his own. If my luck had so willed
Many questions of lordship I had heard him tell – old
Names, rumours. But my pain to more moving called
And him to some barn business far in the fifteen acre field.

Cut Flowers

Not in blue vases these,
Nor white, cut flowers are seen
But in the August meadows
When the reaper falls clean –

And the shining and ridged rows
Of cut stalks show to the eye
As if some child's hand there
Had ranged them, and passed by
To other rows, other swathes.
Moondaisies, pimpernel,
Eyebright, sorrel, the paths
Are shining, the heaps as well.
Violets in spring are,
In vases, a sweet heap.
Better leave them by far
Under hedgerows or banks to keep.
Daffodils, wallflowers, daisies
Of Michaelmas-time, let still
Also, no gathering-crazes
Should spoil the sweet springtime's will.
Daisies best left alone,
Chrysanthemums of chill
Evenings of autumn, gone
Soon to cold winter's will,
All the full garden-folk
Leave in their beds; but if
Under the steely yoke
They must be gathered with
Cruelty of no need
Then lay them in wide pans,
Or open jars – agreed
Best pottery that is man's.
Wallflowers, violets,
Sweetest of flowers bring in
To the four walls, the china-sets
And table clean as a pin.
By books and pictures lay
These wild things cruelly tamed –
Taken from the blowing day
Exiled, uprooted, hurt, lamed,
That the hedgerows miss and the copse.
O if flowers must be cut
To spoil an earth plot's hopes
Take them with eyes shut.

Or give a small coin or two
To children who may not care
So much as grown-ups should do –
Cut flowers in vases rare –
Pottery rounded with these
(Best of all) or with no care
Ranged in mayhap degrees
In wide pot or any jar –

Gather them, pluck not, please.

The Dream

There had been boat-sailing on Severn river,
And when London was reached, it seemed most easy –
Of right – to look for such joy as to see sails quiver
And pull the rudder hard round, against the breezy
Wind out of Essex, or off Kentish shores.
So to Rotherhithe blue as to dancing water,
Seeing the cleaving water before prow scatter,
And the moving surface so wonderful like bright floors.
And doubtful of all things, asked an owner there
Whether a boat might be had cheap, but little hoped
Since money was not mine, and such chance escaped
Any but those with twenty pounds to spare.
It was worrying a good man, but there was that one
Hope in me of getting a sail up, to see foam run.

War Poet

I know that honour is
Because I follow it.
I know that love is
My heart does cry for it.

The sun? I dare not watch.
The stars? I was night-walker:
My friends in the high arch —
By Cranham or high Crickley

They hurt like unsought kisses
From a love one dare
Not love — they are the water-hisses
From a cooled iron, red-bare.

Greatness? I have sailed
A boat in March daring. . .
And made a music, called
All March to my caring

Whether I made well
Or no — and Vermand knows
Colour of my blood — Neuve Chapelle
Courage — as war's courage goes.

Love? A hundred know it.
Men have seen my eyes.
Women have watched love, though it
Failed at actualities.

Steel-bound to my service
Earth, blood and all.
Only England refuses. . .
Only life does not call. . .

Only meanness hurts her heart
Only rust her steel. . .
Only. . . She is coward, coward. . .
And I suffer agonies, rightly unheard,
Because she likes sin too well.

The Depths

Here no dreams touch me to colour
Sodden state of all-dolour:
No touch of peace, no creation
Felt, nor stir of divination.

Friend of stars, things, inky pages –
Knowing so many heritages
Of Britain old, or Roman newer;
Here all witchcrafts scar and skewer.

Coloured maps of Europe taking
And words of poets fine in making,
I march once more with hurt shoulders,
And scent the air, a friend with soldiers.

Devil's dooms that none guess,
Evil's harms worshipped no less,
Grind my soul – and no god clutches
Out of darks god's-honour smutches.

While I Write

While I write war tells me truth; as for brave
None might challenge Gloucesters, save those dead who have
Paid prices for pre-eminence, perhaps have got their pay.
But the common goodness of those soldiers shown day after day,
And the sight of each-hour beauty brilliant or most grave,
Stays with me yet. While I am forbidden to write
Tale of the continual readiness for a bad bloodiness,
And steadiness against hell-fire; and strained eyes with
    humour bright.
War told me truth: I have Severn's right of maker,
As of Cotswold: war told me: I was elect, I was born fit
To praise the three hundred feet depth of every acre
Between Tewkesbury and Stroudway, Side and Wales Gate.

It Is Winter

It is winter, the soon dark annoys me –
Who cannot remember Severn her warm dark lights;
And am too tortured to remember old ploys the
Gloucesters used to please themselves in the straits
Of poverty and idleness of French villages.
Then before opening-time they would walk house-bordered
Or leafy ways – hurrying, keeping off the fierce cold.
Then when the lights showed, the estaminet's time came,
They would hammer on the door; they would shout out
    good-mannered
Rudenesses; enter, sit within, and as careful
As old ladies of knitting would drink beer or more
    honoured
Wine, trembling at the expense, which to them was fearful;
Bask in the warm, dream poetry of the gold flame.
While the poet watching their faces, and envying noble
Poetry of Long Island – strong, human, star-bannered –
Sat also, accusing time for his music, lost in service,
    refusing all blame.

Prelude

Will you not give me
Before I go in
To music, with my fingers
A new thing to win –
Of tune?
Hours are no gifts
Past my worth
To make my own.
At whispers, at hair-lifts,
In me is moving
The power that is equal
To your natural
Courtesy of giving.
(Labour after finding.
Set teeth, back's hefts.)

Give me out of truths
Of wide sight of valley
Fore Severn, far Severn,
Spinney or water sally,
Valley or plain,
My feet's place or far region,
Truth's matter, for my having.

For me to be turning,
Wresting and changing
Into black notes
On white pages
Should stand for ages,
Such hearts burning
As are like mine, ranging
All their hearts' thoughts.

I am that am certain
Of my desire's truth,
And challenge my own
Failures and doubts –
All things claim,
Being all things without.

All things assert
Most sacred to be said –
Your water proves it, your dirt,
To the sense in my head,
To the soul in me hidden.

Great allies me serve –
Shakespeare, Beethoven,
Shelley's friend, the unproven
Works of Walt Whitman
And Fletcher, a tune's serf –
Jonson, an age's freeman –

Let me but have a room
Of golden night quiet –
Peace in a lonely gloom
Mixed of mixed rich light
And dark; and remember some
Height of Cotswold, plough of valley. . .
June, refuse not – it is a shame
To be denied your chivalry –
When did Gloucester ask but right?

Farewell

What? to have had gas, and to expect
No more than a week's sick, and to get Blighty –
This is the gods' gift, and not anyway exact
To Ypres, or bad St Julien or Somme Farm.
Don Hancocks, shall I no more see your face frore,
Gloucester-good, in the first light? (But you are dead!)
Shall I see no more Monger with india-rubber
Twisted face? (But machine-gun caught him and his grimace.)
No more to march happy with such good comrades,
Watching the sky, the brown land, the bayonet blades
Moving – to muse on music forgetting the pack.
Nor to hear Gloucester with Stroud debating the lack
Of goodliness or virtue in girls on farmlands.
Nor to hear Cheltenham hurling at Cotswold demands
Of civilization; nor west Severn joking at east Severn?
No more, across the azure and the brown lands,
The morning mist or high day clear of rack,
Shall move my dear knees, or feel them frosted, shivering
By Somme or Aubers – or to have a courage from faces
Full of all west England. Her God gives graces.
There was not one of all that battalion
Loved his comrades as well as I – but kept shy.
Or said in verse, what his voice would not rehearse.
So, gassed, I went back to northlands where voices speak
    soft as in verse.
And, after, to meet evil not fit for the thought one touch to
    dwell on.

Dear battalion, the dead of you would not have let
Your comrade be so long prey for the unquiet
Black evil of the unspoken and concealed pit.
You would have had me safe – dead or free happy alive.

They bruise my head and torture with their own past-hate
Sins of the past, and lie so as earth moves at it.
You dead ones – I lay with you under the unbroken wires once.

It Is Near Toussaints

It is near Toussaints, the living and dead will say:
'Have they ended it? What has happened to Gurney?'
And along the leaf-strewed roads of France many brown shades
Will go, recalling singing, and a comrade for whom also they
Had hoped well. His honour them had happier made.
Curse all that hates good. When I spoke of my breaking
(Not understood) in London, they imagined of the taking
Vengeance, and seeing things were different in future.
(A musician was a cheap, honourable and nice creature.)
Kept sympathetic silence; heard their packs creaking
And burst into song – Hilaire Belloc was all our master.
On the night of all the dead, they will remember me,
Pray Michael, Nicholas, Maries lost in Novembery
River-mist in the old City of our dear love, and batter
At doors about the farms crying 'Our war poet is lost.
Madame – no bon!' – and cry his two names, warningly, sombrely.

The Storm at Night

I have left my work. I stumble, go out on the roads.
The Thunder-god gathers his moods, great anger waits,
Sultry air warns – not far off a white lightning floods –
And sudden a fixed molten shape hurtles from out of the clouds.
I can see Longford's elms, it is near the Past's high gates.
Let fall, then – let fall great spearthrusts by Wainlode's,

And frighten sacred Maisemore in annoyed slumber,
Light up all Severn valley, all the white trees number,
All the cattle. Me – I shall walk till the rain comes, spates
Of straight water, lit with white electricity and amber:
Crying 'King Lear' out, if it is fine enough, or dumber
Than Edgar or blunt Kent if, from magnificence, magnificent
It fails – or like Poor Tom go read in my lamplit room-corner.

The Battle

The Gloucesters were to go over I was not one –
Glad because of the terribleness, ashamed because of the
    terror,
I saw in the loveliest azure mist September had shown
Great spouts of white, heard thunders and knew that
    somewhere
Gloucesters were moving, men for three years I had known,
Perhaps to see no more – fallen from thought of their shire
Even. High over all, guard on a machine-gun
Which yet might be needed (doubt at Ypres the surer)
I saw blue mist and white smoke, but never fire,
Who heard two days after such names I had sworn
Had long ago saved me – of men fallen by battle torn,
Whether alive or dead – I had sworn to their power.

Regrets After Death

True on the Plain I might have seen Salisbury Close,
But how that would have repaid there is no one knows,
True at Epping I might have thanked kindness more,
But we were for France then – scarce a week to be here.
At Chelmsford, true I might have kept my first lodging
Despite of cooking 'cause she did my washing.
But since no more of France I saw than three
Weeks, and had no more honour of battle than the
One name, the still line of East Laventie,

Regrets and hopes and accusations are all vain.
Chelmsford was bad, Hell-upon-Army the Plain,
Epping had compensations, Northampton kindness,
    invitations.
They buried me in Artois, with no time to complain.

Serenade

It was after the Somme, our line was quieter,
Wires mended, neither side daring attacker
Or aggressor to be – the guns equal, the wires a thick hedge,
When there sounded, (O past days for ever confounded!)
The tune of Schubert which belonged to days mathematical,
Effort of spirit bearing fruit worthy, actual.
The gramophone for an hour was my quiet's mocker,
Until I cried, 'Give us "Heldenleben", "Heldenleben".'
The Gloucesters cried out 'Strauss is our favourite wir haben
Sich geliebt'. So silence fell, Aubers front slept,
And the sentries an unsentimental silence kept.
True, the size of the rum ration was still a shocker
But at last over Aubers the majesty of the dawn's veil swept.

Butchers and Tombs

After so much battering of fire and steel
It had seemed well to cover them with Cotswold stone –
And shortly praising their courage and quick skill
Leave them buried, hidden till the slow, inevitable
Change came should make them service of France alone.
But the time's hurry, the commonness of the tale
Made it a thing not fitting ceremonial,
And so the disregarders of blister on heel,
Pack on shoulder, barrage and work at the wires,
One wooden cross had for ensign of honour and life gone –
Save when the Gloucesters turning sudden to tell to one
Some joke, would remember and say – 'That joke is done,'
Since he who would understand was so cold he could not feel,
And clay binds hard, and sandbags get rotten and crumble.

Don Juan in Hell

I heard a soldier tell, frozen out of all patience,
Tales of girls he had kissed, whose bodies touched, when a
    trench
Was a name of potatoes, gun a thing for crows,
And Somme a river, distant far, by no chance to be his.
But pained to talk, he told me how one had kissed
Him out of anger before his anger was wist,
Another his impudence out of all harm, by charm. . .
It was the talk of Shakespeare – the sound of a farm –
Gossip before the world by fire was turned bitter and
    spurned
All that the day's labour in sin had earned.
'Now that I've stood my turn, and have right of all
I ask, I wonder what end – if it come – will befall
My asking – O at least not the last
Battle, not the last day of all.'

The Bohemians

Certain people would not clean their buttons,
Nor polish buckles after latest fashions,
Preferred their hair long, putties comfortable,
Barely escaping hanging, indeed hardly able;
In Bridge and smoking without army cautions
Spending hours that sped like evil for quickness,
(While others burnished brasses, earned promotions).
These were those ones who jested in the trench,
While others argued of army ways, and wrenched
What little soul they had still further from shape,
And died off one by one, or became officers.
Without the first of dream, the ghost of notions
Of ever becoming soldiers, or smart and neat,
Surprised as ever to find the army capable
Of sounding 'Lights out' to break a game of Bridge,
As to fear candles would set a barn alight:
In Artois or Picardy they lie – free of useless fashions.

Autumn

Autumn, dear to walkers with your streaks and carpets
Of bright colours, spread like a boy's gift for the true boy,
Sacred for the love flowing over and unuttered even in making –
Have you too left me?

Never was trust so equal between man and his dear mates
Of tree or watercourse flowing by Cranham or past Hartpury.
Eternity promised: what unfaith could cause any shaking
In that love, near bereft me?

Earth spaces breathing dark incense (as the kind shower wets)
And woodlands stirring to blood-light, the heart all ready –
Could you not, with your untouched power, save me from
    this breaking
Tyranny; not Severn have safed me?

Signallers

To be signallers and to be relieved two hours
Before the common infantry – and to come down
Hurriedly to where estaminet's friendliest doors
Opened – where before the vulgar brawling common crew
Could take the seats for tired backs, or take the wine
Best suited for palates searching for delicate flavours
(Or pretty tints) to take from the mind trench ways and
    strain,
Though it be on tick, with delicately wangled sly favours.
Then having obtained grace from the lady of the inn –
How good to sit still and sip with all-appreciative lip,
(After the grease and skilly of line-cookhouse tea)
The cool darkling texture of the heavenly dew
Of wine – to smoke as one pleased in a house of courtesy –
Signallers, gentlemen, all away from the vulgar
Infantry – so dull and dirty and so underpaid,
So wont to get killed and leave the cautious signallers
To signal down the message that they were dead.

Anyway, distinctions or not – there was a quiet
Hour or so before the Company fours halted, and were
Formed two-deep, and dismissed and paid after leaden, dilatory
Hanging around, to bolt (eager) to find those apparently
Innocent signallers drinking, on tick, at last beer.

To Y

What! to have come to the shortest village of all Europe.
We, mere Gloucesters, a thing so noted and thus famed
In the curiosity books and statistic books.
Shattered like all the rest: we crossed the rough ford,
(Lovely in cold March with all April's shining looks)
And reached a half-left house, probably left full-mined,
Lay down exhausted, ridded of our damnèd packs.
Well, Fritz, you've turned at last, that is some true hope.
But queer we should reach such a short name of double crooks.
It might have been Havrancourt, or Hauracourt, or Achiey
    the Grand,
Instead of this one tiny thing, in which we may be flung
As well to Heaven as in any long-named, tongue-twisting
    place.
They left no wood, nor shape, nor too much space.
Nor comfort; fires in this March-end would be welcome.
But since we've come to Y, the world's shortest thing
Let us make short work of necessity and accept the thing
As if coming to There we had got There.
And having arrived were to accept the thing in dumb
Acquiescence, and be there indeed, having arrived indeed,
Not to wonder at the strangeness more than might be
    called blunder.
Walking in hunger, or making verse with a hungry head,
Of the Somme running under broken arch, its late winter
    April-like wonder,
Or of the strange places in the chalk slopes on ahead
Which were Caulaincourt, Vermand and another to be said.

Portraits

Looking at Washington, Lee and Jefferson,
And the Scottish pride of Andrew Jackson;
Many more; one believes in the Nation that left
Men of so human a sort to manage the believed-
In States, through freedom's struggle, and the settling;
But why ever to trouble, much less to battling,
Since freedom was so young and hard a gift?
(Grant's face serving a bad cause on condition,
And success – and loathing.) It is best to turn
To those of Thomas Jefferson, or Dolly Madison
(So pretty), or Mrs Derby almost as beautiful
Or James McNeill Whistler's of an unknown girl
Out from Jane Austen or the Mozart Concertos,
Looking from the pages, unembarrassed, life-cool;
Or Miss Curtis of the farmhouses, dairies
Of Gloucestershire . . . . A happy, but too lazy life
When there were few books (out of the world's glorious
Many) to be had – whose goodness and whose foolishness
Shows on every page – and whose pain on one –
The Stuart portrait of General Washington.

The New Poet

Out of the dark north and the easy south –
One with saga strung against the bitter cold,
The other with happiness and homely songs of gold,
Let there be born a new poet – and let him sing
Of all the States, let his home be the town watching
Mississippi flowing southward with names untold,
And waters numberless hidden in her flowing.
More honouring masters old than one Walt Whitman,
Nor like Longfellow falling from his true matching
Of the nobility of earth with the nobility of words –

But out of Greece, Rome, middle England and the all-honouring
Provinces of France, and the Indian tradition,
A new poetry of all lights, all times; wherein swords
Are not honoured more than the shares ploughing
The coloured earth to furrows, dry or wet shards.
Let him say all men's thought nor sleep until
Some great thing he has fashioned of love inevitable.
For the rest, may he follow his happiness' true will.

To Long Island First

To Long Island first with my tortured verse,
Remember how on a Gloucester book-stall one morning
I saw, brown 'Leaves of Grass' after long hesitation
(For fourpence to me was bankruptcy then or worse)
I bought, what since in book or mind about the dawning
On Roman Cotswold, Roman Artois war stations,
Severn and Buckingham, London after night wanderings,
Has served me, friend or master on many occasions
Of weariness, or gloriousness or delight.
At first to puzzle, then grow past all traditions
To be master unquestioned – a book that brings the clear
Spirit of him that wrote, to the thought again here.
If I have not known Long Island none has –
Brooklyn is my own City, Mannahattan the right of me,
Camden and Idaho – and all New England's
Two-fold love of honour, honour and homely grace.
If blood to blood can speak or the spirit has inspiring,
Let me claim place there also – Briton, I am also hers,
And Roman; have more than Virgil for meditations.

Walt Whitman

With more knowledge of the poetic things, of the manly things –
But with no knowledge of Greek care in fashionings:
Forging out great thought like Beethoven, yet caught
In ignorance, not honouring makings of generations.
Not square to form of truth; thought to clear-of-thought
Always vowed – the maker, the companion of true kings,
(Whose page is coloured with earth's and his heart's blood).
Born of Paumanok, son of responding kisses,
Whom all the earth or sea-surge desires or blesses;
Praised by Gloucesters in trench or marching mood
For his courage, colour or master-in-action mood:
(Bought of me just a hesitater in old Gloucester)
Never so much as now by me beloved, acknowledged.
What 'Song of Myself', or 'Drum Taps' or 'Brooklyn',
'Calamus', or 'Paumanok' strikes out or clean misses
Is best known by those who have to Death's face gone;
Or on a sentry post at last discovered 'This Compost' –
Shivering in March sleets, faithful in drearinesses.

Henry David Thoreau

Henry crowned in Gloucester, David my father's name
And Thoreau sign of the clearest of all prose.
Lovely and water-tasting, or like an apple
Laid till the frost of winter in the loft's straws.
Little I know but 'Walden', it is well enough
For love – I have seen Gloucester all lights, and all veil;
And know his goodness like Bridges', or Bartholomew's Chapel
Norman and sure of admiration – shaped so well,
That stands today in Gloucester mourning for me.
After Whitman, Thoreau in France was my praise,
And though from Thoreau breaks not the terrible flame
Of poetry, only truth and beauties loved,
It is enough. In New England there is no farm
Blessed not by his spirit moving in easy ways,

To see no spirit come nor no coppice to harm.
(Also at night I have watched his page with delight.)
Where he was born my book says nothing, nor died,
But Concord knows her memory and grows to his ways.

Washington Irving

To the joy of Bach, and 'Under the Greenwood Tree',
Folk songs, and legends also was added this:
The 'Sketch Book' with its pictures of Bracebridge Hall
(Miss Mitford is better and Farquhar does not miss),
Nevertheless for simplicity and love writ free
A writer may earn love, be under the earth's pall
Because truth has a way of earning honour's pay.
New York – (to me Mannahattan) – and newer Irvington,
Let me not before evil still have to pray – the day
May not be too black-bitter: or a salvation to see . . .

It was long ago, with a friend who gave me the book,
I would sit with him and read till, remembering Belloc,
Scott and Shakespeare, I put aside him, then to be
More at my love truly – more in truth's way.
Only – one would have met him; he has a good talking way.

Masterpiece

Out from the dim mind like dark fire rises thought,
And one must be quick on it, or scratch sketches, a few . . .
And later, three weeks later, in fashion sedater,
See, the night worker writing his square work out,
Set to the labour, muscle strained, his light hidden under.
Half-past two? Time for tea. . . half-past, half-past two . . .
And then by degrees of half hours see how it shows:
The pages fill with black notes, the paper-bill goes

Up and up, till the musician is left staring
At a String Quartett nobody in the world will do . . .
And what Schumann would say there's no one to be caring.
Now, had it been a joke or some wordy, windy poem
About Destiny or Fatal-Way or Weltmüth or Sarsparilla,
London would have hugged to it like a glad gorilla . . .
Happy to know its deepest heart told out so,
Deepest conviction, or maxim driven so home
(To the next door neighbour). But since the new making is
      still a
Mere Quartett for Strings after the Beethoven way
With no aspiration to say more than ever was said
By Beethoven, expecting such treatment and casual pay,
The musician is left to turn over Shakespeare and to find
Favourite passages when the dim east shows blind;
Get rid of his drink how he may, blamed for such drinking;
Leave his MS there, wondering what neighbours may be
      thinking
Of people who write a week through without end
And neither Lyons, Lipton or the London String Quartett
To care much what high glory from the light glory came to
      command;
Or . . . see how the two tunes into one English picture came
      linking.

An Appeal for Death

There is one who all day wishes to die,
And appeals for it – without a reason why –
Since Death is easy if men are merciful.
Water and land with chances are packed full.
Who all day wishes to die. How many ages
Have denied Death so – who reads old-written pages
And finds 'This man suffered and prayed for Death,
And went beyond this, desire of life beneath'?
Bitterly, bitterly, and though he feels his wrongs,
And once took pride in verse-making and in songs,

181

Yet now, yet now would wish to rest, and be
Out of pain, out of life, quietly, as quietly
As pained men ever were meant to rest.
Humanity knows earth to have as quiet a breast
As ever mother's to a longing child.
Therefore in mercy let rest, let rest this wild,
Or show hard torment, or of fear of such
Let rest, out of the fear of any pain's touch.
If men will not honour, nor find employ,
Will common mercy not forget what was wrong,
Remember what was good – a maker of song
Asks, desires, has prayed for mercy of Death
To end all, lie still, quiet green turf beneath,
Since promises forgotten are, and friendliness
Between so many men and him? The address
Of courtesy to casual wayfarers,
Small presents, courtesy of peace and wars –
To rest from pain, to trouble no one more –
Under green turf-mound, or by friendly shore
That will with rocking water lull his peace
That cannot now find hope nor strength nor ease.
To be let rest in mercy – to know an end
Of surety, Death's quiet surest of friend,
And what men would not, let calm Nature mend.

The Betrayal

Some men may take a pride in honour.
Not I, so beaten by a witchcraft power
The hour grinds me, I lie beneath,
Helpless, accusing to God each breath.

Not last determination may pride me,
Not any angel to stand beside me,
Beauty a torture of electrical like
Music, their manner of my soul's spite.

The earth's glad things are terror to me,
Truth and endurance are error to me –
My country's tales, hidden or forgotten,
Are the way my heart is most thrice-broken.

God so absent, no blink but accuses
Of lighten-torture, his black arrogances
In creation, his wilfulness to men's hurt.
How shall our saints save against treacheries
Smuts-in-insult accusing, the very earth's dirt?

Bach – Under Torment

Lovely, brave, affectionate things they were,
Strong handled and sure touched to their strong end,
Protestant devoutness *loved out all fear*,
Youthful remembrance to a grown man still friend.
Artist of four strands, eight, with a hedger's deft
Sure-moving purpose, O, were that spirit to meet
In Europe's common-ways; the Father of great
And small since, would Time were, and storm had a rift.

*

O, will not Gloucester, nor Aubers, nor Ypres save?
I paid a price of love there could not be said
Anyway but huge of any thought of my sternest god.
Golden firelight or racked frost hurt me to the nerve.
O Bach, O Father of all makers, look from your hidden
Hold where you are now and help me, that am so hard
	hurten.

The Lightning Storm

Heaven's fire bursts the clouds – the god of the air shows
	his moods
Or obediences – for no lightness in such indignation
Or in any light rain is shown by the gods of the heavens –
Majesty fills all poetry's hearers with right floods.

But what shall I do, or say – whose wrongs cry to Heaven?
My right a Europe's right, my wrongs of Europe's anger.
But though for a whim of conquest a nation makes shout and
    clangour,
For an honour of God – that's mine – none breaks voice,
    silence ever.

Snow

There's not a sound tonight.
I look out and am beaten
In my face by curious, white
Unexpected flakes
Of snow in a daze fleeting.

And retire shivering to
The warm room and the lamplight,
Where my music waits, and O
Ben Jonson lies . . .
To delight my man's nature with his great spirit.

O warmth! O golden light!
O books behind me waiting
Their turn for my love's thought . . . .
Turning from work
To wrap myself in a past life of golden lighting.

Music must flow with his power, I
Bend over my task and am hard
At wrestling with the stuff for mastery
That is dumb music now –
My spirit and I wrestle, you may hear us breathing hard.

Was there ever any Love could draw me
Out of my true way of work and action?
Yes, one there was, but Time has dared show me
(A soldier and maker)
That Time dares all things, and defies ever question.

To Clare

There are Westlands there died down to the calm
Of night, but still, still
Remembering the afterglow orange and friendly warm
Gone dusk over the hill.
There men that think like me have finished work
And go to their places
About farm-kitchens where the fire makes shadows lurk,
And there are young children's faces.
It is I have been reading Irish poetry that runs on
In anger, beauty, sorrow.
And all that passion lights in me *my* passion
Which gets no good – though
Many my great friends – I range books before me
To firm my thought.
Witchcraft, black witchcraft does overbear me;
In Hell's far nets I am caught.
They, who took hillside, stars and first light away,
Deny me with torture
All that my desperate need myself to justify
Desires – they make soul unsure
With doubt of each hour, 'What will Hell allow tomorrow?'
It is nearly nothing.
Anguish, and bearing up destruction and, after sorrow
Like torture, so bare a making.
It is dark now, there is no light; now if I came
To Ireland by the sea there,
How with my practised fingers would I love to proclaim
Many lands' nobility there –
Songs of the Islands, Germany, and even France,
And much poetry,
France, America, Roman and Greek in another dress,
Homelove and chivalry.
And share my maker's delight with those that love
To listen, and will after
Tell tales of the land which would my delight move,
And sorrow and laughter.

Long we'd sit, late we'd drink, and about the dark ways
Soft winds making trouble
Would delight also, for Gloucestershire is any county's
Friend, may have love double.
(Was it not I said, against Beethoven's persuasion,
Only the Irish knew
Truly the sense of earth, man's love and even salvation?
And Shakespeare the year through.)
How the folk in my own places fare, I know not,
Hell had them for a time.
Hell boasted power, after vile evil, vile might
Had all that county in shame.
Which may none Irish know, but never worse any
Than work paid for a life free –
Freedom by free price got, and always the good company
Of the air and the earth and the sea.
For God that made had no right unless the thing were
Honourable to his creatures. . .
It is false faith that says 'God is God'. Before the austere
Or passionate soul that measures
By faith all things god-like, sees in men's faces
Good past the right of love –
Accuses the eternal and the accursed high-set disgraces
This time's woe doth prove.
Ireland, Ireland, one of so proud a county's
Most affectionate sons,
Of Gloucester, used to holiness, and the time's bounties,
Cries because of your honour in new and old poetries,
Your renowns, and songs, your people of old chivalries –
For a man's good; for death's or the sun's.

First Poem

O what will you turn out, book, to be?
Who are not my joy, but my escape from the worst
And most accurst of my woe? Shall you be poetry,
Or tell truth, or be of past things the tale rehearsed?

Like Hebridean

Great sea water surged to its green height of white,
Clamouring in the stone arch, ages on ages all
Had made — turning at last to sea's natural delight,
Water from the deep playing first its great free game here.
(Zennor Head grim it was, granite of old Cornwall.)
So long the sea had been toy-thing to hearing and sight,
After great poetry music — it was mere relief great
To watch and hear rage of sea water hammering on granite
    stone here.
So the Sagas were not lies, chanties, and certain loved
    music . . .
Men had told truth. December in strong despite
Battered with wind and water old county of Cornwall.
(Seagulls uttering drear, flying momently, their strange call.)
Until now ploughland had kept my truth; colour, mystery of
    ground,
Rise to hide heaven of earth, or sudden white or green fall;
Before this tame thing, sea, was honoured for all virtue.
Yet now the white uptossing surge, great hoarse-voiced
    sound,
Compelled admiration — surf in leagues all of elation . . .
The poets were not liars, here also was glory to-praised and
    found.

The Coin

It is hard to guess tales from the sight of a thing
Brought up suddenly to the light, though one may have blood
Of Rome, and as I, all instinct, quick to one's high mood.
So Constantine's coin suddenly upward turned here, ploughed,
Still left me dumb of word as to what the loser seemed
(Only in music my spirit rightly mused or dreamed)
And the Roman that lost this small penny-thing was most
A wonder to me, though Plutarch I had read, Virgil and others
(English). I could not get to comradeship of him, nor make ring
The coin on stone as once he might have — but stared and stood
Far-off watching the valley, the Welsh hills, with a sting
Of regret (that I, war poet, had lost this high good

Of knowing one of my infinite dead generations of brothers).
My arms might have laid friendly on his walking shoulders;
His spirit spoken to spirit of my deepest pondering . . .
So following the plough under the lovely and ancient wood
A coin was ploughed up, heating thought till it sudden grew
    ruddy and glowed.

Varennes

At Varennes also Gloucester men had their stay.
(Infantry again, of my soft job getting tired.)
Saw wonderful things of full day and of half-day:
Black pattern of twigs against the sunset dim fired;
Stars like quick inspirations of God in the seven o'clock sky.
Where the infantry drilled frozen – all all foolishly
As on the Plain – but to the canteen went I,
Got there by high favour, having run, finished third,
In a mile race from Varennes to the next village end.
Canteen assistant, with a special care for B Company –
And biscuits hidden for favour in a manner forbidden.
Lying about chocolate to C Company hammering the gate.
Pitying them for their parade all the morning through
(Blue to the fingers, to all but the conscience blue)
Uselessly doing fatheaded things eternally.
But keeping (as was natural) Six Platoon ever in mind.
And one evening, drowsed by the wood fire I got lost in the
Blaze of warm embers, green wood smoking annoyingly;
Watched deep till my soul in the magic was rapt asleep:
Grew to power of music, and all poetries, so, uncared,
Became a maker among soldiers – dear comrades;
Which is the hardest of all wide earth's many trades;
And so proved my birthright, in a minute of warm aired
Staring into the woodfire's poetic heart, lost a tide deep.
(Until the anger of fire caught all, all in rose or gold was lost.)

Epitaph on a Young Child

They will bury that fair body and cover you –
You shall be no more seen of the eyes of men,
Not again shall you search the woodlands – not ever again
For violets – the wind shall be no more dear lover of you.

Other children shall grow as fair, but not so dear.
And the cold spirited shall say 'It is wrong that the body
Should be so beautiful' – O puritans warped to moody!
You were the true darling of the earth of your shire.

And all the flowers you touched, but would for pity not pick,
In the next spring shall regret you and on and so on –
Whether you are born again your love shall not be done –
In the most wonderful April or October your spirit shall be
     mystic.

Dear body (it is an evil age) that so enclosed
So lovely a spirit, generous, quick to another's small pain:
Is it true you in the dark earth must be down-lain?
Are there no more smiles from you in the house, sunlight-
     drowsed?

I must find out a love to console my hurt loneliness,
Forget your children's beauty in the conflict of days –
Until there come to me also the sweetness of some boy's
Or girl's beauty – a western spirit in a loved coloured dress
     of flesh.

Christopher Marlowe

With all that power he died, having done his nothing . . .
And none of us are safe against such terrible proving
That time puts on men – such power shown – so little done . . .
Then the earth shut him out from the light of the sun.

All his tears, all his prayers to God, and Elizabethan loving
Gone to a nothing, before he was well of age –
Having seen Cornwall, perhaps visited a loved Germany,
Known all London, read in many a poet's page –
Brave and generous, braggart and generous in doing,
Poet born and soldier, sobering to his elder age;
The earth covered him, and wrought wood was his clothing.
'Tamburlane' half glorious, then 'Faustus', half victorious,
He left us, chief, an ache that a poet true man of men,
Should be stabbed cold, like any mean half gallant frothing
    nothing.
Other men honoured, great ones made a tradition true,
But we curse luck for silence in manners various –
The courage and youth and virtue of Christopher Marlowe.

Song of Autumn

Music is clear about such freshness and colour,
    But how shall I get it?
There is great joy in walking to the quarry scar,
    And glory – I have had it.

Beech woods have given me truest secrets, and the sighing
    Firs I know, have told me
Truth of the hearts of children, the lovers of making.
    Old camps have called me.

It is time I should go out to ways older than tales,
    Walk hard, and return
To write an evening and a night through with so many wills
    Aiding me – little now to learn.

The Nightingales

Three I heard once together in Barrow Hill Copse –
At midnight, with a slip of moon, in a sort of dusk.
They were not shy, heard us, and continued uttering their notes.

But after 'Adelaide' and the poets' ages of praise
How could I think such beautiful; or utter false the lies
Fit for verse? It was only bird-song, a midnight strange new
   noise.

But a month before a laughing linnet in the gold had sung,
(And green) as if poet or musician had never before true tongue
To tell out nature's magic with any truth kept for long . . .

By Fretherne lane the linnet (in the green) I shall not forget
(Nor gold) the start of wonder – the joy to be so in debt
To beauty – to the hidden bird there in spring elms elate.

Should I lie then, because at midnight one had nightingales,
Singing a mile off in the young oaks that wake to look to Wales,
Dream and watch Severn – like me, will tell no false adoration in
   tales?

Dawns I Have Seen

Terribly for mystery or glory dawns have arisen
Over Cotswold in great light, or beginning of colour,
And my body at them has trembled, for beauty enraptured
   shaken.
(My spirit for so long beauty's friend, truest follower.)
It seemed the right of Severn to call from the east-heaving
Of Cotswold, nobleness his own for his right of honour;
And the birds have exulted as if newly let from prison.
To those dawns have I read Shakespeare, and the grand
   wide reason

Of Milton, the childlike wonder of Chaucer – almost on grieving
At the beauty of dewy daisies in the May-time season.
Dawns overpowering me past my own power of making;
Glorious as west country dawns show, day's first most-sacred
    hour.
No music in me to fit that great life-in-flood awakening,
To walk only in other men's poetry
Saying my heart in passion out, or deep musing.

The Last of the Book

There is nothing for me, Poetry, who was the child of joy,
But to work out in verse crazes of my untold pain;
In verse which shall recall the rightness of a former day.

And of Beauty, that has command of many gods, in vain
Have I written, imploring your help, who have let destroy
A servant of yours, by evil men birth better at once had slain.

And for my county, God knows my heart, land, men to me
Were dear there, I was friend also of every look of sun or rain;
It has betrayed as evil women wantonly a man their toy.

Soldiers' praise I had earned having suffered soldier's pain,
And the great honour of song in the battle's first grey show –
Honour was bound to me save, mine most dreadfully stain.

Rapt heart, once, hills I wandered alone, joy was comrade
    there, though
Little of what I needed was in my power; again – again
Hours I recall, dazed with pain like a still weight set to my woe.

Blood, birth, long remembrance, my county, all these have saven
Little of my being from dreadfullest hurt, the old gods have no
Pity – or long ago I should have got good, they would have
    battled my high right plain.

St Sylvester's Night

The moon is clear, the winds have blown clouds away –
And my thoughts are out to better than these east lands
Though an Earl lived here: Christopher Marlowe was
Born in Canterbury city on a promising day.
The light on Randwick Hill must be silvery
As fairy now, Severn will show with silver strands
Heaving waters in the power of this great moon –
Swinging Atlantic like a draught in her hands.

The Poets of My County

One was a happy serious boy on lands
Of meadows – and went to France, and kept his hands
For bayonet readier than the pen, being likely
To dream into a poem men should not even see.
And one was sailor by Horn and Valparaiso, wrote
Such tale of Pompey as showed him rightly the great.
Another, the first, of St Thomas wrote imagining,
Of whom cuckoo flowers brought immortal lines and did sing
Like water of clear water – like April's spirit of spring.
But what of Taylor, water-poet, who left desiring
The Roman town for the rich one, fame his heart so firing
He'd not heave cargoes nor draw wages by Severn?
And one wrote worthy verses indeed of the Four-ways,
Coming in, watched of high clouds, for commercial days,
And military: another saw Ryton and wrote so –
Another yet wrote sonnets none so fool should forget.
(Of Rupert Brooke – gold winter on the sheets
Where light made memory of history of the room's happenings.)
The love of Edward Thomas in night-walkers' promise.
But I praised Gloucester city as never before – and lay
By Tilleloy keeping spirit in soul with the way
Cooper's comes over from eastward, sees Rome all the way.

Gloucester

Many have praised dancers
As folk of fine pride –
And I have seen foreigners
Dance, beauty revealed.

But on sombre ruddy
Lit lands of Gloucester –
Suddenly in March, suddenly
Gold princesses were master

Of lovely and emerald lit fields
Winter saw desolate . . .
They sang to far hills melodies
Like Easter water in spate.

They were like young children come
To a century-lonely house –
Heralds of a glory should soon foam
And glitter beside the hedgerows.

The Love Song

Out of the blackthorn edges
I caught a tune
And before it could vanish, seized
It, wrote it down.

Gave to a girl, so praising
Her eyes, lips and hair
She had little knowing, it was only thorn
Had dreamed of a girl there.

Prettily she thanked me, and never
Guessed any of my deceit . . .
But O Earth is this the only way
Man may conquer, a girl surrender her sweet?

Small Chubby Dams

Small chubby dams banked in the water
Flowing half as clear quite as the soft air,
Going placid westward, a small daughter
Between Crickley and Severn, and only there.
Short childhood, early youth, but dead primal fires
Set limits to a flowing thing's girl's desires.
The one thing was to live that short course sprackly;
Therefore nuthazels and ashes hanging all slackly
Regarding boughs, he drew to familiar plants round him
As foxgloves dusty purple with serrate rim
And willow-herb and lady's mantle and dark flower dim
A hundred dainty watchers of clear eddies
Ladies of common soil, and fine mould ladies;
To perfect himself, and comfort such a one as I;
Too ill for walking plans, left but to try the uplifted
The instant medicine of the smooth sky.
Chancing on this (not written) as shapely Slow Movement as
Brahms he made ever, but native to more grace.

Of Cruelty

From the racked substance of the earth comes the plant and
That with heat and the night frost is tortured:
To some perfection that grows, man's thought wills his hand –
Roots rent, crown broken, grub-holed, it is drawn upward.

A hundred things since the first stir have hunted it,
The rooks any time might have swallowed ungrateful.
Caterpillars, slugs, as it grew, have counted on it,
And man the planter bent his gaze down on it fateful.

The thing will go to market, it must be picked up and loaded,
The salesman will doubt it or chuck it anyway in,
A horse must be harnessed first, or a donkey goaded
Before the purchaser may ever the first price pay for it.

Who may be now trembling with a vast impatience
And anxieties and mixed hopes for a resurrection
Out of the mouldering soil — to be new form, have perfections
Of flowers and petal and blade, to die, to be born to clean action.

War Books

What did they expect of our toil and extreme
Hunger — the perfect drawing of a heart's dream?
Did they look for a book of wrought art's perfection,
Who promised no reading, nor praise, nor publication?
Out of the heart's sickness the spirit wrote
For delight, or to escape hunger, or of war's worst anger,
When the guns died to silence and men would gather sense
Somehow together, and find this was life indeed,
And praise another's nobleness, or to Cotswold get hence.
There we wrote — Corbie Ridge — or in Gonnehem at rest —
Or Fauquissart — our world's death songs, ever the best.
One made sorrows' praise passing the church where silence
Opened for the long quivering strokes of the bell —
Another wrote all soldiers' praise, and of France and night's stars,
Served his guns, got immortality, and died well.
But Ypres played another trick with its danger on me,
Kept still the needing and loving-of-action body,
Gave no candles, and nearly killed me twice as well,
And no souvenirs, though I risked my life in the stuck tanks.
Yet there was praise of Ypres, love came sweet in hospital,
And old Flanders went under to long ages of plays' thought in
    my pages.

For Mercy of Death

I suffer racking pain all day, and desire death so —
As few desire. Where is man's mercy gone?
Did ever past generations such torment know
Who lived near earth, and joyed when the sun shone,
Or when sweet rain came on

The earth; and the afterglow
Of sun and flowers in show
Of golden sweetness gladdened earth's dear son?
Where is that mercy now
That palpably took pleasure in the sweep
Of hedgerows – high to deep –
And houses in the making, man's own dear
Vesture and shelter here?
O sure it is that if those olden-time
Builders of farm and byre
Were here again, my pain should pity receive –
Death should make no more to grieve
My spirit with such pain it knows not how
To endure. O show
Such olden pity on poor souls in pain.
Let rest again –
As would our fathers, friends of wind and rain.

Hell's Prayer

My God, the wind is rising! on those edges
Of Cotswold dark glory might swing my soul –
And western Severn and north of water sedges
Mystery sounds, the wind's drums roll.
None will care to walk there. Those prefer to tell
Tales in a warm room of gossips, gettings, wages,
While I would be cursing exultant at the wind's toll
Of bell, shout of glory – swiftness of shadows.
My birth, my earning, my attained heritages,
Ninety times denied me now thrust so far in hell.

I think of the gods, all their old oaths and gages –
Gloucester has clear honour sworn without fail –
Companionship of meadows, high Cotswold ledges
Battered now tonight with huge wind-bursts and rages,
Flying moon glimpses like a shattered and flimsy sail –
In hell I, buried a score-depth, writing verse pages.

To Crickley

My soul goes there crying when
It is hurt by God far . . .
It is hurt too far, and moves again
By green and quarry scar.

Ages and ages dreaming there
Speak their heart to me –
Generations of tried men honour
My broken good with pity.

'Such good', they say, 'your blood had
At birth, and in this
Land was given you music in mood
Noble, true, clamorous.

And what has broken England to such
Evil is not guessed
Nor those old sentries rustling grass rough
Know, nor the rest.

Soldier that knew war's pains, poet
That kept our love –
The gods have not saved you, it is not
Our prayers lacking to move

Them to you – deep in hells now still burning
For sleep or the end's peace.
By tears we have not saved you; yearning
To accusation, and our hopes' loss, turning.
What gods are these?'

The Coppice

There is a coppice on Cotswold's edge the winds love;
It blasts so, and from below there one sees move
Tree-branches like water darkling – and I write thus
At the year's end, in nine hell-depths, with such memories;
I guess that rocks and heaves like west Irish seas;
Where the kite is this evening, that loves rock and hover
About the thin wood growth, I shall not know, cannot discover
Only guess dark ridge edge, and the gloomed valley's
Magnificence below them first night does cover.

The coppice of thin and great trees as nobly set
Against Wales for Cotswold, as it were the gate
Of Britain watching Britain, refusing ever
To acknowledge Rome; great shapes by older barrows;
That longs for me tonight as if my name were great
And owner of that swift fall, that wind-beaten swerve:
Were sayer of what the wood's heart could never forget.

The Elements

A writer thought, 'How lovely to rise and lave
My smooth fair body with water clear from earth drawn.
Ponder on it, and dig the garden, so little garden,
Drink tea, and smoke, write, thanking my aunt's kindness
(Hoping to return work-chance and all, as doubtless
I did – a friend of mine, and beyond thought kind
Often . . .) It was a chance of work past my hopes, save she
Would force tea, and trap to food, so it was terror to me.
So I'd go walking by Cotswold streams set a-talking
By a short course and steep from hills azure, green
Through the hawthorn hedges, and orchards dimly seen,
There by Haw Bridge and Forthampton, and the hill whose name
Is gone from me – where the silver brook earth bore and laughed
        silver,
By the landslide, to Hartpury, Maisemore and so where I came

(To see Great Peter's like 'Leonora' over Severn meadows).
To talk and work, returning courtesy with company,
Till she'd go upstairs, then no more talking in lamp shadows
Golden and black on gold, I'd work hours untold
Reading Goethe and Shakespeare, seeing Longford meadows,
And getting notes on paper, and verse square bold,
Till the days tardied out over Kingsholm, and light soaked up
    gloom.
Quartetts and tea, tobacco, Elizabethans – none better of those.
My aunt would come down fresh-cheeked for all her years,
To find me writing, and I'd smile and talk my thanks,
Lie down, covered with a rug for one hour, with eyes clear as
    on high Cotswold there'.

December 30th

It is the year's end, the winds are blasting, and I
Write to keep madness and black torture away
A little – it is a hurt to my head not to complain.
In the world's places that honour earth, all men are thinking
Of centuries: all men of the ages of living and drinking;
Singing and company of all time till now –
(When the hate of Hell has this England's state plain).
By the places I know this night all the woods are battering
With the great blast, clouds fly low, and the moon
(If there is any) clamorous, dramatic, outspoken.
In such nights as this Lassington has been broken,
Severn flooded too high and banks overflown –
And the great words of 'Lear' first tonight been spoken.
The boys of the villages growing up will say, 'I
Shall leave school, or have high wages, before another January –
Be grown up or free before again December's dark reign
Brightens to Christmas, dies for the old year's memory.'
May to them the gods make not all prayers vain.

Cotswold edge, Severn Valley that watches two
Magnificences: noble at right times or affectionate.
What power of these gods ever now call to you
For the folks in you of right noble; and of delight
In all nature's things brought round in the year's circle?
Pray God in blastings, supplicate now in terrifical
Tempestuous movings about the high-sided night.

Men I have known fine, are dead in France, in exile,
One my friend is dumb, other friends dead also,
And I that loved you, past the soul am in torture's spite
Cursing the hour that bore me, pain that bred all
My greater longings; Love only to you, this last-year date.

Poem for End

So the last poem is laid flat in its place,
And Crickley with Crucifix Corner leaves from my face
Elizabethans and night-working thoughts – of such grace.

And all the dawns that set my thoughts new to making;
Or Crickley dusk that the beech leaves stirred to shaking
Are put aside – there is a book ended; heart aching.

Joy and sorrow, and all thoughts a poet thinks,
Walking or turning to music; the wrought-out links
Of fancy to fancy – by Severn or by Artois brinks.

Only what's false in this, blood itself would not save,
Sweat would not heighten – the dead Master in his grave
Would my true following of him, my care approve.

And more than he, I paid the prices of life
Standing where Rome immortal heard October's strife,
A war poet whose right of honour cuts falsehood like a knife.

War poet – his right is of nobler steel, the careful sword –
And night walker will not suffer of praise the word
From the sleepers, the custom-followers, the dead lives unstirred.

Only, who thought of England as two thousand years
Must keep of today's life the proper anger and fears:
England that was paid for by building and ploughing and tears.

VI

1926 and after

Music Room

There is best no sound near starred midnight
Save the falling coals, and a wind's stir outside –
Shakespeare open, master of lonely delight,
And candle, firelight, flickering the room wide.

Many memories there are not fit for work's aid –
But if a friend, a woman, now dead, has given
Pain for the sake of this, lit room and still haven,
Remember, and by Townshend her name be said –
Nor go less to watch Sirius or Mars in Heaven.

I Read Now So

So I read now, dull verse in hidden measures,
Great of the earth or earldom, or of abbeys,
So I listen now or scan to find great pageant treasures
Fall in infinite depths of terror, heights of Hell.
Love all persuading, powerful, tender, infinite –
Of the world's, blessed Mary's children's, friends;
And then again my verse or the verse of my friend.
By a city or a library, or in post betrayed,
Stolen else, to be a pride of a torturer in torture:
The devils barren to cheat the rich right forepaid.
Ruin and empty work made of our fine,
Our fine work, signed under another's trade –
And the master of us all a trap; corrupted, made
A peril for boys, a book for the cunning, that's said
To be the tender and high book of England's drawing –
Terrible and secret, when rich asking pain over-paid.
Danger in masters and slick thieves at the trade.
So read I now, on thin ice or on spiked reserve to go,
Or leave my thoughts of county or of music's bounty –
The spear of the gods bent into a trident and a bow
To shoot the poisoned arrow unmoving frozen shining slow.

Poets' Affection

Reckoning good in time, how ruined and how fine the high poets
    stood,
And seeing what I saw there, the blossoming meads of apple and
    pear, with rough bark-clothed wood,
I knew a thing not human killed the good of man and woman
    were it glory or straight making
Of fine eloquence or rhyme.
Then knew the high gods helpless save they took a power was
    dangerous
For aid for man his great plan fit to crown and traverse time.

Then all the men that walked there did I list in my thoughts,
Watching to hills and valleys that they listed for their pleasures
Made small symbols like rare treasures of, bediamonded rich
    small fraught.
Their dawn looks and their day-falls from the north where
    Raphael Bredon falls
To Michael's hold, Crickley, Nicholas, Cooper's guard and glory,
Uriel's English story and sway to valley of old that Randwick
    taught.
Cried: May the angels weakened care as much for England sickened
And the straitened poets beaten as those lovers for Severn's
    land's
Hollow hand. When the blackbird cried out 'Fealty to thee',
And the linnet, 'Obeisance, obeisance, O, Obeisance' from his tree.

Skylark, plover, rook, robin scarlet like a book
Wagtail shaking, making pointings joyous at first look,
Cried, 'Joy to thee, poets loved to be, may our service come to
    suffice to thee'.

Friend of the Mists

    A thing of the field that loves the air between,
    And azure between grey branches,
    Bird of your own
    You have that's known

With songs of romances
Of your age vast –
Unguessed age in a frosty morning
Known all green.
No word of the godlike
Beautiful kind friendliest
Holy one that died . . .
Sing all in mourning phrases
Clear as the light in fruit-closes
The orchard's tune sing with his own best . . .
Oath from all folk's lips
Save this strange one . . .
Kept from his knowing.
O the runes perished!
And dark days soon finished
And armour all tarnished –
The last bird's silence.

Traffic in Sheets

Silk colour and lit-up candlelight the sheets I saw
By Severn's bridge that day . . .
O the lost history . . . O ladies and pageants of the mystery
Of February here and miles away.

I could have sung, but knew no fitting tunes
(For all my lore) of the spread
Of coloured sheets of the floods that ensure all June's
Dark fan-grasses of the pretty head.

The Shelter from the Storm

And meantime, fearing snow, the flocks are brought in.
They are in the barn where stone tiles and wood-shelter
From the harm shield; where the rosy-faced farmer's daughter
Goes to visit them.

She pats and fondles all her most favourite first,
Then after that the shivering and unhappy ones,
Spreads hay, looks up at the noble and grey roof vast
And says, 'This will stop storms.'

Her mind is with her books in the low-ceilinged kitchen
Where the twigs blaze, and she sees not sheep alone
Of the Cotswold, but in the Italian shelters, songs repeating
Herdsmen kind, from the blast gone.

The Two

Hearing the flute call
Of my country's meadows still through March blasts,
There have I hurried out and farther to the amethyst
Changes of the willows small.

And at home at night
Quiet through poetry the day's roaring shaking and rising
Me has driven to music, great mood to iron-twisting changing:
Withered leaves at next seeing.

That at least gave dawn
When to the upper windows of the house all else still
Climbed I, saw magnificent dawn-pageant of the daffodil
And rose-on-thorn come on.

The Pedlar's Song

Now dust is on the roads,
And the blue hills call to distances,
On my shoulders I take my fancies
And travel where good shows –
To places of grey stone and water
Where a squire and his lovely daughter
Come once to talk with old Richard Spragg
And give tea, for the heart's glows.

The squire with his old right
And the lady with half a bookful
Of names for homage's delight,
They are my patrons and like-council.
I travel through frosty weather warming
The blood that shall lie in a barn at evening –
And that's their bounty with farm-hands company,
The blaze and converse of nightfall.

I never travel without
A pipe for company, nor books
Of tunes that delight heart,
And ancient honest wood-cuts –
Skill enough but there's love in my fingers,
The harpsichord is served by my prayers,
And many a house and manor of music
Has learnt from my crammed pack.

In sweet lands making travel,
With money for taverns, at luck's time,
Or to lie on the straw with a double
Roof on my head, hostel of rhyme –
And never a rough word from seven demesnes,
For I carry them treasures they'd else miss.
Till I die I will serve Middle Ages honour;
Then die, and be a faithful name.

Going Outwards

The men have left their twisty taverns behind,
The mates have put their sweethearts' thought from mind . . .
And go from ridge to ridge of the Channel's skymarks,
Till they feel the open sea, and the rough-breasted, kind
Vasty affection of swift-lilting ocean.
Now they sing, and their chanties are ports to come,
Strange kindly people, black laughers, with all new notion
Different from the grey or ruddy left roofs' cover over
In the comfortable villages of England touching ocean.

Now childish and too-valiant before Father Wet-face,
Amorous of nymphs, more at home than dolphins allowed,
They sing old rant of sea battles, ruddy sailed and proud;
Meetings of fleets long scattered, and the frowning oaky-browed
Pride of the Spanish galleons the north-west scattered;
And keep their quiet tunes for the illimitable slow watered
Plains of the middle ocean – regret for the diapered
Tavern blind, gold lighted like Darien within doors . . .
And girls as pretty as wild-roses, slim and music-voiced.

Musers Afar Will Say

Soon will blow the changed leaves on the Malvern road
Hurtling in tiny charge; and the streams will be strowed
With arrows and shields of a hundred affectionate fields . . .
But who to dear desiring Gloucester will bring good?

Men afar off by strange rivers will say, 'Now the year
Will be storming and crying triumphant before death there
By Gloucester.' But who will bring Severn any heart's good,
Full-heralded bright river? They will fear, and they'll remember.

December Evening

The windy curtains blew there, it was a closed room
And winter howled outside, but no poetry could come . . .
Only staring blankly at old rhythms of Lombardy
Lost and in tapestry found, or cunning lies of poets –
Dumb in December, with weather savage in a lit room.
The waste of time . . .
To my friend at last looking
(He right if any to praise Avon-land and secret Frome,
Musing and moveless, hoping in an hour's right to come,
A week, a year of his deserving) . . .

Caught at what I did not see, infinite wrongs uselessly breaking
Against evil, and our own trapping like past men of rhyme
From the bold and chivalrous storm . . .
And the nobleness of its vasty shaking . . .
And from faces in the fire's ruin.

No, Come Not, Swallows

Swallows, those our meadows love, come not hither
To our loved walls at heights of summery pride warm,
We speak no word to other, it is hard to keep from harm,
No love between ourselves . . . O, if the shelves
Of Apennine may please you, or famed Venetian border
Come not to our unhappy lands now with friendless hands,
But swerve above south meadows and the richer verdure
Children to delight. O, visit not our city famed Princes
Praised. But for a time choose Adriatic and the Hellenic wharves.

The Dancers

The dancers danced in a quiet meadow
It was winter, the soft light lit in clouds
Of growing morning – their feet on the firm
Hillside sounded like a baker's business
Heard from the yard of his beamy barn-grange.
One piped, and the measured irregular riddle
Of the dance ran onward in tangling threads . . .
A thing of the village, centuries old in charm.
With tunes from the earth they trod, and naturalness
Sweet like the need of pleasure of change.
For a lit room with panels gleaming
They practised this set by winter's dreaming
Of pictures as lovely as are in spring's range . . .
No candles, but the keen dew-drops shining . . .
And only the far jolly barking of the dog strange.

I Would Not Rest

I would not rest till work came from my hand
And then as the thing grew, till fame came,
(But only in honour) . . . and then, O, how the grand
Divination of ages grew to faith's flame.
Great were our fathers and beautiful in all name,
Happy their days, lovely in considered grain each word,
Their days were kindness, growth, happiness, mindless.

I would not rest until my county were
Thronged with the Halls of Music; and until clear
Hospitality for love were e'er possible . . .
And any for honour might come, or prayer, to certain
Fondness and long nights' talking till all's known.

Madness my enemy, cunning extreme my friend,
Prayer my safeguard. (Ashes my reward at end.)
Secrecy fervid my honour, soldier-courage my aid.
(Promise and evil threatening my soul ever-afraid.)
Now, with the work long done, to the witchcraft I bend
And crouch – that knows nothing good, Hell uncaring
Hell undismayed.

If I Shall Praise

If I shall praise honour with dark hair,
And azure eyes with courtesy bright under,
My friend, and many's, of the delightful room,
Where Holbein challenged glance with Bechstein,
And there was talk of history and of the loom
Weaving it . . .
        Such skill as befits well
The handmaid of the gods, fierce fighter at turn,
And swift as birds to discover what to learn;
Lovable one to visit, and longed for long
On the moor's or quarry's edges – the start of a song,
Or duty to be followed after joy halloed . . .

Her voice musical so to remind of water
Seen on the hills, and dresses the seasons learn . . .
And natural grace to be hostess.
                                        She, Cotswold's daughter,
Perhaps in many things was the hidden wonder,
And fashioned fate too in that lighted room . . .
History, and written portraiture, newspaper matter . . .
For her let there be worn
Rosemary, sweet marjoram, violet, beech,
An acorn in its season, and chestnut too.

(For well she kept that faith which never slept)
Autumn crocus, and wonderful trefoil, harebell
In whose hill power the lovers know themselves well.
There are terrible things to silence always kept,
And tears past right, a scar on meadows mapped;
Not the high gods she served can yet right who
The lists mayhap declared, and stretched her reach
In far lands . . .
                        Her right was love, and that
Came against Ocean's and Europe's gates to beat.
Her tale, death taken from her, and after . . . honour.
Till, devils gave, a terror at terror's ending
Gave her a peace she will not hurry in spending.

Now silence and the wrong intolerable has
All things – Evil bitterly persisted in
Keeps gods and devils fatally set on sin . . .
And sorcery-torture gives never any grace
But evil acknowledgement, nets for claims, Hell-sent:
Messages of thieves that broke her treasuries in.

The Pleasance Window

Now light dies from the pleasance
With rich look of colour
About the lawn, and winter
Whispers of leafless trees . . .

Of orange sunsets soft dying
And chill in the air at morning,
When friends will delight also
To speak of Artois' friends

Warm straw after freezing ditches.
And soon will come long dark
Starry when the poet goes
Content with his masters out to stars.

Sea-Marge

Pebbles are beneath, but we stand softly
On them, as on sand, and watch the lacy edge
Of the swift sea

Which patterns and with glorious music the
Sands and round stones. It talks ever
Of new patterns.

And by the cliff-edge, there, the oakwood throws
A shadow deeper to watch what new thing
Happens at the marge.

What Was Dear

What was dear to Pan is dear to him no more,
He answers prayers never, nor ever appears —
And so sore a loss is this to his lovers
They play never, the sweet reed sounds no more

In the oak coppice, or the seven-poplar shade
Silver hearted . . . softly wailing at eve.
The silent country folk no more bring gifts
They delighted in — nor the new pipe greenly made.

Rather I Would . . .

Rather I would have a cup of red clay
Sparkling with bright water, because there
I might think of my kinship and friendship with
    many.

Unless the mighty aged tree were felled, and
Fairly made the sweet white of the wood cut,
Rhythmed by the spirit of argent clear water.

This Christmas Morning

This Christmas morning, once to the gods given,
We shall go sit amid stone where music wraps
Infinite cloaks companionable round people
That the dear Morning Star saw for sign of Christ.

Waking in our panelled rooms with no straw
And the content passion of Sebastian Bach
Soaring by clear and coloured windows to be
Heart of thought, this Christmas of clear shining.

Wood-Gathering

The gatherer will not go too far,
For fearing of taking too much store,
But picks the bits of branches there
Where they lie, and looks at hills the more.

Returns, and who cares if the flare
Does not burn deep against the frore,
So merry mist-brave heat does stare
Against the folk, and roar up there.

When dusk veils all, they'll heap the spare
And noble wood, heap on heap without care,
For the noble frost will call for such cheer
Shining in white stars most royal in air.

The House of Stone

This is the house of stone and coloured
Glass of the City of Duke Humphrey.
At Michaelmas at All Hallows' forget not
What courteous low kindness his was

Nor forget, taking those great ensigns in
Of age and honour like the sound of brass –
What sort of friendship lasts when the tomb goes
Or who of lowness will care speak in centuries.

The Bridge

Ceremony that the boys loved is no more
About those white walls fallen –
Nor will any
At All Hallows' Even cry out Humphrey's ensigns.

At the gate none will praise the well-wrought
Heraldry of the long bridge, sun-silver, all-honour –
A dirty water drifts between crampt
Borders, lies and goes past the shadow.

In far ravines and on heights love delights in
The trees will pity the haggard Half-Lady
Of crystal-sprung Severn,
The flowers beneath accuse angels betraying.

The Poet

In nature's paid discernment
Quick and as steady still
As a bird or a beast of the grassment,
The poet learns his will,
Not by learning, not in obedience – but to fulfil.

And all he sees or hears
Will teach him, if he never
Lie in his reverence, for
Affection pays itself ever,
May go far on without chart or friend or cares.

If he know the song of the lark,
Rudely, as a brat calls it,
And the dawn, and water's teasing spark
Rushing in flood-time, and leaves' look
Week by week the year through it –
He will not harm book nor bark
But love, with lack, and golden truth, while devil spoils it.

Near Spring

Now the strong horse goes loose at last,
Free for his strength, in the February's end –
Floods have left the meadows and gone past
To the broader river's rocks and sand.

Musing on old tunes, ploughboys go
Hoping to catch the lilt forgot
Of a tune their fathers recalled in glow
Of talking, or after cricket hot.

The year stirs wing and watches skies
Deep-in again; the girl is happy
With her white apron showing in the doorway's
Frame; daffodils thrill in hedgebanks ruddy.

Where the Mire

Where the mire was thick from winter's sledges,
By the woodside, there I walked and mused
On the deep music floating there out of reach,
Just out of arm's length . . . It was December,
West country . . . Orange, low, the riband gleamed
Of the sunset, on it tangled twigs in teasing
Show, and the scent of the breath of the earth
Might have borne in me music to stir the silent
Folk of London; disowned, forgot of birth.
I thought that . . . and turning south to my end,
The farmhouse that too brought aid to my making,
Forgot much in tea's desire, by a hearth
To be sitting, talking countywide, or till limned
Pictures in the fire glow – talking to world's ends . . .
In friendship hiding sorrow, in long thoughts of poetry
As gave us lines and reality of the apple orchard.

The Wood of August

The wood gathers strength of green in mid-August
Calling from the deep all store of April water
And later, to be triumphant while the time serves;
Golden-rod, orchis, guelder rose and scabious
Grow near him, and he watches the three swerves
Of Cotswold Edge, South Severn and Malvern Sideways.
Soon he will change, the nuts will ripen, and tideways
Turn greater to the equinox, and brown and brittle
His leaves, save the little, will change, and he'll dream
Of two things: how in rich music is fixed his glow
(Ruddy and bronze), and in All Hallow his August title
With vanished days to it, is held as high as any
(Poor un-named English company),
That haws last through November and dare winter's battle.

In December

In December the stubble nearly is
Most loved of things.
The rooks as in the dark trees are its friends
And make part of it ...

Now when the hills shine far
And light and set off
That darkness, all my heart cries angrily
That music to fashion

For if not so, one must go
To the stubble every day
For comfort against such emptiness
As lost treasures make.

Cruelly scare the choughs from
Fallows and trees alike –
Though dim in love, or bright far
With the hills heroically they ally.

The Old Walnut

The old walnut the children have loved so long
Must come down. The squire needs a fine furniture,
Having things of honour, a chest and other
Must hold music – pictures of the land, for
The land made, and after death the tree
May be more honoured yet than in greatness
There by the lawn, showing the red brick wall ...
But in this November yet there is none to take
Truly its place, nuts but no monarch-show
Undoubted of one field's demesne.
His sons and daughters will grieve not after a little,
But follow duty, and the children will climb them
As honouring and friendly ... True, the sweet music
Drawn out of the chest will sound there, and
Hospitality come ...

Here, If Forlorn

When to Mediterranean the birds' thoughts turn,
Watching the lessening days
And the softer glow
Of sunset, 'Goodbye' shall I say
And praise their beauty, and pray winter stern
To hurt nothing those feathers and fairy grace.
But after a week, in a place
Of coppices
I will count the kinds of birds that do not go
But for a Shakespeare and rare courage
Keep here, if forlorn
Despite sleeting scorn, and bitter hate of snow.

Soft Rain

Soft rain beats upon my windows
Hardly harming.
But by the great gusts guessed farther off
Up by the bare moor and brambly headland
Heaven and earth make war.

That savage toss of the pine boughs past music
And the roar of the elms . . .
Here come, in the candle light, soft reminder
Of poetry's truth, while rain beats as softly here
As sleep, or shelter of farms.

The Wind

All night the fierce wind blew,
All night I knew
Time, like a dark wind, blowing
All days, all lives, all memories
Down empty endless skies —

A blind wind, strowing
Bright leaves of life's torn tree
Through blank eternity;
Dreadfully swift. Time blew.
All night I knew
The outrush of its going.

At dawn a thin rain wept.
Worn out, I slept
And woke to a fair morning.
My days were amply long, and I content
In their accomplishment –
Lost the wind's warning.

As They Draw to a Close

As they draw to a close,
These songs of the earth and art, war's romanzas and stern . . .
The seaboard air encompasses me and draws my mind to sing
    nobly of ships . . .
Or the look of the April day draws anthems as of masters from
    me –
(O, it is not that I have been careless of the fashioned formal
    songs!)
For rough nature, for gracious reminder, I have sought all my
    days:
For men and women of the two-fold asking, for democracy and
    courtesy wherever it showed –
For the honour of flags well-borne at the head of regiments
    digne . . .
Of what underlies my songs, the precedent songs, as they draw
    to a close I think,
Of failures rough crude half formless (yet I understood rarely
    why)
Of the blurred pictures of rare colour here and there shown on
    my pages . . .
Yet I have deserved well of men, and the book *Leaves of Grass*
    will show it –
Their homes and haunts nobler that I lived. (Hear the laugh
    ringing from the tavern . . .)

The meeting in market-place or hall, the workers together will
   remember me.
(In their talk are words like earth or panelled rooms, Baltimore,
   forced-march, page and maker-look —
The winds of the north still stir their eager questing minds.)

The seed I have sought to plant in them, trefoil, goldenrod and
   orchard-bloom,
These O precedent songs you also have helped plant everywhere
   in the world —
When you were launched there was small roughness in the touch
   of words,
A woman's weapon, a boy's chatter, a thing for barter and loss:
But I have roughed the soul American or Yankee at least to truth
   and instinct,
And compacted the loose-drifting faiths and questions of men in
   a few words.

EDITORIAL NOTE ON THE
PRESENT EDITION

THIS collection is not a 'complete Gurney', even less a complete variant edition, as is explained in greater detail below. It is, however, the most substantial and representative collection of his poems to date; and the annotation, consisting of details of the sources in the Gurney Archive, and indicating the existence of alternative versions and significant variants when appropriate, is intended to guide the Gurney student through the Archive as well as containing material of interest to the general reader.

THE GURNEY ARCHIVE (GA) (The Ivor Gurney Collection, Gloucester Library)

All number references are to GA, sole source of unpublished verse material for this edition.

An Index of all copies of poems found in GA, compiled in the course of making this edition, is now in GA (64.13).

GA now contains (1982) 66 listed groups of material. These include separate notebooks, collections of MSS (with other notebooks) and TSS, music, letters, medical records, photographs, catalogues, cuttings, etc. Verse of some kind is contained under the following numbers:

Notebooks: GA 1, 2, 52. (1,2,7), 64.1–10. Some early pocket-books of pencil notes; middle and late period exercise books.

Collections of MSS: 15, 42, 44, 45, 52, 53, 55, 64.11–12. Boxes or folders mainly of loose MS pages; some with TSS and Scott MS copies; letters, appeals, prose essays, etc. The 'asylum' papers are often folded to form booklets addressed to public figures and institutions. Most are without corrections and in regular verse lines; almost all completed, signed, and many dated (often several on the same day). There are few dates after 1926, though the prose notes, etc., seem to be later. The latest date is 1933.

Collections of TSS: 16–21A (spring folders); 12, 66 (carbons and copies); 60, 65 (collected sets). Some TSS are grouped according to origin (e.g. 'from the 3d. Exercise Book "To Hawthornden"') but most do not correspond to notebooks or groups now in the Archive.

Various MS verses: to be found among other material: 4, 5, 46, 61.

The seven spring folders of TSS (16-21A) form the basis of Edmund Blunden's selection in 1954. In 1960 they were added to by Mrs Joy Finzi, who gathered further material from various sources; and it is these augmented TSS, with the MS material then in the Archive, that Leonard Clark used for his larger selection in 1973.

In 1976 a further ten MS notebooks came to light, with two collections of MSS and copies (64.1–12). Some of these contain copies or versions of poems already in the Archive, but there are also poems of which no other copy exists. The history of this material before 1976 is unclear; Edmund Blunden certainly saw one of the notebooks (64.2) because he describes it in his Introduction. Since 1976 the material has been consulted by Michael Hurd for his biography, and by Geoffrey Grigson for his selection in TLS (1978). It has been invaluable for checking printed versions taken from TSS, and also for dating of poems.

Not all the poems selected by Blunden still have TS copies in the Archive (hence 'no original' noted when there is no MS to hand either). The seven TS folders are chronologically a mixture but have been used for what help they can give when there is no other clue. The collections of loose sheets can be in any order. A large proportion of the verse in the 'asylum' boxes (e.g. 44 and 45) consists of autobiographical appeals ('for Release or Death'), some very long, addressed to the Metropolitan Police, the Prime Minister, Rudyard Kipling, most of the States of America, Iceland of the Sagas, the People of France, etc. Few are without interest, but they are very repetitive. Examples printed here are 'To Clare' (p.185) and 'Chance to Work' (Appendix, p.265); there are other examples in Hurd's biography. There is also at least one verse play, and much writing in the manner of, or on themes of, Shakespeare and Walt Whitman.

Altogether there are upwards of 1,700 items of verse material of all kinds now listed.

SELECTION

In 1954 Blunden printed 78 poems. In 1973 Leonard Clark printed 140, including 43 of Blunden's selection. The total number of Gurney poems collected since his death in 1937 was therefore, until this edition, 175. I have wanted to include all these (whether agreeing with the choice of previous editors on every occasion or not) for the sake of completeness. However, I have placed 6 of Blunden's selection and 9 of Clark's in the Appendix, either because better examples of that kind of poem have since been found, or because, now there is more material to choose from, they did not seem to earn their place in the main body of the text.

To the poems repeated from Blunden and Clark are added 117 poems, hitherto uncollected, from the Archive. From *Severn and Somme* (1917) and *War's Embers* (1919) are included 23 poems, 11 more than in Clark (Blunden included none), to provide a base from which Gurney's development can be observed.

It would hardly be possible, and certainly unfair to Gurney, to print everything he wrote, because of the way he worked. From quite early on (although there may be drafts lost or destroyed, and the exceptions being the 1925 revisions referred to below), it appears that rather than work on an existing poem, he preferred to write a new one on the same theme or incident. Sometimes these poems are sufficiently different to justify printing two ('Crucifix Corner' and 'New Year's Eve'), but he would surely not have published all his attempts; on some of them he writes 'unsuccessful'. The task of an editor is often, in Gurney's case, to choose the most successful from many similar poems; and to ensure that no side of Gurney goes unrepresented.

TEXT

Many poems have several TS versions (as well as Scott MS copies) in which there are minor variations, often a single word, or a line omitted. As these were presumably not typed by Gurney, the guiding principle has been to return to MS source when this is possible. The two previous collections were it seems, taken wholly from TSS; now that more MSS are available it has been possible to check a high proportion of the TSS and they are not always reliable (see examples quoted in the Introduction).

When there is no supporting MS of a TS or printed poem, and there appear to be misreadings of the kind now known to have crept in elsewhere in TSS, changes have been made and noted (e.g. in 'War Books', p.196).

Various typists attempted to regularize Gurney's MS punctuation, which became increasingly a matter of dots, dashes, and semi-colons. When it has been thought helpful the poems have been lightly repunctuated, with only the most significant changes from previously printed versions noted. Most of Gurney's capitalization has been abandoned; some idiosyncratic spellings have been retained, but obvious mis-spellings have been silently corrected, and house style adopted in unimportant instances.

In 1925 (see below, 'Chronology'), Gurney went back to some of his earlier poems and added to them: usually a group of lines at the end, sometimes with additions in the body of the poem. Occasionally these additions are improvements ('The Not-Returning'), sometimes they are not. This is also true of alterations in the text of the poem, which can complicate and obscure what was originally clear. In such cases one of three courses has been followed: (*a*) The later (known or presumed) version has been printed entire, with an asterisk before the additions when appropriate ('Mist on Meadows'). (*b*) The additions have been considered unhelpful, omitted, and placed in the notes ('Looking Out'). (*c*) In a few cases, the earlier lines have been returned to their earlier MS. form, and the added lines which almost form a separate poem, or at least a postscript, printed after an asterisk ('Imitation', 'All Souls' Day'). 'The Not-Returning' is the exception: no space has been placed before the 2-line addition for fear of spoiling the poem.

Titles of poems have been standardized. Double titles retained. Titles have been supplied from other versions, or from first lines, when lacking in original source.

CHRONOLOGY

Gurney dates few poems (other than the Appeals) but they can usefully be put into sections to correspond with the approximate period of composition, although about some poems an element of doubt must remain.

I, II. *Severn and Somme* and *War's Embers* make an obvious first section. There are also poems known to have been written about the *War's Embers* period (1917–19), because of letters, datings, etc. These make a second section.

III. After the publication of *War's Embers* Gurney prepared a third selection, to be called *Rewards of Wonder*. There is a series of TSS in the Archive under that title, to which we can attribute a rough date 1919–20; these make a third section. We have no guarantee that these TSS are in fact the selection as rejected at that time by Sidgwick & Jackson, but from tone and style it seems probable.

IV. The fourth section, 1919–22, contains the work of the most fruitful period. There must be doubt about the dates of some of these poems, as in all the later sections, but what seems certain is that they cannot be dated by internal evidence alone. Poems that describe mental disturbance do not necessarily belong to the asylum period, or even near it. 'What Evil Coil' was noted by Marion Scott as an asylum poem (Gurney may have sent her a copy from Dartford), but it is in a fairly early notebook (64.4) and in early handwriting.

V. Late 1922 marks the beginning of the fifth section, for it was then that Gurney was committed to Barnwood House, where he wrote poems a number of which he signed and dated. A selection of these, when not specifically dated presumed to be of the same period by paper, writing, and tone, are placed together; followed by poems written after he was transferred to Dartford.

1925 is a difficult year chronologically as in other ways (see above, 'Text'). 'Mist on Meadows', the example quoted above of an earlier poem with later additions, has a MS (64.1) of the lines up to the space in the text, but neither MS or TS of the version printed in Blunden and reprinted here. Probably as in other, surviving, examples of TS/MSS, the earlier poem was typed and later altered in handwriting, then possibly retyped. The later lines of this particular poem, as in other examples, darken the mood repetitiously: the poem as printed therefore not only belongs to different periods but to different moods. Each poem of this kind presents its own chronological problems. The principle followed had been to place the poem in an earlier section if the original mood predominates (as with 'Mist on Meadows') and (more rarely) in the 1925 section if the later mood has overtaken the earlier one (as, e.g. with 'Bach').

VI. In 1926 Gurney had another burst of original energy and began again to date some of his poems; these therefore form the sixth section. The last poem of all is not possible to date confidently, though it is late, and is placed where it is for reasons of content.

The Appendix contains two examples of poems of extra-literary interest; and 15 poems included because they were previously collected by Blunden or Clark (see above, 'Selection').

THE NOTES

The notes on individual poems give the following information:

1. Source of poem in this edition (in italics), followed by TS, or MS draft of same version where appropriate.
2. * indicates previously uncollected.
3. Editorial changes, other than minor punctuation (see 'Text', above).
4. If previously collected, a reference to Blunden and/or Clark, as appropriate, followed by TS, their presumed source, in brackets.
5. Other information: dates, previous printings in magazines, major anthology choices, etc.

Many poems are in 2 or 3 MS or TS copies, with minor differences often due to typists' misreadings. 'Version' indicates such minor variations.

'Different version' indicates the same poem (i.e. with same opening and subjects), but substantially rewritten.

'No MS this version' indicates no MS in GA is identical to the text named.

'No original' indicates no TS or MS in GA. Printed versions only known.

ABBREVIATIONS

MS	Throughout refers to Ivor Gurney's handwriting.
Scott MS	Marion Scott's handwritten copies.
IG	Ivor Gurney.
Scott	Marion Scott.
GA	Gurney Archive: the Ivor Gurney Collection, Gloucester Library.
SS	*Severn and Somme.* By Ivor Gurney, Private, of the Gloucesters. London: Sidgwick & Jackson, 1917.
WE	*War's Embers* and other verses, by Ivor Gurney. London: Sidgwick & Jackson, 1919.
RW	*Rewards of Wonder.* Poems of Cotswold, France, London. TS collection (GA 16).
RCM	Royal College of Music, London.
Squire SMP	J. C. Squire: *Selections from Modern Poets.* Secker: London, 1921 and 1924.
Squire YPT	—— *Younger Poets of Today.* Secker: London, 1932.
Haines	'Poems of Ivor Gurney's which appeared in various periodicals between 1915 and 1926.' (30 TS poems, from Robin Haines collection).
Blunden	*Poems by Ivor Gurney.* Principally selected from unpublished manuscripts. With a memoir by Edmund Blunden. Hutchinson: London, 1954. (76 poems.)
EB	Edmund Blunden.
Auden	W. H. Auden: *A Certain World.* A Commonplace Book. Faber & Faber: London, 1971.
Clark	*Poems of Ivor Gurney, 1890–1937.* With an introduction by Edmund Blunden and a Bibliographical Note by Leonard Clark. Chatto & Windus: London, 1973. (140 poems, including 42 from Blunden.)
LC	Leonard Clark.
Hurd	*The Ordeal of Ivor Gurney.* By Michael Hurd. Oxford University Press: Oxford, 1978. (Biography.)
TLS	*The Times Literary Supplement*: six poems by Ivor Gurney, previously unpublished, selected by Geoffrey Grigson. (Coinciding with publication of the biography, with a review by Samuel Hynes.) 13 October 1978.
PJK	P. J. Kavanagh: the present edition.

NOTES

I. *Severn and Somme*

Selected from 46 poems published in 1917. No MSS known of any of these.

Page

31   *To the Poet before Battle*] SS p. 17. Clark. RCM Magazine, 1915. Squire SMP, 1921. Hurd, p. 56.

31   *Strange Service*] SS p. 23. Clark.

32   *The Mother*] SS p. 27. Clark.

32   *Bach and the Sentry*] SS p. 29. Clark.

32   *Song and Pain*] SS p. 36. Clark ('Song of Pain').

33   *Song ('Only the wanderer')*] SS p. 42. Clark. Set to music by IG as 'Severn Meadows'. Hurd, p. 51.

33   *Ballad of the Three Spectres*] SS p. 43. Hurd, p. 115.

34   *Time and the Soldier*] SS p. 45.

35   *After-Glow*] SS p. 47. Clark. Hurd, p. 116.

35   *Praise*] SS p. 49. Clark.

35   *Song of Pain and Beauty*] SS p. 52. ('In Trenches, 1917'). Clark. RCM Magazine, 1917. Squire SMP, 1921.

36   *Requiem*] SS p. 62. Clark. *Faber Book of 20th Century Verse*, ed. Heath-Stubbs/Wright, 1975 (3rd edition).

36   *Pain*] SS p. 66. ('Sonnets 1917. To the Memory of Rupert Brooke').

37   *Servitude*] SS p. 67, as above.

War's Embers

Selected from 49 poems published in 1919.

41   *To His Love*] WE p. 45. Clark. MS draft 55 (32–33) (on army canteen paper). Hurd, p. 117.
     F. W. Harvey, Gloucester poet and early friend of Gurney, was taken prisoner (reported missing) in August 1916.

41   *De Profundis*] WE p. 91. Clark. MS draft 64.5.

42   *Turmut-Hoeing*] WE p. 21. MS 64.9 (St Alban's, Sept. 1918).

43   *Ypres – Minsterworth*] WE p. 33. MS 64.9. Also 'Robecq – Minsterworth' (TS 64.11).

44   *Old Martinmas Eve*] WE p. 48. No MS. Scott MS 64.11.

44   *Companion – North-East Dug-out*] WE p. 56. MS draft 52.1.

45   *The Poplar*] WE p. 76. MS draft 64.5.

46   *The Battalion is now On Rest*] WE p. 86. MS draft 52.1. *The Spectator*, Dec. 1918.

46   *Photographs*] WE p. 87. MS draft 52.1. Hurd, p. 118.

II. 1917–1919

Poems contemporary with *War's Embers*.

51 *The Old City – Gloucester*] *Scott MS* 64.11. Clark (TS 20). No MS. 3
   extra lines printed in Hurd (p. 29) are cancelled in Scott. Scott/LC have
   note: 'written at Buire-au-Bois, July 1917.'

52 *To the Prussians of England*] *TS 20, dated 'Bangour, October 1917'.
   No MS.

53 *Above Ashleworth*] Clark (TS 20). No MS.

53 *Memory, Let All Slip*] *Scott MS* 64.11, with note: 'written at Bangour
   1917'; and line 7 corrected IG. Clark (TS 20).

54 *Song ('My heart makes songs . . .')*] *TS 20. MS draft 52.1.

54 *Song of Urgency*] *Scott MS* 64.11, which has note: 'Seaton Delaval,
   Jan. 1918'. Clark (TS 20). MS draft 52.1.

55 *Excursion*] *Scott MS 53 (45)*. TS 20. MS draft 52.1. 'Hospital Pic-
   tures' group.

55 *Crickley Hill*] *MS 64.9, marked IG: 'Warrington, July 1918.' No TS.
   Scott MS 64.11. Possibly omitted from *War's Embers* by mistake; in
   64.11 is a letter from Marion Scott:

'"Crickley Hill". I am rather doubtful about including this poem, unless it is
rewritten. If you do rewrite, could you make the rhyme pattern of the first verse
agree with the others? At present verse 1 is *ABBACCA* and all the other verses
are *ABABCCB*. I am inclined to think that verse 5 would be better omitted – it
would knit the poem closer.'

At the bottom of her remarks IG has written: 'Please take out'. Whether
he meant the poem or merely the offending stanza is unclear; at all
events, the whole poem went.

56 *O Tree of Pride*] *MS 64.9 only, dated 'St Alban's 1918'.

57 *Equal Mistress*] Clark (TS 21). No MS this version. *Music and Letters*,
   1920.

58 *Crocus Ring*] MS 64.4. Blunden/Clark (TS 12). Scott MS 52.11 has
   note: 'Gloucester 1919.' *Music and Letters*, 1920.

58 *North Woolwich*] MS 64.4. Blunden (TS 12).

59 *The Companions*] MS 64.4. Blunden (TS 18).

60 *Michaelmas*] *MS 64.4. TS 19.

61 *London Dawn*] *MS 64.4. Line 5 'to' inserted from other versions.
   Many different versions. MS 55 (34–5) (longer) printed by Hurd,
   p. 137.

Lines 20, 21: comma moved from after 'million' to after 'clever': PJK.

63 *Tobacco*] MS 64.1. Blunden/Clark (TS 12) has minor changes and
   additional 8 lines:

But by Laventie or Ypres or Arras the thing
Kept heart and soul together, and the mud out of thinking.
There was no end to the goodness, and Raleigh who journeyed
Far over waters to Virginia – and risked life and there did

Things like the heroes' things – but felt want never as we
Carefully guarding the fragments, and finishing the half-spents –
Knew joy never so, nor pain; two hours and miles over sea.
How tell the poetic end and comfort of pain past any sustain?

As an example of the kind of change made by Gurney when he approached an early poem in a later mood, see line 25, where the *London Mercury* version replaces 'A Woodbine breakfast inspiriting the blood' with 'For Woodbine breakfast or the spilling of blood'. (See 'Old Thought', p. 123n. below.) *London Mercury*, 1924. Squire YPT.

63 *Above Maisemore*] Blunden (TS 12). MS 64.1 lacks line 9.

64 *When from the Curve*] *MS 52 (139)*. TS 21. TS has Scott note: 'This poem was written in 1919 or 1920 by Ivor Gurney and he gave me a copy, but would not let it be published in the RCM Magazine because he said it was too intimate.'

64 *There Was Such Beauty*] MS 42.7 (pencil draft). Blunden/Clark (no TS). LC notes: 'Original given to MMS [Marion Scott] by Ivor's mother, June 1939.'
Line 2, full stop added: PJK.

65 *If I Walked Straight Slap*] *TS 21 A. No MS.

65 *Advice*] Clark (TS 21). No MS. *London Mercury*, 1923.

65 *March*] Blunden (TS 18). No MS.

III. *Rewards of Wonder*

Selected from 83 poems in TS collection (GA 16), probably submitted to Sidgwick & Jackson in 1919.

69 *First Time In* ('After the dread tales...')] *TS 16. MS 64.1 is shorter by 4 lines. This notebook has 2 poems on this subject, see (same title) 'The Captain addressed us ...' (p. 85n. below).

69 *La Gorgue*] *MS 64.1. TS 16, with minor changes, has 3 additional lines at end:

God bless the honourers of boy soldiers and the folk generous
Who dwell in light clean houses, and are glad to be thus
Serving France with Love generous, in the light, clean house.

70 *June Night*] *TS 16. No MS this version. Title from MS 64.3.

71 *Blighty*] *TS 16. No MS this version.

71 *The Bargain*] *TS 16. No MS this version.

72 *Songs Come to the Mind*] *TS 16. No MS this version.

73 *That Centre of Old*] *TS 16. No MS this version.

73 *Possessions*] * TS 16. No MS. See 'Sand has the ants' on the same theme (p.98).

74 *Billet*] * TS 16. No MS this version.

74 *The Soaking*] * MS 64.3. TS 16. *London Mercury*, 1934.

75 *I Saw England – July Night*] *TS 16. No MS this version.

75 *First March*] *MS 64.1. Line 16 'the one way not to die' is cancelled and 'the one thought under by' substituted; original reading retained. TS 16 has later changes and added final couplet:

> But words are only words and the snowdrops were such
> Then, as some Bach fugue wonder – so some Winter Tale touch.

76 *What I Will Pay*] *TS 16. No MS this version.

77 *Thoughts on Beethoven*] MS 64.3. Blunden/Clark (title 'Beethoven'); no original this version. *Music and Letters*, 1927.

77 *Laventie*] Blunden (TS 16). No MS this version. Several versions; also similar 'Laventie Front'. Blunden version retained as it improves on earlier MS 64.1, despite the unhelpful last 2 lines added.

79 *The Touchstone – Watching Malvern*] Blunden/Clark (TS 16). No MS this version. Other versions have title 'The Comparison'.

79 *Glimmering Dusk*] *TS 16. No MS this version.

79 *New Year's Eve*] MS 64.3. Clark (TS 16) prints:

> Aveluy and New Year's eve, and the time as tender
> As if green buds grew. In the low West a slender
> Streak of last orange. Guns mostly deadest still.
> And a noise of limbers near, coming down the hill.
> Nothing doing, nothing doing, and a screed to write,
> Candles enough for books, a sleepy delight
> And the warm dug-out, day ended. Nine hours to the light
> There now and then now, one nested down snug,
> A head is enough to read by, and cover up with a rug.
>
> Electric! Clarinet sang of a Hundred Pipers
> (And hush-awe mystery vanishes like tapers
> Of tobacco smoke), there was a great hilarity then.
> Breath and a queer tube magicked sorrow from men.
> Here was no soul's cheat, friends were of love over there –
> How past thought, returning sweet! Yet the soldier must dare.

London Mercury, 1924

80 *Crucifix Corner*] Blunden/Clark (TS 16). No MS this version. Last line corrected from dash to hyphen, as Scott MS 64.11. (Marion Scott's handwritten hyphens were unusually long and often became dashes by typist's misreading. This happened in several Blunden versions, e.g. 'Smudgy Dawn'.)

81 *Darkness Has Cheating Swiftness*] MS 64.3. Clark (TS 16). *London Mercury*, 1933.

81 *Half Dead*] Clark (TS 16). No MS this version. Several very different versions.

82 *Daily—Old Tale*] MS 64.12. Clark (TS 16). *London Mercury*, 1924. Other versions have lines 6–7:

> . . . they sheath a cart
> With iron, I'll sheathe my own – my mind must be made . . .

83 *The Poet Walking*] Clark (TS 16). No MS this version.

83 *Near Vermand*] Clark (TS 16). No MS this version. First 10 lines only in MS 64.1.
Final question mark: PJK.

84 *After War*] MS 64.1. Clark (TS 16).

84 *Brimscombe*] MS 64.3. Clark (TS 16). *London Mercury*, 1924.

84 *Riez Bailleul*] MS 64.1. Clark (TS 16) has minor changes and different fifth stanza:

> So why muse more in the way of poet?
> Lonely – when wine of estaminets
> Was red to the spirit as to the gaze,
> Golden the lamplight and the boys who knew it,
> Poets leave stars then, go human ways.

85 *First Time In* ('*The Captain addressed us . . .*')] Clark (TS 16). No MS this version. MS 64.1 and MS 64.3 are shorter versions; the more sombre ending presumably added later. Gurney went back to several middle-period poems and darkened their mood (see 'Tobacco'). Clark version retained here, with gap before later addition.
See also 'After the dread tales . . .' (same title), p.69n. above.

87 *Canadians*] MS 64.1. Clark (TS 16). *Faber Book of 20th Century Verse*, ed. Heath-Stubbs/Wright, 1975 (3rd edition).

IV. *1919–1922*

Poems placed between the *Rewards of Wonder* collection and IG's committal to Barnwood House in September 1922.

91 *Drachms and Scruples*] MS 64.1. Clark (TS 17). Later TS version titled by IG 'Depression'.
Drachm: pronounced 'dram'.

91 *April Gale*] *TS 21A. No MS.

91 *Personages*] *TS 21A. No MS.

92 *Compensations*] *TS 19. No MS.

92 *April – Dull Afternoon*] *TS 21 A. No MS this version. Titles from MS 64.4 and TS 19.

92 *Silver Birch*] *MS 64.1. TS 17.

93 *The Garden*] *TS 19. No MS. Hurd, p.201.

93 *Tobacco Plant*] Blunden. No original this version.

94 *Mist on Meadows*] Blunden. No original this version. MS 64.1 of first section only.

94 *The Awakening*] Clark (TS 18). No MS this version. Several different versions.

95 *Walking Song*] Clark (TS 21A). No MS.

95 *Cotswold Ways*] MS 64.4 (untitled). Blunden/Clark (no TS this

version). Another version *London Mercury*, 1922. Squire YPT. Hurd, p. 201.

96 *Quiet Talk*] *MS 64.4. TS 18. TLS, 1978.

96 *Water Colours*] MS 64.12. Blunden/Clark (TS 42).

97 *Generations*] MS 64.4. Blunden/Clark (TS 18). Hurd, pp. 5, 202.

97 *Going Out at Dawn*] *MS 64.4 only. TLS, 1978.

98 *Possessions*] *MS 64.4 (no TS this version). *London Mercury*, 1934. See 'France has victory', same theme, p.73.

98 *Changes*] *MS 64.4 (no TS this version). TLS, 1978. Line 3, repunctuated: PJK.

98 *When I Am Covered*] MS 64.4. Blunden/Clark (TS 19). *Music and Letters*, Jan. 1938.

99 *Leckhampton Chimney Has Fallen Down*] Clark (TS 17). No MS this version. Earlier MS 64.1 has line 8: 'Not all the good influences will pass away.'

99 *The Change*] *MS 64.4. TS 19. TLS, 1978.

100 *Stars Sliding*] MS 64.1. Blunden/Clark. TS 42 (2) has extra stanza added in MS:

> But these were less to me had not Beethoven made
> (For Rasoumoffski—his name) a worship of recognition.
> Or Shakespeare, Whitman, not walked night of road and glade –
> To lose their hearts in worship – to wait dawn – feel wind freshen.

100 *Of Grandcourt*] *TS 21. No MS. Hurd (extract), p.94.

101 *Between the Boughs*] Clark (TS 18). No MS.

101 *Rainy Midnight*] *TS 64.11. No MS. TLS, 1978.

102 *The Silent One*] Blunden/Clark. No original this version. Full stops at ends of lines 10 and 14: PJK. Hurd, p. 203.

102 *The Telegraph Post*] MS 64.4. Blunden/Clark (TS 18).

103 *Fragment*] *MS 64.4. TS 19. TLS, 1978.

103 *The Lock Keeper*] MS 55 (8), with slight punctuation changes: PJK. Blunden/Clark (TS 12). Hurd, p.47, also from MS 55. There is a much shorter poem with the same title, 'to the memory of Edward Thomas', in *War's Embers* (not included here).

106 *Longford Dawns*] *MS 64.4. TS 17. Hurd, p.31.

106 *London*] *MS 64.1. TS 17.

107 *Brown Earth Look*] MS 64.1. Clark (TS 17).

107 *Time to Come*] *MS 55(31). TS 19. Hurd, p.211. The church of St Nicholas is a prominent Gloucester landmark.

108 *Midnight*] *MS 64.1. TS 17. Hurd, p.106.

108 *Saturday's Comings*] MS 64.4. Blunden (TS 12).

109 *Song ('O were there . . .')*] *MS 64.4. TS 18.

109 *Behind the Line*] MS 64.1. Line 10 'fear' altered in MS to 'moan'.

Original reading restored for sake of rhyme. Blunden/Clark (no TS this version). TS 42.8 has extra stanza added in MS:

But I hope, still, they remember us kindly, and me
Sitting watching, silent in a talking company.
To understand Europe, and the great pride of France that Valmy proved.
And as men of Valmy I too have watched faces, – land's faces and loved.

110 *We Who Praise Poets*] *MS 64.4. TS 18. MS 64.12 has title 'Apprentices'.

110 *Yesterday Lost*] MS 64.4. Clark (TS 17). MS 64.1 has title 'The Miracles'.

111 *On the Night*] *MS 64.4. TS 19.

111 *Robecq Again*] MS 64.1. Blunden/Clark (no original this version) have a last line not in MS: 'O Margaret, your music saved me. I also made beauty.' *London Mercury*, 1934.

112 *Towards Lillers*] MS 64.1. Clark (TS 17). *London Mercury* (LC note) as two poems. Last 14 lines are also in TS 17 as a separate poem, with title written by IG: 'Aeroplanes Over Aubers'. However, these lines are on facing page of MS notebook, untitled, and appear to follow on; in 64.1 IG almost invariably heads a new poem with a title. Possibly he separated the two parts as an afterthought. See 'Near Vermand' (p.83) for an opposite case, treated as separate poems.

113 *The Hoe Scrapes Earth*] MS 64.4. Clark (TS 18). *Music and Letters*, Jan. 1938.

113 *Schubert*] MS 64.1. Clark (TS 17). Scribbled in pencil in an otherwise clear, ink-written notebook. Prose?

114 *Imitation*] MS 64.1. Clark (TS/MS 17). Last stanza not in 64.1, but added in MS to TS 17. IG in MS 64.1 appears to try rhythmical notation in lines 9–10: '. . . To a . smooth going / And . flowing . . .'.

115 *Old Dreams*] MS 64.1. Blunden/Clark (TS 17). *London Mercury*, 1933.

115 *Looking Out*] *MS 64.1. TS 17 has added MS stanza:

Which were of War
The only comfort, the agonized
After . . . that Duty stilled
And the Dawn surprised.

116 *Poem*] MS 64.1. Blunden/Clark (no TS): title 'Horror Follows Horror'. Line 6 question mark: PJK.

116 *East Wind*] MS 64.1. Clark (TS 17).

117 *The Escape*] Clark (TS/MS 17). Repunctuated, partly from earlier MS 64.1: PJK.

117 *On Foscombe Hill*] MS 64.1. Clark (TS 17).

117 *Autumn's Flame*] MS 64.1. Clark (TS 17).

118 *Up There*] Clark (TS/MS 17). Line 5 'pigsties' and line 8 'topple of crests' corrected from MS 64.1, which does not include line 11.

118 *The Sea Borders*] Clark (TS 18). No MS. Line 16 omitted in Clark.

119 *The Dearness of Common Things*] MS 64.4. Clark (TS 18). Another TS ends three lines earlier, on 'curves'.

120 *Friendly Are Meadows*] MS 64.3. Blunden (no original) prints:

> Friendly are meadows when the sun's gone down in
> And no bright colour spoils the broad green of grey,
> And one's eyes rest looking to Cotswold away, the northline away,
> Under cloud ceilings whorled, and most largely fashioned
> With seventeenth-century curves of the tombstone way –
> A day of softnesses, of comfort of no false din.
> Sorrel makes rusty rest for the eyes, and the worn path
> Brave elms, and stiles, willows by dyked water-run
> North-France general look, and a sort of bath
> Of freshness – a light wrap of comfortableness
> Over one's being, a sense of strings music begun –
> A slow gradual symphony of worthiness –
> Quartets dreamed of perfection achieved masterless,
> As by Robecq I dreamed them, and to Estaires gone.
> But this is Cotswold, Severn; when these go stale
> The universal and wide decree shall fail –
> England, her natural love shall fall to be
> The admirer of the strange false thing – the freak of beauty
> Or strength – a rainbow or eclipse – or lightening riven tree,
> And Elizabethans be no more remembered for plain truth and glory.

This, certainly a later version, is a perfect example of Gurney off-form, returning to an earlier poem and blurring it by bringing in two preoccupations which do not belong to the original poem: war-time France and the Elizabethans.

120 *Andromeda over Tewksbury*] MS 64.4. Clark (TS 18).

121 *The Bare Line of the Hill*] MS 64.4. Clark (TS 18). Some added punctuation: PJK.

122 *Had I a Song*] MS 64.4. Clark (TS 18). Hurd, p. 193.

122 *Quiet Fireshine*] *MS 64.1. TS 16 has two added MS lines:

> Yet turning to music for duty, making black or white
> To achieve beauty like poplar, or stark strength like oak.

123 *The High Hills*] MS 64.1. Blunden/Clark (no TS). Auden, *A Certain World*, 1971.

123 *Old Thought*] *MS 64.1. TS 17 has last line changed in MS to: 'In my mind. White Cotswold, with the breathing earth, and leaves hurting, bloodwet.' An example of IG returning to an earlier poem and changing its mood. (See 'Tobacco', p. 63n. above)

124 *Kettle Song*] *MS 64.1. TS 17.

124 *Hedges*] MS 64.1. Clark (TS 18).

124 *When March Blows*] Clark (TS 18). MS 64.1 has last line without 'infinite', which is added in MS to TS 18. *London Mercury*, 1934.

125 *All Souls' Day 1921*] MS 64.1. Clark (TS/MS 17). Last verse, not in MS

64.1, added (1925?) in MS to TS 17, retained here after gap. Title from TS.

125 *Sonnet to J. S. Bach's Memory*] Clark (TS 21). No MS. *RCM Magazine*, 1938; also (Scott note) *Daily Telegraph* (edited version).

126 *Song* ('*Past my window . . .*')] Blunden/Clark. No original. Possibly early.

126 *Kilns*] Blunden. No original this version. Auden, *A Certain World*, 1971.

127 *George Chapman – The Iliad*] *MS 64.1. TS 17.

128 *The Cloud*] Blunden/Clark. No original this version. Punctuated from shorter MS 64.3. *London Mercury*, 1924.

129 *Early Spring Dawn*] MS 64.1. Blunden/Clark (no TS).

129 *Tewkesbury*] MS 64.12. Blunden/Clark (TS Haines). *Gloucester Journal*, June 1922 (cutting in GA 12).
Line 8 'where a cricketer was born':(?) A. E. Dipper (1887–1945), Glos. and England, a great local character.

130 *On a Two-Hundredth Birthday*] Blunden (TS Haines). No MS. *Gloucester Journal* (bi-centenary), 1922.

131 *Clay*] MS 64.4. Blunden (TS 12).

131 *Wandering Thoughts*] MS 64.4. Blunden (TS 12).

131 *Larches*] MS 64.1. Blunden (no original this version). Auden, *A Certain World*, 1971 (first 8 lines).

132 *Near Vermand*] MS 64.1. Blunden/Clark (no original this version) has lines 8–9 defective: 'Where April is pattern of living not merely guest pressed. / And we were in forced marches after an enemy.'; and 6 extra lines after 'racks':

> Winds are driving rain sheets in white deep lines over
> Country to Malvern perhaps, but what use to that
> Body which cannot be of spirit the mover,
> And is still, when swift speed is right to be at.
> Clean life is round, wind in elms, driving glorious
> To the night hills, when October is friendly and furious.

In MS 64.1 'racks' is the last word on the page. These extra lines, untitled and incomplete, are overleaf in dissimilar writing with a different pen.

133 *The Bronze Sounding*] Blunden/Clark (no original this version). MS 64.1 lacks last line.

133 *February Dawn*] Blunden/Clark (TS 60). No MS.

134 *Moments*] MS 64.4. Clark (TS 19).

134 *Remembrances*] *MS 64.1. TS 17.

135 *Early Winter*] MS 64.10. Reworking of an earlier love poem. Blunden/ Clark ('I Love Chrysanthemums') (TS 12) print:

> I love chrysanthemums and winter jasmine
> Clustering lichened walls a century old,

Ivied windows that the sun peeps in
When dawn an hour gone sees the level gold.
But for my Love, Sweet William, snowdrops, pansies,
To else she is cold.

And all the host of tiny or mighty things
Scattered by April, daring Autumn frost.
Or of man's hand scarcely her imaginings
Touch, being save to these three careless almost
And save to me. This knowing should I envy
Princes of proudest cost?

135 *The Valley Farm*] *MS 64.4. TS 18.

136 *Winter Has Clouds*] *MS 64.4. TS 19.
     Enyopean: formation from Enyo, Greek goddess of war(?).

136 *The Dark Tree*] *MS 64.4. TS 19.

136 *Felling a Tree*] *TS 21. No MS this version.

139 *The Noble Wars of Troy*] *TS 21. No MS this version.

139 *The County's Bastion*] *TS 21. No MS this version.

140 *Roads—Those Roads*] *Blunden/Clark*. No original this version.

140 *Strange Hells*] Scott MS 64.11. No MS this version. Blunden (TS 12).
     The Oxford Book of Twentieth Century Verse, ed. Philip Larkin,
     1973.

141 *The Songs I Had*] MS 64.4. Blunden/Clark (TS 18). An example of the
     difficulty of dating: TS 18 has note 'written at Dartford', i.e. after
     1922, but MS notebook 64.4 almost certainly precedes that date, and
     its first part, where this poem is found, certainly does. See 'What Evil
     Coil' (p. 146). TS 42.2 has 2 last lines as: 'Well to go quiet/Into the
     night.'

141 *From the Meadows – The Abbey*] *Blunden*. No original. Date uncer-
     tain.

142 *Looking Up There*] *Clark* (TS/MS 17). Line 4 'seemed' for Clark
     'seem', from MS 64.1, which lacks last line, added in MS to TS 17.

142 *Townshend*] *Blunden/Clark* (no original this version).

143 *Smudgy Dawn*] *Blunden*. No MS this version. TS 12. Clark (TS 66)
     prints first 10 lines with another poem as second part. *London Mer-
     cury,* 1924. Squire SMP, 1924.

144 *Thomas Heywood*] *Clark* (TS 17). No MS this version. Lines 11–12
     repunctuated: PJK.

144 *Lovely Playthings*] MS 64.12. Blunden (TS 64.12).

145 *Schubert*] *Blunden/Clark* (TS/MS 42.7 (3)). Several different versions.
     Music and Letters, 1925.

145 *By Severn*] See Corrigenda p. 244.

146 *The Not-Returning*] MS 64.1. Blunden/Clark (no original this version).
     Last 2 lines, not in MS, from Blunden/Clark: example of a later
     addition which is an improvement.

146 *What Evil Coil*] MS 64.4. Blunden/Clark (TS 18). TS has note: 'written at Dartford', copied by LC. From MS 64.4, this would seem unlikely; the notebook is marked by IG with a Gloucestershire address, contains poems dated 1919, and has in it no asylum material. See 'The Songs I Had', p. 141 above. Hurd, p. 162.

147 *Swift and Slow*] * MS 64.4. TS 18.

147 *Looking There*] TS/MS 17. Clark. MS 64.1 has 1st 8 lines only. Example of poem altered in 1925 (?), placed earlier.

148 *When the Body Might Free*] MS 64.1. Blunden/Clark (TS 17). *London Mercury*, 1934.

149 *In the Old Time*] MS 64.4. Clark (TS 19).

149 *Sonnet – September 1922*] MS 15.7 (2–1). Blunden/Clark (TS 42).

V. September 1922–1925

Poems written in asylums.

153 *There Is a Man*] * MS 15 (78) only. Marked by IG 'Barnwood House, Gloucester'. Gurney was confined in Barnwood Mental Hospital between September and December 1922, before being transferred, for the rest of his life, to Dartford. This is therefore one of his first descriptions of his fate, his conditions, the relief to be found in writing ('The act of writing is a distraction in madness' he later noted), and an attempt to describe his mental condition itself. To this period also belong the next 13 poems, selected from perhaps three times as many, greatly varying in quality, written in pencil on apparently the same lined paper torn from a block.

153 *The Incense Bearers*] * MS 15 (50) only. Barnwood. 5th verse: uncompanied (*sic*).

154 *There Have Been Anguishes*] * MS 64.12 only. Barnwood.

155 *Riez Bailleul*] * MS 64.12 only. Barnwood.

155 *Old Tunes*] MS 64.12. Clark (TS 21A), with note: 'written Oct. 1922'. Barnwood.

156 *The Shame*] MS 64.12. Clark (TS 21). Barnwood.

156 *To God*] MS 15 (86). Line 11 'Orders' for 'orders': PJK. IG has 'is' before 'orders', presumably military 'Orders of the Day' intended. Clark (TS 21A). Barnwood. Hurd, p. 162.

157 *On Somme*] *MS 64.12 only. Barnwood.

157 *After 'The Penny Whistle'*] *MS 64.12 only. Barnwood. Similar in rhythm and tone to 'The Penny Whistle' by Edward Thomas; hence title?

158 *The Golden Age*] *MS 64.12 only. Barnwood.

158 *The Interview*] *MS 15 (243) (2) only. Barnwood.

160 *A Wish*] *MS 15 (235) only. Barnwood.

160 *Hazlitt*] *MS 64.12 only. Barnwood.

161 *Hedger*] *MS 15 (47) only. Last in Barnwood group.

162 *Memory*] *MS 64.7 only. Title from MS 64.8, a different version.

162 *Song* ('I had a girl's fancies')] *MS 64.7. TS 21.

163 *The Mangel-Bury*] *MS 64.7 only.

163 *Cut Flowers*] *MS 44 (51) only. In pencil, signed 'I. B. Gurney, Stone House, Dartford, Kent. Appealing for Chance of Death. Pains of Life worse than Death.'

165 *The Dream*] *MS 44 (49) only. 'For the London Metropolitan Police Force. Praying for Release or Death.'

165 *War Poet*] *MS 44 (165–6) only.

167 *The Depths*] *MS 64.10. MS 52 ('Sodden Depths') different version.

167 *While I Write*] *MS 64.7. MS 64.8 different version.

168 *It Is Winter*] *MS 64.8 only.

168 *Prelude*] * MS 64.7 only, this version.

170 *Farewell*] *MS 53 (46) only. Page finishes '. . . one touch to dwell on.' Next 4 lines sideways in margin; last 3 lines on verso.

171 *It Is Near Toussaints*] *MS 53 (44) only. From a booklet of exercise-book pages.

171 *The Storm at Night*] *MS 53 (44) only. From same booklet as above.

172 *The Battle*] Clark (TS 21A). No MS. This and the following 5 poems are from a TS set headed 'Memories of Honour. March 1925'. (No MSS.) Placed here for that reason; possibly earlier.

172 *Regrets After Death*] *TS 21A. No MS. Line 8: 'more' added: PJK.

173 *Serenade*] Clark (TS 21A). No MS.

173 *Butchers and Tombs*] *TS 21A. No MS. Hurd, p. 203.

174 *Don Juan in Hell*] Blunden (no original; TS listed 21A).

174 *The Bohemians*] Blunden (no original; TS listed 21A). Repunctuated at end of lines 4, 7, 11, 16: PJK. Hurd, p. 90.

175 *Autumn*] *MS 1 only. (Red MS notebook, dated 1925.)

175 *Signallers*] *MS 1 only. As above.

176 *To Y*] *MS 1 only. As above. 'Hauracourt' uncertain reading.

177 *Portraits*] *TS 21A. No MS. From a TS group of (7) poems headed 'Six Poems of the North American States' among others dated 1925.

177 *The New Poet*] Clark (TS 21A). No MS. From same group as above.

178 *To Long Island First*] *TS 21A. No MS. From TS group headed 'Poems to the States. March 1925'. Line 14 'Mannahattan' (as with Whitman and elsewhere in Gurney) changed from 'Manhattan': PJK.

179 *Walt Whitman*] *TS 21A. No MS. From TS group headed 'In Praise of Poets. Poems of the States'.

179 *Henry David Thoreau*] *TS 21A. No MS. From same group as above.

180 *Washington Irving*] *TS 21A. No MS. From same group as above. Line 8 changed to usual Gurney version, 'Mannahattan': PJK (as in 'To Long Island First', p. 178 above).

180 *Masterpiece*] *MS 44 (189–191) only.

181 *An Appeal for Death*] *TS 21A. No MS.

182 *The Betrayal*] *TS 18. No MS.

183 *Bach–Under Torment*] TS/MS 17. Clark. MS 64.1 has first 8 lines only. Lines after gap are later additions. Included in this section as later mood dominates. IG's italics.

183 *The Lightning Storm*] Blunden (TS 42). No MS.

184 *Snow*] Scott MS 64.11, dated by her 2nd Jan. 1925. No other MS. Clark (TS 18). Placed here because of Scott dating; probably earlier.

185 *To Clare*] *MS 64.12 only. Successful example of Gurney's dozens of Appeals, written on small sheets of paper folded into booklets.

186 *First Poem*] MS 64.2. Blunden/Clark (TS 21A). Quoted by EB in his Introduction. The first poem of 64.2, a notebook marked by Gurney 'The Book of Five Makings. Feb. 1925 (in torture)'. The 10 poems selected from it are printed here in a sequence which concludes with the last poem of the notebook, also quoted by EB: 'There is nothing for me, Poetry, who was the child of Joy.'

187 *Like Hebridean*] MS 64.2. Blunden (TS 12).

187 *The Coin*] MS 64.2, one of 2 different versions in this notebook. Clark (TS 21) prints the other:

> It is hard to guess tales at once from sight of a thing,
> Suddenly brought to the light, though one may have blood
> Of Rome, all instinct, and quick to the makers' mood
> So I could not tell, Constantine's coin, being up ploughed:
> What manner of man had lost it, with what regretting,
> And not till music began in my mind it seemed
> Possible to find out from a heart that dreamed
> Day long of Rome, majesty and mildness in setting
> Of Crickley curves against Severn, and clouds that streamed.
> So though it might have been the farmer that had lost,
> Or mere private from the hillside missing beyond his cost
> The casually* let fall coin that not till now had gleamed
> Above the shear of the plough, shown in the rubble of cutting.
> Him I might have saluted, or round his shoulders
> Put my arm – now could not be imagined, the horses' surges
> Went up and down the field, great bodies at strength held.
> And the coin given me lay in my pocket, urges
> Continual to take out the thing, and watch its so bold
> Countenance of an Emperor, dust with all his friends that were,
> But this symbol suddenly gathered from the many coloured mould.
>
>   * (LC 'Casualty' a typist's misreading.)

188 *Varennes*] * MS 64.2 only. Clear until line 16 ('. . . Six Platoon ever in mind.'). At this point there is an insertion mark on the opposite page,

below an otherwise cancelled draft. Taken literally this would demand the omission of lines 17–18; but these mark and explain the change of mood in the poem and have therefore been retained. Last line added in pencil to ink draft. A marginal note ('Loved') added by line 21.

189 *Epitaph on a Young Child*] MS 64.2. Blunden/Clark (TS 12). Line 12 in MS has '. . . shall yet be mystic' with 'yet' deleted in pencil.

189 *Christopher Marlowe*] MS 64.2. Blunden/Clark (TS 12). 2 lines on opposite page of MS may be marked for insertion after line 7 ('a loved Germany'): 'Gloucester will send heart out to like Canterbury./In the makers heart was some likeness of clear striving.'

190 *Song of Autumn*] * MS 64.2. TS 21.

191 *The Nightingales*] * MS 64.2. TS 21.

191 *Dawns I Have Seen*] * MS 64.2. TS '21.

192 *The Last of the Book*] See Corrigenda p. 244.

193 *St Sylvester's Night*] Blunden (TS 60). No MS.

193 *The Poets of My County*] Clark (TS 21). No MS.

194 *Gloucester*] Clark (TS 18). No MS. Line 8, full stop at end of stanza omitted: PJK. Date uncertain; possibly later.
　　Foreigners: non-native flowers, as opposed to the 'princesses' (daffodils?). See 'Early Winter', p. 135, for same idea.

194 *The Love Song*] Blunden/Clark (TS 18). No MS. TS has note: '1925'.

195 *Small Chubby Dams*] Blunden (no original this version). MS 64.3 is a different version, in a notebook marked by IG: '1921–22. Corrected 1925'.

195 *Of Cruelty*] Blunden (no original this version). The different version 'Of Garden Stuff' in 64.3 is less successful.

196 *War Books*] Blunden (no original). Lines 10–11 in Blunden are:
There we wrote – Corbie Ridge – or in Gonnehem at rest
Or Fauquissart or world's death songs, ever the best.
Last 'or' a possible typing error, changed to 'our': PJK. Hurd, p. 191.

196 *For Mercy of Death*] Clark (TS 21A). No MS.

197 *Hell's Prayer*] Clark (TSS 42.2 and 65). No MS. TS 65 differs from TS 42 in three words: line 10 'tones' (42 'times'); line 11 'oaks' (42 'oaths'); line 16 'buried' (42 'burned') – all likely misreadings followed by LC. While the first two ('times' and 'oaths') seem clearly better in TS 42, 'buried' from TS 65 seems preferable in tense and meaning and has been retained.
Last line repunctuated: PJK.

198 *To Crickley*] Clark (TS 12). No MS. Final quotation marks closed: PJK.

199 *The Coppice*] * TS 18. No MS.

199 *The Elements*] Clark (TS 21). No MS. All between brackets probably later additions.

200 *December 30th*] Clark (TS 18). No MS. Line 17 'Brightens' from TS 60. Line 23, final ?: PJK.

201 *Poem for End*] Blunden/Clark (no original). No indication of date. Placed by EB as final poem in his selection.

VI. *1926 and after*

Late asylum poems.

205 *Music Room*] * MS 64.10 only. MS marked IG '1919–1926'.

205 *I Read Now So*] * MS 64.12. TS 20. This and the following poems, up to the last two in this section, are selected from over 180 MSS in similar hand-writing on a few recognizable types of paper, some dated IG 'September 1926'. (The first 6 are from 45 on thick pages from a block, watermarked 'Mimosa'.)

206 *Poets' Affection*] MS 64.12, signed IG 'Sept. 7th, 1926'. Clark (TS 18).

206 *Friend of the Mists*] MS 64.12. Clark (TS 18).

207 *Traffic in Sheets*] MS 64.12. Clark (TS 18). Title words recall Shakespeare's 'The Winter's Tale', IV, iii, to which IG often refers.

207 *The Shelter from the Storm*] MS 64.12. Clark (TS 20).

208 *The Two*] * MS 64.12. TS 18.

208 *The Pedlar's Song*] MS 64.12. Blunden (no TS, listed 20).

209 *Going Outwards*] * MS 64.12. TS 20.

210 *Musers Afar Will Say*] *MS 64.12. TS 20.

210 *December Evening*] *MS 64.12. TS 20. Line 10, bracket closed: PJK.

211 *No, Come Not, Swallows*] MS 64.12. Blunden (no TS).

211 *The Dancers*] MS 64.12. Clark (TS 20).

212 *I Would Not Rest*] MS 64.12. Clark (TS 20).

212 *If I Shall Praise*] *MS 64.12 only. Title supplied: PJK.

213 *The Pleasance Window*] MS 64.12, signed IG '24–25 September 1926'. Clark (TS 65).

214 *Sea-Marge*] MS 64.12. Blunden (no TS, listed 20).

214 *What Was Dear*] MS 64.12. Blunden (no TS, listed 20).

215 *Rather I Would . . .*] * MS 64.12 only. TS listed 20.

215 *This Christmas Morning*] MS 64.12. Clark (TS 20). Title supplied: PJK.

215 *Wood Gathering*] MS 64.12. Clark (TS 20).

216 *The House of Stone*] * MS 64.12. TS 20.

216 *The Bridge*] *MS 64.12. TS 20.

217 *The Poet*] *MS 64.12. TS 20.

217 *Near Spring*] MS 64.12. Blunden (no TS).

218 *Where the Mire*] * MS 64.12. TS 20.

218 *The Wood of August*] MS 64.12. Clark (TS 20). In line 5 all versions have 'swerve'; rhyme as well as grammar seem to justify 'swerves': PJK.

219 *In December*] MS 64.12. Clark (TS 20). Title supplied: PJK.

219 *The Old Walnut*] MS 64.12. Clark (TS 20). Title supplied: PJK.

220 *Here, If Forlorn*] MS 42.5. Blunden (TS 42.2). No title in MS.

220 *Soft Rain*] * MS 15 (270). TS 18, with note 'RCM Magazine 1938, written at Dartford 1926 or 27'.

220 *The Wind*] * MS 15 (156) only. Signed IG 'Valentine Fane' (unidentified). Written on the back of an Oxford University Press letterhead, dated March 6th, 1929. On this evidence, the latest poem of Gurney's that we have, if, that is, it is composed by him.

221 *As They Draw to a Close*] * MS 15 (231) only. A Whitman title from his 'Leaves of Grass'. Gurney wrote much verse in the manner of Walt Whitman, including his own 'Leaves of Grass' referred to here, of which there are many fragments in GA. This is signed: 'Walt Whitman./ (Ivor Gurney here./probably all-altering/F W Harvey's *Ironical* work)'. That it is an apologia for himself is confirmed, if it needed to be, by his last remark about irony. Date uncertain.

CORRIGENDA

145 *By Severn*] *Blunden*. No original this version. Line 15: 'meeding' from MS 64.3. Repunctuated: PJK.

192 *The Last of the Book*] MS 64.2. Blunden (preface; 1st line 'for my Poetry')/Clark (title 'There Is Nothing'); no TS. Lines 1, 12 repunctuated: PJK.

APPENDIX

I Saw French Once

I saw French once – he was South Africa cavalry –
And a good leader and a successful, clever one to me.
A knight of Romance – for the knight of Veldt was about him
Who outwitted Boers – few could – who laid traps and got him.
Egypt and Aldershot – Commander of the Forces
And Mons Leader – and Ypres of the Worcestershires.
Now Captain of Deal Castle – so my book advises.
We were paraded for six mortal long hours of shoulders strain
And after hours of cleaning up of leather and brasses –
(O! never, never may such trial be on soldiers again!)
And it was winter of weather and bitter chill,
Outside of Tidworth on a barren chalk slope – Wiltshire Hill.
Six long hours we were frozen with heavy packs –
Brasses cleaned bright, biscuits in haversacks.
At last horses appeared hours late, and a Marshal
Dismounted, our shoulders so laden we were impartial
Whether he shot or praised us – Whether France of the Line
Or soft fatigues at Rouen or Abbeville or Boulogne.
Slow along the ranks of stiff boys pained past right use
Egypt and Veldt – Ulster – Mons, Ypres came
And none to shout out of Ypres or cry his name –
Hell's pain and silence gripping our shoulders hard
And none speaking – all stiff – in the knifed edged keen blast.
He neared me (Police used electricity) Ypres neared me
The praises of Worcestershires, Joffre's companion Captain he
Who the Médaille-Militaire – the soldier known of France wore,
Scanned me, racked of my shoulders, with kind fixed face
Passed, to such other tormented ones, pain-kept-in-place
To stare so – and be satisfied with these young Gloucesters
Who joined to serve, should have long ago seen Armentières,
As Ypres, but at least Richebourg or near Arras.
But they would not send – youth kept us rotting in a town
Easy and discipline worried – better by far over by Ovillers –

245

Or Béthune – or St Omer – or Lys, Scarpe, those rivers
To keep a line better than march by meadow and down.
Chelmsford army training to bitterness heart turning
Without an honour – or a use – and such drear bad days
Without body's use, or spirit's use – kept still to rot and laze,
Save when some long route march set our shoulders burning
Blistered our heels – and for one day made body tired.
Anyway, on the chill slope we saw Lord French, Commander on the hill
Of short turf, and knew History and were nearer History
Soon for scarred France – to find what Chance was to be feared,
To leave those damned Huts and fall men in shell blast and shots.
To live belt-hungry – to freeze close in narrow cuts
Of trenches – to go desperate by barbed wire and stakes
And (fall not) keep an honour by the steel and the feel
Of the rifle wood kept hard in the clutch of the fingers, blood pale
The coming of French after freezing so long on the slope.
Tidworth was Hell – men got Blighties – at least equal hope.
This was March – in May we were overseas at La Gorgue –
And the Welshmen took us, and were kind, past our hoping mind –
Signallers found romance past believing of War's chance.
But the leader of Mons we had seen, and of History a mien,
South Africa and the first days, Mons, Ypres and between.

What's In Time

What's in Time that it should frighten
The newborn child just awaken
Out of some other life – from a woman's loins?
What's in Time, it should cry for its fear and pains?
The first pains, and the new breathing.
The strange coming to personality,
The growing boy, the mother leaving,
Insurrection and desire to be one's own and free,
The birth of creation in the heart, the touch of poetry.

'But these are not to be feared, they grow
Equal with use – as I and the world know!'
The coming to making and the finding the
Noblest string needs mastery.
The waking next morning to one's own scorning –
Dead leaves instead of the high unwondered tree.

To return, and labour and pain, and be
Broken by torture, in labour, to last effort.
And, the lover of God, be turned to smut
Because one man needed an evil gold;
And clean with hunger, dirted with eating,
Because some devil had mistaken in betting.
To make the time's greatest song, and be given
Dust on the covers for all the pain striven.
To cast out a shout of love to a far
Country, long loved, and be given bare
Silence, and cold unhonouring there.
'This is enough to break the heart
Of David the King set royal apart
The singer, the soldier, the maker of laws,
So he took Bathsheba to his hurt
And healed a heart-terror against cause
Of allowing.'
　　'True David had many sorrows,
Care hurt his forehead with lasting furrows.
I cured some bearing the fire and steel
Of a hundred cannons battering wheel against wheel,
Battering huge violence down from the air,
With raining steel, and furious red fire
Hurtle of mass, Hell's insurrection furious.
Weight of unthought horror roused courage there.'
'You make me curious.'

'Yes, and the Death song men had waited
A thousand years for, and the all wanted
Hunger of home song wrote I in War. . . .
The song of a thousand years of passing,
And an age's song of home-despairing.
And lay in the darkness up against wires,
Watching the dark and the enemy's fires,
Feeling the bullets whizz past my tin helmet
(The Gloucesters impatient behind me) and set
Cold trembling fingers at order spoken
Against the damned wires, and to find them unbroken.
And to sing Homelove at Caulaincourt.
To praise faith from Aubers to Ypres there,
And Wenlock Edge over Arras chalk looking.
To cough gas, and get recommended and be
Stopped of shoving by Richebourg, wading

Three feet of water past fire to the bones
For Hell cold east of snow-sleeting Chaulnes,
Missed death, at Fauquissart, and St Julien –
Sniped to a hair's-breadth souvenir-hunting
At Ypres – and frightened a hundred ways
Through all hours – of all summer and winter days.
A soldier is all to be honoured surely?'

They gave me to Hell black torture as surely
As God – if He judge them – shall judge for it.
They tortured my last nerve, and tortured my wit.
True later I wrote the noblest poem of Cities
And music the instinct of all the Pities
Tragedy, wonder, and of all home beauties
That Severn or Cotswold showed of their merely
Wonderful half-hour changes of watches
From Bredon to Berkeley, and Crickley to Staunton –
Loveliest Country lost to all honoured Duties. . . .
'But England's honour was assured of old blood
And sacrifice by Crecy and by Vermand wood. . . .
Tears of poets, masters of music their gladness,
And if She turned, like this fiend to madness
Scotland, Scotland surely would cry or hear her God!

'I wrote Her best songs, and some verses.
I loved Her writers as men love their own born
Children from loins of love called for love's service.
And Ireland I loved like my heart's current.
Songs made I worthy of Aran or Narain Island,
Mused poetry with Synge, or with "Baile's Strand"
Made my thought fine when my own thought failed,
Heard Deirdre and Emir Conal call my command.
Ireland I loved, served Her as few have proved.
Tara, Connemara, Antrim, Mayo, left me
To be the easy prey of a Hell unaccountably
Let to the light free.'

'And Wales?'

'Welsh soldiers received us with tales
And songs, and courtesy like the Earth's and I
Have made Her great Song; and loved Her vales
And Mountains, Her song and poetry –
Heard voices that mazed and that magicked me.'

The virtue is gone out of land and water
Houlihan's Daughter nor Britain's Daughter,
Nor Daughter of Gael, or West Severn lover
Have friended me, nor with steel nor freedom –
Past High God to most high God against me
Men have offended – their wives are whores
For their men's baseness not cast out of doors.
And the bastards born of their lust's embraces
Are hated of Hell for their concealing faces
Of shame better dead, and life better still,
A stuff of body lecherous from foul earth brought by will
Of evil to enact, or craft, or to endure all evil.
Cowards to live when Death cries to their courages . . .
And the scared separate Four-land honour of Islands –
The smut of vile branding their forehead brands.
Earth looks up, Heaven cowers to curse.
The water shrinks at them, the air with them withers.
Who leave a soldier, and a war poet,
A maker and lover, in Hell, for doubt
Whether Hell's evil is cured by Hell's repentance, or if
Their fathers with steel rose insurrections together
To risk a soul out of body so England
Should not have such dung guilt stuck to Her hand.
And ran upon Death so England should not be whored
By the lyingest devil, and lewdest with a word
Of anger – and no more, and rushed on any sword.

'You are in a temper.'
'I am.'
God curse for cowards; take honour and all damn
For bastards out of good blood, last leaving of diseases,
The rulers of England, lost in corruptions and increases
All mean, foul things they lap up like (powderless) jam –
While the cheated dead cry, unknowing, 'Eadem Semper'.

The Dance of the September Birds

O! how the maidens sing in the dance of the birds!
This is their delight. Robin and linnet now sing.
A childlike grace of dancing,
Most ancient words.

Hark, do you hear Europe's phrase ring?
'Lord, Lover'.
So, with the flocks of the world's meadows
All air's songs they sing,
The shrill and lonely plover,
Lark's chanting,
And all poetry's hid shadows,
The tiniest reference in heraldic stanzas they
Have caught and sing,
'They are all our friends'.
O, hear the sweep of sound pass the crest of the
    meadows!
They sing like priests at amends.
High up, low; as birds fly; voices ring.
The silver
Of the hallowed morn on them droop in pleasure.

The Anger of Samson

What! with bad Orchestras and bad audiences
To say immortal things as if all free
(As in Quartetts). To please the unskilled as the dunces,
And yet translate his own beliefs, or of Shakespeare
Into a shape of sound to satisfy the imaginary
Hope? Long labour of scoring, pages on long pages
Insignificant means, infinitely dreary in the
Doing; and after all only ten, twelve seconds to be
In sounding; and received as right by such hearer's fear,
Politeness; faint liking brought to his concerts. Chances,
Certainties shameful against him. Now the praises
Of truth in clearer making are forgotten; men choose
The sounding elaborate structure than the reticences
Of quieter lonely things . . . So Ries ears violently
Were boxed; and Prima Donnas got impolitenesses
Furiously at last said . . . at midnight, solitary
Anger died down to sorrow; still some part of his clear
Behest he had accomplished — and men grew wiser . . .
Pain had balances.

O Tan-Faced Prairie Boy

O friend who took a double stand for me
Signaller, who white-faced, stayed on post never disgraced
Buzzing and tapping messages in the strafe's devil's-glee
And walked by Crucifix Corner; and the canal still in summer,
Was almost smashed when the mine went up by Tilleloy the malign
And got to Blighty, and was officer (and got honour of degree)
And you who gave me kindness and lie at Chaulnes
And you, true Gloucester, of whom Ypres has the bones.
A Company almost of true friends tried to the courage ends –
The dead with living equal – and living lucky alone,
(Having taken Dead Man's many chances and still for other ones)
A verse of love for you – and the others who chattered
Gloucester and talk of girls when the shrapnel shattered,
And cursed a fate that had never wine nor beer;
That is not less than six kilometres, and perhaps further:
Love endless for you – though I win to rapt, and mapped
Music, and to my deep thought get great sound shaped.
You knew my mind – what it hoped – not to keep body unhurt,
Nor to save life so much as to return to the heart;
To find my heart again in some candle-lit room
And work out music till the true shape and soul should come.
I left not you – why have you left me to fall
Into the hands of evil lying lies to the truth of Hell.
(I was a war poet, England bound to honour by Her blood)
Why have you dead ones not saved me – you dead ones not helped
   well?
Or is it even Michail, my master, strict; forbidding a good?
But why you, Gloucesters, O dead ones, my dear companions,
Laventie – Vermand – Ypres, why have you not given
Courage from beyond the grave to your comrade so driven
By torment from his heart to call for you, friends under the guns?

Is there not honour of war poet at rebirth, or in Heaven?

A Madrigal

Trees, men, flowers, birds, nuts, sing one choir,
One madrigal shout far: scatter clouds with brass:
Scholars, leave your books folded, run, scat, follow here,

Harvest is done, the year's high set in flower . . .
Michael and his armed press, Raphael, all chivalry here,
Echo beat the tympan of the woods, cry all clear –
Blast, dray, bellow deep sounds for the Master of the Year.

Old Tavern Folk

Five feet ten and fond of the sea, and glad
To sit the night through drinking, making merry,
Talking infinite sea yarns and widest like-things,
Till dawn stole in and showed masts, ships and wide
Headlands stretching outwards into grey mists.
They knew their craft and all such things as English
Might care for, thickets of interest like the masts
And spars of the swaying harbour-crowd outside,
Hugh, Michael, Nicholas, Sargeant and Barthelemy,
There was no craft nor hid thing but they had a touch
Of it and could smooth or touch a man on the rough:
Lies were a start of irony, only honour could
Hide its sight, or let loose what honour could hide.
Their dawns reached out to sights of all scheming Europe,
Name led on to name, they knew difference and every land's
    hope,
Drank the last time and went to their untired business
Getting the honest good of life with the largest scope.

Then I Heard

Then I heard a tramping in the winter leaves
And a knight rode from the clearing and stood beside
Me, this All-Hallows, silent with the day's pride
And reckoning. He looked on a thousand things,
Honour and honour again, villages and many cottages
Had borne the famous banner to where battle believes
True things of stolen record – lit up in murderous griefs.
Roland, Charlemagne, Arthur with silver sign
Blown to the mists, to the coppice-edges scattered . . .
He besides me, and of the chronicles speaking that
Were no more than ashes in the minds of men
Gone long withering gyring on careless soft breezes

With snatches of song, old earthy like his old russet
Jerkin – and weather coloured like his fine face,
The burrs on his legs, the drifted beech on his shoulders,
And frost touching the face promising winter soon –
He praised the year's height, but I thought rather of
Long winter book evenings with the fire drifting on panels,
Books on the shelves, tobacco drifting, a friend talking
Shadowy all-hallowed memories drifting there.

William Byrd

Friend of Ben Jonson, or if not friend, equal
In his great strength, but with tougher and less plastic
Material – and no instruments like to the English sense
Of words to use. . . . Byrd master and squarer of sound.
Well I remember walking down Farringdon Road
Finding the well printed loose binded Book inch thick –
And hastily fumbling for the shilling charged – a shilling was all.
And going home; working, occasionally scanning
The noble words, music not yet truly found:
In my own work in middle night glancing for rest
At the 5 part or 6 part Motetts – to be stirred
By nobleness of look and music – and mind made sound.
To wonder, and to accuse Time of having withheld him from me –
    opprest
By certain disliked things of old praised Palestrina.
Joyed by loved things praising loved Gloriana.
That page and this shape . . .
And to walk at night and to guess how he too walked
Musing on Thames' look or talking late night
With Jonson or with friends of Johnson or Heywood . . .
Greeting apprentices honour'd, the honoured master
Of Organ and singer – to God's praise giving delight.
Or merchants saluting courteous in midday mood . . .
To wonder where he was born, honoured William Byrd . . .
In what woman the desire for more life grew faster,
Where what loins in whom the life seed felt and stirred
(For thought of comradeship with Warwick and Hertford)
And what Church blessed with a cross that infant forehead . . .

O glory that shape to square the shapes wandering;
O courage that makes the dumb spirit to submit and sing . . .
O age of Greene and Shirley, Ford and Christopher
(That young one) beloved for airs at the difficult wicket
Swiping over the boundary with accustomed swing . . .

What boys must have passed under that clement mastery;
Loved, and let the opportunity pass over,
To tell his conversation, and how he looked;
What tried for them the Chapter would not have liked;
Hid all up; and wrote till night's veil was nothing –
Square and the human beauty, proving and proving . . .
Winter and first April and loved October,
Firelight or candlelight – that music sober.
After long talking with friends at the day's ends;
Such friends as Gloucesters were to me in France; now,
By some imagined lost, but the natural friendliness
Of such as know the days twenty-four hours moving;
And on with wine till labour some high glory sends;
Some 'Such I would have' no less . . .
O Byrd, London lies a filth very low and low!
Could your great spirit clean it, she would be happier . . .
But to all Christian purpose she is hog-slow
And for the dead, honours with graven stones and ceremonies.

'Girl, Girl, Why Look You So White?'

'Girl, girl, why look you so white?
    Is it death has you taken?'
'No, no, you must not question me so,
    Out of the air is this shaken'.

'Sickness out of the air can be cured
    By simples or one night in the open
But on you – heart's threat so as you stared
    Some power for you bad forelooking has shapen.'

'It is my dead love, who whispers me now
    I loved him well. I love you far better
That is not borne; anger, hurting, and scorn,
    I can take, but not to be of Love the debtor.'

254

'Yes, but for my love of him, he has called
  Me to his side, quick as maybe.
It was never so — it is lies; so enthralled
  Never I was, what'er day's tale be.

'My own heart's master I was and he
  The taker of what I spared
Out of the richness of my fancies (much less
  Of his worth) I dared.

'Shall the dead leave the deep clay to mind
  The living of a love year covered?
Does Death presume so? And out of the blind
  World of spirit a known one hovered.'

'Dear, let deny your heart, come kiss
  That past love out of fancy until
He as the morning mist on our hill
  Of delight be, bathed in sun bliss.

'Dear, let the dead one let you rest.
  My heart is as rich with earth's love
Loving with poetry from the upturned fresh
  Ploughland, with small weeds above.

'He had no more — let the terror slide out
  (Of your eyes and heart) I too, beloved
Of earth — have such right of
  Honour of the soul, delight of
Earth, you should be moved.'

'Though your girl's virginal naturalness
  To the secretest wood be dear
(Or the ploughland) there are gods shall confess
  I, too, the poet, have right here.

'May and September, the clear, the romance — one
  Put fear away
That you have unfaithful been or looked deathly . . .
  To the earth's yea or nay.

'Only put out the blind terror from your eyes,
  For one by dear earth chosen

For service, poetry, and love's ways
    Of reward for service and for night seeking.
Wandering to music's heart after the day's
    Common wonder (but never losen)
The common wonder on wandering and making.
    Make love for me your solace for eyes
Feared awhile, and be calm to admire and see
    There's evil in death does so awaken.'

Watching Music

Watching music – guessing the sounds set down.
How on the real instruments they would sound, when
Gathered in a small room, lit with gold firelight thrown
Lovely about the room, the gloom riching again.
Strings should sound all man's heart ever found,
Or piano dearly touched tell truth's tale of pain
Or Beauty . . .
        Seeing the black
Notes on the page, cursing the sounds' lack
To tell such imagination its true creation
To realize sound's beauty under the look
Of crotchet, minim, quaver on the page,
So as to hear, as to the true musician's dear
Shakespeare's words moving under the music –
Elizabethan clearness under the dumb sound,
Heart's-love to wound;
'Anthony' or 'Winter's Tale' moving under the fall
Or rise of sounding strings telling all out,
As a man to a woman will, when the first doubt
Of love accepted glows into love exalted.
('Beauty's ensign yet' – 'Wilt thou be Lord of the whole
World – that's twice.' – 'and take the winds of March
With beauty' – 'Girdle with embracing flowers' – 'My nightingale'
'In cradle of the rude imperious surge.'
All these things moving under like unknown names
Of deep love only spoken out by eternity's urge.)
Strings singing soft the heart's solace of grief,
Or exulting high forcing from weighted strings the belief
Of high Cotswold undaunting in morning sun.
Looking away past Severn and meadows of Up-Leadon
To surging Malverns or Welsh mountains by Brecknock known.

Night mystery, the unmatched glory of Orion.
Milky Way's dazzle, on North East skies hazel
Or dark azure at midnight or dawn heralding on.
These things but music only spoken and under
Shakespeare's or Jonson's or some French poet's equal wonder
Only in words told, not in music's gold.
These things of eternity, catching up to immortality,
Guessed in the trenches after ages of courageous cold.
Or on Cotswold walking alone, the God-chosen one.
Or the determined fray after Ypres' Hell-battering day.
'This shall pay, I shall have music – music shall pay this pain;
Barrage, stray shrapnel, machine-gun traverse and hurting
Terror of black danger, never ending, incessant starting.
Past men's bearing – this chosen for chosen price . . .
To hear strings tell out love's thoughts with tender voice
(O friends, O heartache – dead are you or estranged.
God pity has changed
Towards me who was his worshipper, devoted server.
In all England I the one, I the one . . .)
These black notes then, watching desperate out of my pain
To guess the content, to know what the maker meant
Realizing such beauty, schooled to such discipline.
With equal art realizing what dreams did make begin.
Black notes, to be moving arms, a bow on the strings,
Beauty matchless like twilight's unfelt wings.
Or talk of Roman sentinels on the high Camps
Before are clear night's contemplative high aloof lamps.
These I should be playing with dearest friends in rooms
Lit with glooms, dark with firelight's gold power.
Taking pay for Laventie, or Vermand's hour.
Or of Ypres, Tilleloy the complete terror.
Who, first war poet, am under three Hells and lie
(Sinned against desperately by all English high-sworn to Duty)
Out of music, out of firelight – or any joy.
A tale of heroic courage, made pains' mark.

The Motetts of William Byrd

Nobly I saw them first
On great paper black printed, . . .
And their strength showed, and more
Behind yet hinted.

257

It was in Faringdon Road
On a dull Day of London weather,
Small money had I, the day
With me, poor together.

After first puzzling glance,
The friendlier and comprehending . . .
Greatness showed from the page,
Mastery, square shaping.

Till my most critical
And searching spirit could not
Resist. 'How much' I turned and said.
'How much? Not a lot?'

It was only a shilling and
My heart sprang higher to be found
In company of the great friends of Jonson,
The makers of that old ground

On which I stood, for long
Had doubted more than worthiness
And beauty to the madrigals,
Not starkness, not greatness.

And I thanked. 'This book is
What I have long sought. Palestrina
Is lesser than this great strength is
A mystic, a dreamer.'

And talked of Missa Brevis
Praised Wilbye, Morley and others –
With greedy heart fears it be taken:
And envious fear smothers.

Thanked him, and went
Up North and West to Oxford Street, in glancing
At a great thing only a shilling found.
Passers-by romancing

Perhaps of one who had
Found a rare copy on some dusty barrow.
Late I worked that night, and had more peace
Before the tomorrow.

O what shape, what squareness
Over strong Latin moving powerful to its close.
Here was a new work companion, with Borrow,
   Chaucer,
Shakespeare, the wise knows.

And 'Sartor' stayed the longer
On its shelf – for once I might help my plans
Not with the poets; burning all-lovely candles
With dead and brave musicians.

Improvisation

City of my delight in the water meadows
Though they grime history and change all colour grey
Yet will a thousand memories of Europe's cities
Strive to guard you – yes, though even as they
Arthur and Guinevere you fall to soft renown,
But even so, with bad heraldry they cover high realities
In a thousand ways bond that should not feel one
You are held serfwise – and if from your light skies
You would clear your heart or brow, they hide those over . .
Nothing earth's helps, shallow Severn, jagged countryways.

But, though the music or poetry in your name
Was done (for ages, ages by your renown called out),
Withers and is lies, destroyed, and is of evil fame,
Yet that is only part of a whole usurpation;
None doubts but that kings and masters have had exaltation
High as the swerve to East in Cathedral and Hall,
Nor that Gloucester trumpets first rattled out Shakespeare's fame
As a thing achieved. (The pools were glad of the rhythm).

Nor that all England travelling to Wales or Severn
Desired that to fairer Westminster a new foil might be given
More riches everywhere but chiefly here
A ford of army and market music and poetry's contest
That had the overlordship of Frome and of Avon,
These things are not doubted, the grater that all smooths out
Has not yet ground out faith in Arthur – and a million.

The Scent of That Country

The scent of that country is in many songs
Its desires are gone
On the winds of prayer and desire to the world's ends –
That Triumph, that has come.

So far, that when men sing afar off . . .
In any place of the world –
Though they are labour's own, or earls of time's proof.
Yet honour must give, and the word.

To Gloucestershire

To my own County where I was born, and the earth
Entered into my making and into my blood –
Which I praised better than any ever of Her birth,
(The City of Gloucester finding in me Her true mood.)
Where Southey only of the great makers was born
And I beat, because of the love of Earth in me –
He desiring books, and I truth rather than the
Writing continual – who saw Cotswold glorifying God,
And the eastern stars, pale out under the paling morn.
And saw Andromeda a sky-wonder over Tewkesbury –
And praised Gloucester, and Tewkesbury and Brimscombe, so
In all their centuries no man from any century.
And after making – with small chance – with no late working,
Came to a London Town which was worse, and to be
Only comforted by the Thames dusk and the City dawns –
The stars of night and the paled east hour-pass marking.
(To lose heart, and health, a night walker's soul to electricity.)
Who served in trenches as many a famed soldier
Unfamed of Caesar's Legions never had served –
Having read Plutarch now, and known the bolder
Lies of Historians – Whose spirit there never swerved . . .

2. Examples of autobiographical poems

This long autobiographical poem, one of many, is included because Gurney begins to describe his front-line experiences – even the shooting at people – in comic terms. This is typical of a certain vein in Gurney (perhaps typical of certain aspects of war) and he would not be fully represented were it to be left out.

The Retreat

After three weeks of freezing and thawing over
Against Chaulnes, mud dreadful, with water cover
Of gumboots in the low places, and ice of nights,
They marched us out sore footed to far billets,
Straw and warm tea, more bread; letters more. . . .
Where for a week we recovered; and now less sore
Our feet were – beer there was, a little bread, wine;
But not the strength they asked of making roads fine
With weak bodies, sore feet, and hungry bellies.
Warmth there was, and sleep – the barn a Palace.
When suddenly the news came, Fritz has retreated. . .
What! from Chaulnes wired yard-deep – where a shot greeted
Any patrol at midnight moving strict ways,
None else to take? It was a most strict terrible maze.
It was true – we marched three days – to our old place,
Passed through a hedge of No Man's Land and saw far
Other lines, pillboxes, headquarters, and further,
Artillery wired positions, Heads of Divisions.
Passed, came to Amiecourt, found billets; it was but the fractions
Of farms – but wood in plenty, and water pure,
Fire warm; billets warm while the North wind sheer
Tore a space round corners of our one small room.
There was a Mass book, great Plainsong in the gloom
Of the broken church with German Journals and such. . .
I found a score of postcards in a billet, to catch
All of them, and to be sorry afterwards. . . .
But first finding den and souvenirs as rewards.
After that, onward slowly till roads we had mended;
Weak, hungry, feeling the heart labour bended;
To come to the last rise, see Somme azure of blaze

(Soft March. . . it was warm of sun), and go onwards, across
The pioneer mending of the arch broken; by planking
Laid across, rattling but standing strain, Transport clanking,
Artillery. We passed Y, and another huge, mined, destroyed
    place,
(Terribly huge) and on till Caulaincourt valley of grace.
Home of the dead men, of Napoleon's men
Lay in the Mausoleum, expecting never invasion,
Nor to see Gloucesters guarding a place that few
Should touch, but of the old rule Rousseau or Le Sage knew –
But Caulaincourt glad enough boys were there who had stuff
Of such within them communion with the smooth and rough
Of road and valley gleaming with lit sapling water
Young Artois' sister to become Somme's one daughter
Glimmering beauty before 'Lights Out' stirring heart out
To tears. (I climbed weak-kneed, I saw fallow unploughed
And the darling valley. . . .) German prisoners passed, defiantly:
One gaily: and we went on to artillery before the town,
Vermand; where (road mending) our Captain rode too far shown
And got a blast of gun barrage – frightened his horse – A
    Company
Took Vermand – two prisoners; and our first trophy
A machine-gun . . . So further to high banks France had raised
Long ago against the Eastward threat, nobly placed
To be the guard of Vermand, Caulaincourt, Somme's Land;
Free men making, cursing arms-taking to Hell out of hand:
Digging with sulky vigour; or in furious paced
Frenzy: promised dismissal and an early end
(We knew). Fine mounds of Roman sort we saw looming
First through the dim night. Then one miserable week,
Through displeasure of the weather, body-sick, heart-sick,
Saw change from green to white, white to golden,
With sleet and sunshine changing, with storm and sun frowning.

First night I lay forward freezing, while others dug pits,
A lump of panged ice. Two hours watching keen for Fritz,
Who saw no more than flurries of snow against the spinnies
Or bare ridge . . . Next day rested, at night advanced
To the near wood, searched and left; nothing but fancies
Of shadows; nothing but dry leaves rustling fortissimo.
Left again, spent one day of before-Spring sun.
But next to be bombarded by Fritz while guarded
Our own feeble guns with a third of such.

So we dug in, under the trunks and brush.
Stayed – in holes – with a sheet to get warmth and shelter
(On which the winter leaves pattered helter skelter,
And the trees dripped.) I was sentry – with two others;
When suddenly, two-hundred off, three great Germans
Appeared. . . the sentry (duty) ran quietly off
To warn the others. His friend went off in the smothers
Of embarrassment. . . I alone (good shot) in the foreground?
Now, Ivor Gurney lonely, make no sound, wait.
The others are at the wood-end; now waste no shot.
No noise, no noise. . . To find (as once: a mine)
My equipment tangled up in my right ear: the bayonet
Hurting my ribs; the fore-sight; O where the fore-sight
Against the woods gunmetal, most lovely, shine?
They touched the wood. I fired straight at the middle one.
No move; now at the right side of the left one.
No move; again between the right one and middle one . . .
When up there dashed my Platoon, crashing branches down;
And off went Germans as swift as deer, as soon
To turn. Great, well-fed men, to our hungry:
Two Corporals; one over-fed, lusty Lance Corporal
I should guess. . . . How did I miss them! How did I miss?
But I refuse to believe (flatly refuse)
And believe that men may be shot through middle bodies
Before enemies without dropping. I, who had hit posts
As hard as ghosts to hit in Verey lights of Laventie. . . .
Posts and any echoing thing. . . . It was, and yet is
Absurd to me to think the belly may not be wholly
Shot through – by a tiny bullet of our Army
And the man not stand up without sign of folly
Or wound. . . . The nicest men I had seen for six
Weeks; to our poor scarecrows of weak pulses. . . .
Moving by will, – hungry, yet comradely;
While these comfortable Burghers came over like country squires
To see the work of the farmhand; happy after white coffee;
And a good gossip before glowing half wood fires. . .
(O! O! Newspapers Anglais, Français Papers daily,
What have you told us of hungry or cowed Bavaria, Saxony?
What yarns of three-course dinners, when here the sinners
Come overland 8 mile an hour, and do it easily?
And walk off indigestion after meals like millionaires
For size (and accomplishment)? O Wurtemburgherie,
Is this the population you fake your figures on?

Is this the beaten horde of conscripts, beginners?
(Two as nice men as I'd ever meet again . . .)

So we talked over. . . they cursed me. . . the little skirmish:
Cursed also and felt excitement and watched them vanish,
Like record-breakers, over the chalk slope borders.

'Goodbye' – 'You chaps, I'm sure I hit them in the guts.
Bang through or near. . . You know I have hit dark posts,
My equipment round my neck. . . .' To which only jests
Were answer; and 'no excuses for a miss at twelve yards, sir!'

Next night to trench again – and they told us we were going
Over the top to take some unseen damned wiring
Over the crest. They bombarded, and our guns cutting were
    trying.
At seven the drizzle began; at 10 we formed in Line . . .
And (they too fast) went over across country,
I grumbling, and half running; while silence sombrely
Hung over all things, the air misty almost rainy,
I weak as a rabbit 'How much longer, dammit?'
They said 'Shut up'. I said 'I wish this were over!'
They said 'Shut up'. When suddenly up went a cheer.
The men on the left had hit it. . . . I stumbled on and struck it
Blind eyed, upfaced. . . fearing wire high and to be scratch-faced.
Hit wire, and lay down . . . seeing fires, whether of theirs
Or ours, cutting the wires I knew not, only from behind
The impatient second line shot past my helmet,
And the machine-guns blazed away, lower, lower
(O Christ, what pain) and lower, till my body did cower
Stuck to the mire, and no holes at all in the wire.
So much for artillery fire . . .

The Company jester and my little lieutenant
Crept about: snipping odd wires. . . ten yards I guessed went
Before us (or over ten foot) and shells came down, and that
    damned machine-gun
Sprayed us . . . O down, further down; Vermand,
You are too chalky a land . . . We retreated. . . dug shallow
Pits – the moon above the mist made a mellow
Light, transfused – we could see an old machine-gun post . . .
And nothing more – we were a little down in the hollow.
Again returning, to catch the same – lighter now, see wires

Thick against dares; and no more forrader; to retreat again;
When suddenly my arm went blazing with bright ardour of pain;
The end of music . . . I knelt down and cursed the double
Treachery of Fritz to Europe and to English music:
Cursed Pomerania, Saxony, Wurtemburg, Bavaria,
Prussia, Rheinland, Mecklenburg, Pomerania
Again . . . (But had forgotten Franconia, Swabia)
Then said 'You chaps, she's beginning to move again;'
(Borrowed a rifle – shot one shot to say 'These things were so.
My arm – she'll stay on yet; I believe it's a Blighty.'
And the stretcher-bearers bound it up carefully, neatly . . .
In the darkness whitely . . . And I left them all, vulgar soldiers to
	brawl;
Passed through reserve in the sunken Road. . . . Oxfords I just
	could
See, who asked me news: 'O wires, wires, wires, sticks, wood. . .
Machine-guns, machine-guns, shells . . . Nothing else.
	Goodnight!'
And went off through a barrage spraying the hill side
(Machine-guns) risking so much. . . tired out and careless:
Having a Blighty; hunger; weakness; by disgust fearless;
And saw the downward slope to Blighty and new hope.

Chance to Work

(For the English Police
For Scotland Yard.)

I have never had chance to work, for when a boy
Small day was mine, bed-time too soon came by –
Few friends were mine who might have taught me books;
Yet loved I Nature with its joyous looks;
Played football hard as most, and the Cathedral
Worshipped surely with its great rise and fall.
Yet later there was one of sweet humanity
Who brought much worthy knowledge free to me.
But sitting still spoiled health, and the great poets
Were still misted with fear and explaining notes.
Too much food, too few hours, yet sunrise I saw
Brighten sweet Highnam woods, and the bright clouds draw
Off from an April sky, strangely roused up.
Beauty brazen and strange; from the sky's top

To the houses' edge unreal, strange. But when
Schooldays were left, a noble man of men
Helped me, my sloth spoilt me and worse was known.
Yet his prayers called on me some goodness down.
One March called me out walking with the natural
Love of joy, and with clean fervour my heart was full.
Gloucestershire called — the western light, the true
Elizabethan surrounding daylight, ever new,
Ever old, satisfying. Knowledge lacked, not
Yet was the time of work by me to be got.
Much of the natural joy that goes with making
Was given me, known to me; Nature set me shaking
In ecstasy of purity, passion true —
That life Marston, Shirley, Greene and Dekker knew.
Now was music seen to be mirror of Life,
Discord like brambles beautiful in wind at strife
Criss-cross, sawing across light; great chords known
As repose of hills against the east fire known.
A woman's love now helped. Great knowledge grew
Of how the makers gathered and guarded to
Endeavour each small thing seen, each great sight felt.
Holiness of Earth was known. But not yet dealt
Life with me fairly. Long night watches were denied —
So needed — and still labour; on Cotswold side
And higher up, at night it was granted me
The quarries white in moonlight, black greenery
Of beech against the moon; graceful tree-stems,
Stars such as Chaucer saw, and still sky-rims;
O high above the valley. Was mist streaked there?
A dawn is remembered also. But night to labour,
To work, read, walk night through — this needed a friend
Guiding more wisely than I knew. But Life did send
Many consolations. Art apprehended, springs
Of true worth known — natural, of divine sendings —
Earth, air, and water the true sources of song or speaking
In high words. Not out of books the awaking
Spirit might gather much save of discipline —
Manners, application of work's rules —
A right weight given to mastership and use of schools.

All this out of love chiefly was taken, and love
Makes rules of nobleness. Nevertheless, above
Love is Law for youth, though Law light-laid —

Friends to me dear, yet rules were right to be made
On me – the legacy of toil out of the past
So pondered, so dwelt upon, formed four-square at last.

London came, with mastership and right rule indicating,
Dull bending to what hitherto had been of Love's rating.
Art in fetters, till limbs had grown strong – City's
Surroundings for Nature's sweetest teachings and pities.
The long streets going onward without much joy.
Mean lodgings, far country, and duty's employ
For all those fires and strong compulsions: the true
Sources of what is worthy, at once old and new.
Ill-health there was, and hardest straining at tasks
Of school sort – a hard term, such that good memory asks
Not to look back upon. Holidays came
To freshen the mind once more; the country-side same
As ever, new-old, old-new, gave life and hope
To heart and soul. Two months of growing; then again
To London – the wonderful mists of autumn with men
Seen small-black in the smother. Work easier now,
With rules understood. Song and the quicker glow
Of Lyric now were mastered, more. The stern forms
Made afraid the pupil spirit; that yet charms
Needed. Walking all day with sketch-books came
Later, the best plan. Clarity of mind; and dream
So was kept. Terms went. Holidays with dear friends –
Sailing, walking. Going as Nature intends
On white ways for discovery of what lay
Unvisited by most; white water, or spray
Of bramble queerly hanging, or new-old farms,
Black timber, or timber unwrought; or runnels in storms
That fill and empty tiny water-courses
Perhaps nine months all dry; or small gay horses
Galloping sham-afraid from frightening trains.
Walking all morning, afternoon too, the lanes
Or high-roads – To return dusty, tea-thirsty
To friends, the piano, sketching ambitiously
Such works as broad country might bring to attempt.
There was hay-making too, how wisps unkempt
Clung to the clothes, the horses strong trampled
And all wide Heaven had cumulus unexampled
With war threatening, falling. At last to strike,
Set Europe's dearest killing, thrusting alike

At life or body's beauty. Too ill for war
Was I, whose life was organist, and more
Writing. But health came, the return home, dress
Changed. A little longer the tenderness
So dear, of friends, after drill, that love which had given
Help to work; shared Bach's thought going to Heaven,
Or Beethoven's music loved in company –
Half-light playings of music, of poetry
Readings . . .

        Training took all strength, none was left
For shaping or word or sound. Forgotten the gift.
Rattle-tattle, bugle-call, button-cleaning, leather-shining.
Midland, East England, South England; digging, hard-
    training . . .
Songs a few; verses few. But overseas better
Chance came. Signallers might, more than the letter
Of Linesmen, Infantry, night-watchers accomplish.
Candles were lit, more time was, and the great wish
Of reading, writing, making was more possible
Than to others of greater danger more honourable.
Nevertheless, Songs and verses. Laventie, by Arras,
Crucifix Corner, Caulaincourt, Rouen, by Ypres,
Something was fashioned out; work in all odd-sort corners.
Yet time there was for dreams, which so often discerners
Are of the future paths, gatherers of old
Thought-wrack; treasurers, hoarders of time's gold.

Chance of work? Yes, but one hoped so in the coming
Peace, the hoped for universal true homing
Of Line and all Force.

        Wound brought on Hospital, then
Was more chance of writing. Some true work. Eastward again
To war-chance.

        Gas brought England, and some hope-fulfilling.
The leave, walking, and friendship; but joy too willing
For hope would not bend down to so short a day
Of labour. Better taste joy, and go quick away
To the hard task. Country seen, friends loved, work's hope
    renewed . . .
Depot again was not of right labour's hope,
Little comforted there; but the kindest fine scope
Of hospitality made bright dun closed-in dull lives.
Dreadful the tale to follow.

                    And the spirit forgives
Best in freedom, horror on horror best put in the black
Oblivion of Time, not ever to be told, or called back.
There was no shadow of happiness, and small chance of
That work my spirit had right of, had learnt to love.
Gloucestershire restored again, though evil forces made
Difficult. The spirit strove for its earlier unafraid
Trust in life. Work at munitions purified, strengthened
Body and spirit. Beauty shone nobly on the well lengthened
Days; but working late was not allowed to me
Or was difficult. Freedom not yet was my legacy
Of right – nor had I learnt yet the worth of an hour,
Or the all-watching night come into my power.
Cornwall, Gloucester again. London to work –
London that held such hopes, but perils lurk
And are dread there. Hopes broke, work was destroyed,
For all my hopings. Evil flowed black like a tide
Of darkness over me.
                    Goodness freed, at the last.
But out of London – West Country; Songs, other work passed
From my hand. Walking, making, living on small
Riches, but friendship helped me. Without any call –
Friendship reached out a hand, or where had I been?
Music shared, book-talk shared, and a serene
Hope gained. Many songs, other things, then a good farm
Took me, and body labour took away harm
With fine muscle-using, wood hewing, labouring with spade.
Hedging, plough-helping, stone shifting, Labour was good.
Gone out was danger, ill longing of unspiritual food.
May-time was more, with poems, or music to sketch;
In the great Roman-trod hill-sides, with water to fetch,
Wood to carry, tasks – then to return
At evening high up where last sunset light did burn
Looking high over to the British borders
Of old, these camps-slopes sentries and true warders,
Guardians of Rome's power. Yet it is difficult
In a house not one's own to work, and the fire felt
Not into much work grew or was forced. Some poems
Captured the sense of Rome; but one's own home's
Shelter, not to disturb sleep – this not yet
Was granted. Chances I remember to have read late –
Sketched often in the open – Quartetts, songs
Where-to the real sense of earth still clings, belongs.

                            269

Much loved all this; but something most evil drove
Me from that place, where desperate work with love
Was mixed. An evil took me; the farm I left –
Beautiful West England of every gift
Dowered, it would seem. London once more, where never
Had stronger been my struggle or hard endeavour.
Success a hundred times deserved, and all
Evil, as best might be, shunned. Work came, but small
Return for so much trying. A war-mourning
Had nobleness, many songs, a violin thing
Pleased my ambitiousness. A good room that was.
Many streets helped me with their width, a place
Of labour London never was more to me.
Little more than tea, coffee; coffee and tea
My fare. To Gloucester again for holidays. Still
Sketching, hoping, poems and lyrics making.
Late staying up perhaps; but always shaking
A little with fear to disturb the sleepers over.
It was not one's own house. Better in streets to be rover,
Sketching at notes easily to be completed
In short time, while the quick mind no-ways waited.
Many times walking in the grimy dark, or
Moonlit streets till the time came: the true working-hour.
No fault was mine save drink, and that kept often
The brain clear – tea preserved me to making then.
But in tea-houses one may not work, there is business,
One may not loiter; and resting places are less
In city ways than anywhere almost.
But a Morley's extract of old time plays; at last
Here were Elizabethans, Greene, Dekker, and Marston –
Shirley, Massinger, Ford, and greater Jonson –
Something of each; carefully in honour reading,
Learning slowly the new mastery, needing
Such swift mastership after the slower
Foreign scholarship of the more modern hour
Of music . . . This was revelation, this new
Guidance to what I hoped for – the saying true
And clear out what truly was to be shown of life.
Then an organist's post gave me once more subsistence.
Walking the flint ways, daylight or darkness dense,
Sketching or trying to think – but again I left that;
Went to the dear loved farm, but illness out
Cast me – and so my life to the finest year

Of all comes; the working, hoping, pain-without-fear.
My aunt with kindest hospitality
To her house and garden made me wholly free –
In her kindness trusting reward which never came –
But honouring work, honouring old poet's name,
And work performed. Hope filled me; papers I read
For that hard work should bring me daily bread,
And finding none, on my few shillings was
(Of pension) content to work and know my place
Of waiting – worker. Tea, fire, my chief desires.
To dawn often I laboured, and with keen cares
Kept sleep away with wary avoidance till
Sun's fire topped the steep of the Eastern Hill.
Employment came, but not long kept – the expected
Body-labour, the cleansing work, directed
Controlled, till work-end came, once more I was free
For thought, and writing, and free artistry
Denied. Denied must be content; on twelve
Shillings and odd earnings I must serve.
So through the winter, the spring, wherein I was reader
Of Midsummer Night's Dream, on that sweet thought the feeder.
On, on to summer; my nights to working so given,
Days to sketching, walking, watching, water, earth, heaven –
Labouring as might be – seventeen miles, home again,
Fair payment of body's usage for using pen,
Back at dusk; talking (scribbling the while) not to lose
Much of the precious work-time. Her habit, use,
Was – bed-at-eleven, when I might settle hard to
Quartetts, or verse, or reading. Summer drew so
To height. Digging, wood chopping, leaping, and such
To increase body's joy, never, never too much.
Night-long often, till others full waking time
Working in strict discipline, music or strict rhyme.
Chaucer, Carlyle, Borrow, Jonson to my aid
Calling. A life of pain, a spirit unafraid
Of duties' costs.
                    Then my misfortunes began.
Influences wrought on me after evil plan.
My body pained, work spoiled, and not my fault –
Since such activity rarely did halt
Rarely falter . . . O little I deserved this thing –
Was I wasting time? Was I playing? Was it slacking?
This life carried onward to one good end,

Yet ready to be abandoned should orders send
Me to some body-using, or money earning.
An office-post for twelve weeks to me turning
By other men's kindness I had; no real fault mine
I lost it — influences drove me, there was much pain.
Still I laved body, still worked when courteousness
Let me so; but worse and worse still my distress
Became. I wished Life's end, because of much pain.
Demanded that — many times, many. But why again
Should I, the striver, be punished? So few men led
Life that so little loved easiness of bed
Or slumber. Fruit pulp, milk, tea, salt, water I took,
Hanging despairingly on many an old book.
Strange things happened, many times death denied
To a spirit that loved working, and had such pride
In achievement, and making's pain. I must leave that
House, where my hopings, strivings had been so great.

I would have gone on tramp. Many hindrances let
Me from this course. Pain. Obstacles, hurt head, the wet
Ending of water I feared, but longed much for another.
A promise failed, a pension that would have saved, rather
Led to destruction perhaps. Friends took me, they thought
Out of danger, but much pain, wrong, was there on me wrought.
Friends helped again; but here I am walking a ward —
A twelve hour day — small comfort for him whose true word,
True thought was labour. Why punish so one who so paid
For success, such worthy strong efforts, why ever denied
To me Chance of Work, Bread-earning, who loved sun and
        stars
More than most others. And saw the bronzed cloud-bars
Between work-spells at cold dawn? . . .
                                O if such pain is
Not of account — a whole life's whole penalties
To cancel . . . Grant pity, grant chance of Work, grant that
Freedom of effort in other days held to be great.
Prices I paid, small rest took. Others slept, still
Warding sleep, I watched meadow and tree and hill —
Farm workers still at slumber . . .
                                Who earned more a good
Fate; how many followed the thing he should
In all England; with such chance?
                                Honour, I pray

And rescue one who worked, knew every aspect of night and
    day.
Would pray for death, beneath which Chance, Change; this life
Is horror, and bad horror. For here now no strife
With self or evil is possible, nor yet is brief
The minute. Pain or Wearing without relief.

NOTES TO APPENDIX

1. *Poems from previous editions by Blunden and Clark omitted from main text*

I Saw French Once] Blunden/Clark (TS 42). No MS. *London Mercury*, 1933.

What's In Time] Blunden/Clark (TS 18). No MS.

The Dance of the September Birds] MS 52 *(11) (5h)*. Blunden (TS 20).

The Anger of Samson] Blunden (TS 42). No MS.

O Tan-Faced Prairie Boy] Blunden (TS listed 21). (A Whitman title).

A Madrigal] MS 64.12. Dated Sept. 1926. Blunden/Clark (no TS). Printed in Blunden as a separate poem, but is almost certainly the final 7 lines, on reverse of MS page, of an unsuccessful longer poem, 'Now September Comes'.

Old Tavern Folk] MS 64.12. Clark (TS 20).

Then I Heard] MS 64.12. Clark (TS 20).

William Byrd] MS 52.10. Clark (TS 18).

'Girl, Girl, Why Look You So White?'] Clark (TS 21). No MS. Title supplied.

Watching Music] MS 52.10. Clark (TS. 18).

The Motetts [sic] *of William Byrd*] TS. 18, dated Jan. 1925. Clark (first 8 verses only). No MS.

Improvisation] MS 64.12. Clark (TS 20).

The Scent of That Country] MS 64.12. Clark (TS 20). Title supplied.

To Gloucestershire] TS 21A (no MS.) Clark: first 21 lines of a much longer poem, from group 'In Praise of Poets. Poems of the States.'

2. *Examples of autobiographical poems.*

The Retreat] * MS 4 *(151–157)* only. Dated April 23rd 1925.

Chance to Work] * MS 55 *(13–26)* only. Hurd, pp. 171–8.

GLOSSARY

'*A Hundred pipers and a*'': Scots song
'*Après la guerre fini*': War song

Barrage: Artillery bombardment along a fixed line
Billet: Place of rest
Blighty: Home. A wound that caused a soldier to be sent home
'*Bread and cheese*': Country name for wild flower, probably Common
   Mallow, or hawthorn blossom
Buckle: Historian (19th-century)
Bucks: Buckinghamshire

Clare: County of west of Ireland
Cross: The ancient crossroads of Gloucester

Dixie: Cooking-pail
Drachms (and scruples): Jewellers' weights (pron. 'drams')
Dug-out: Larger roofed cavity in trench system

Elvers: Young eels, a delicacy
Estaminet: Small French café
Enyopean: (?) War-filled

Fleet: Fleet Street, London
Fritz: A German

Going over: Advancing on foot out of trenches to attack enemy line

Harvey (F.W.): Gloucester poet, friend of IG
Huffler: A sailing barge
Humphrey: 'The Good Duke Humphrey' of Gloucester, son of Henry IV

Leadon: Tributary of River Severn
Limbers: Gun-carriages
Line: Front Line of battle
Lipton's: Brand of tea
Lockhart's: An all-night café
Lyons: Tea-house where popular string-ensembles played

Machonachies: Brand of pickles
Mangle-bury: Thatched heap of mangel-wurzles
Minenwerfers (Minnies, minniewerf(er)s): Like '*tweedledees*' and '*handy-
danders*', soldiers' slang for types of German explosives
Maries: Gloucester churches. St Mary de Lode & St Mary de Crypt

Nicholas: Gloucester church

On Rest: Out of the Front Line
Orders: Pinned-up notice of orders

Pagles: Cowslips
Parapet: Front of trench
Paul's: St Paul's Cathedral
Peter's (Abbey, Place): Gloucester Cathedral
Pippa: In Browning's poem 'Pippa Passes', who sang 'God's in his heaven,
    all's right with the world'
Plain: Salisbury Plain
Putties: Ankle-strappings

Raikes (*Robert*): (1735–1811), proprietor of the *Gloucester Journal* and
    founder of Sunday Schools
'Revally' (Reveille): Waking-up signal
Rood: a measure of land

Sarsparilla: A tonic
Screen: Creeping artillery barrage behind which infantry advanced
Squele (Will): In Shakespeare's *Henry IV, Part II*: 'Will Squele, a Cotswold
    man'
Stand-to: Beginning of day's duty
Strafe: Bombardment

Toussaints: All Saints' Day, 1st November
Townshend: Patron of Ben Jonson – Gurney's type of the ideal host. Sir
    Robert Townshend
Turmut: Turnip
Twyvers: Small river through Gloucester

Verey lights: Illumination rockets fired by pistol

Weltmut(h): 'world-courage' (German)
Wires: Barbed wire
Witan-ring: Anglo-Saxon council
Woodbines: A brand of cheap cigarette

INDEX OF FIRST LINES

MORE OXFORD PAPERBACKS

Details of other Oxford Paperbacks are given on the following pages. A complete list of Oxford Paperbacks, including the World's Classics, Past Masters, OPUS, and Twentieth-Century Classics series, can be obtained from the General Publicity Department, Oxford University Press, Walton Street, Oxford OX2 6DP.

The Ordeal of Ivor Gurney

Michael Hurd

Behind the name of Ivor Gurney lies the tragic story of a composer and poet whose life seemed full of promise but who ended his days in a mental hospital.

In his biography of this exceptional man, Michael Hurd draws on a wealth of material, including Gurney's brilliant and amusing letters and the extraordinary poems that chronicle so movingly his descent into madness.

'Ivor Gurney . . . admirably portrayed here by the composer Michael Hurd, is of compelling and tragic interest.' Anthony Storr, *Sunday Times*

'After this biography, Ivor Gurney's name will never again flicker minimally in the anthologies and song repertoires, as it has for so many years.' Ronald Blythe, *Listener*

The Collected Poems of Edward Thomas

Edited by R. George Thomas

'Thomas's bleak, heart-catching verses have won him a steadily rising reputation and challenge comparison with Hardy, both for their observations of nature and their inner desolation. Killed in France at Easter 1917, Thomas wrote all his 144 poems in the last two years of his life: this pocket-size edition, chronologically arranged and well annotated and introduced by R. George Thomas, also includes his last war diary.' *Sunday Times*

The Heart of England

Edward Thomas

'We are so rich that we do not count our treasure.' Edward Thomas was always aware of the richness of the English countryside, the elusive beauty of the natural world. Everything he saw was something to be treasured. Here is the essence of the England he knew, in all seasons and in all moods: an August day through the haze of corn dust 'when the thresher twists his oaken flail', or a November morning in the 'close, perpendicular, quiet rain'.

Although Edward Thomas was only later to become known as a poet these early essays already reveal the poet's sensitivity for language and the poet's eye for truth.